Illustrated Battles
of the Continental European
Nations 1820-1900
Volume 1

Illustrated Battles of the Continental European Nations 1820-1900 Volume 1

Herbert Russell
John Augustus O'Shea
and
Arthur Griffiths

LEONAUR

Illustrated Battles of the Continental European Nations 1820-1900
Volume 1
by John Augustus O'Shea
Herbert Russell
and
Arthur Griffiths

First published under the title
Battles of the Nineteenth Century

Leonaur is an imprint of Oakpast Ltd
Copyright in this form © 2017 Oakpast Ltd

ISBN: 978-1-78282-632-3 (hardcover)
ISBN: 978-1-78282-633-0 (softcover)

http://www.leonaur.com

Publisher's Notes

The views expressed in this book are not necessarily those of the publisher.

Contents

The Battle of Navarino 1827	7
Brussels, August–September 1830	23
The Battle of Warsaw 6-7 September 1831	49
The Fall of Constantine 1837	61
Moltke's First Battle: Nisib June 23 1839	73
The Defeat of Abd-el-Kadr by the French, Isly August 14, 1844	89
The Battle of Gislikon November 23, 1847	105
The Storming of Brescia March 31–April 1, 1849	125
The Battle of Novara March 23, 1849	135
Omar Pasha at Chetaté and Calafat, 1854	153
MacMahon at Magenta 4 June, 1859	167
The Battle of Solferino 24th June, 1859	187
Spanish Battles in Morocco Castillejos, Tetuan, Guad El Ras 1859-60	207
Palermo: The Coming of Garibaldi May 26, 1860	229
The Battle of Castelfidardo September 18, 1860	247
The Battle of Volturno 1st Oct: 1860	263
The Battle of Aspromonte August 29, 1862	275

The Greek War of Independence
1821-32

The Battle of Navarino
1827
By Herbert Russell

The immediate causes which led to the Battle of Navarin, or Navarino, are of a romantic and dramatic character. On the 6th of July, 1826—the Greeks having risen in revolt against the oppression of the Turks in 1820—a treaty had been signed in London on the part of Great Britain, France, and Russia, having for its object the pacification of the Levant by intervention between Turkey and Greece. Through the indiscretion of some unknown official the treaty found its way to the *Times*, which published it in its issue of July 12th, 1826—six days after its signature. It thus became fully known to all concerned before the official instructions which it rendered necessary could be delivered. As a result, Sir Edward Codrington, the British admiral in the Mediterranean, found himself in a situation of perplexity, and was directed to consult with the French and Russian admirals, and arrange a plan of action with them.

The instructions of the three admirals in question definitely required an armistice between Turkey and Greece, and limited the period for its acceptance to one month. If the result of negotiations should be—as was, of course, anticipated—acceptance by Greece and rejection by Turkey, the admirals were instructed to enter into friendly relations with the former country-, and unite their fleets to prevent all Turkish or Egyptian reinforcements or warlike stores from being transported for employment against the Greeks. Each of the allied admirals had particular instructions to take care, if possible, that any measures they might adopt in restraining the Ottoman Navy should not wear the aspect of open hostilities. They were directed to endeavour to carry their arguments rather by a display of force than by the employment of it. This, briefly, is a review of the situation whose climax was the Battle of Navarino.

Sir Edward Codrington, the British admiral in the Levant, as we have already said, found himself in a situation of perplexity on the publication of the treaty. The French squadron was at Milo, and the Russians had not yet arrived. But with that instant resolution which has always been such a fine characteristic of the British naval officer's spirit, Sir Edward determined to take the initiative, and with three sail of the line he placed himself before Hydra to oppose, "when all other means are exhausted, by cannon shot" the whole of the Turkish and Egyptian fleet. The "general order," which he issued to all his captains on September 8th, 1827, well illustrates the policy which the English commander-in-chief resolved to adopt. He writes from on board the *Asia*:

> You are aware, that a treaty has been signed between England, France, and Russia for the pacification of Greece. A declaration of the decision of the powers has been presented to the Porte, and a similar declaration has been presented to the Greeks. The armistice proposed to each, in these declarations, has been acceded to by the Greeks, whilst it has been refused by the Turks. It becomes, therefore, the duty of the allied naval forces to enter, in the first place, on friendly relations with the Greeks; and, next, to intercept every supply of men, arms, etc., destined against Greece, and coming either from Turkey or Africa in general. The last measure is that which requires the greatest caution, and, above all, a complete understanding as to the operations of the allied naval forces. Most particular care is to be taken that the measures adopted against the Ottoman Navy do not degenerate into hostilities.
>
> The formal intention of the powers is to interfere as conciliators, and to establish, in fact, at sea the armistice which the Porte would not concede as a right. Every hostile proceeding would be at variance with the pacific ground which they have chosen to take, and the display of forces which they have assembled is destined to cause that wish to be respected; but they must not be put into use, unless the Turks persist in forcing the passages which they have intercepted. All possible means should be tried, in the first instance, to prevent the necessity of proceeding to extremities; but the prevention of supplies, as before mentioned, is to be enforced, if necessary, and when all other

means are exhausted, by cannon shot.

In giving you this instruction as to the duty which I am directed to perform, my intention is to make you acquainted thoroughly with the object of our government, that you may not be taken by surprise as to whatever measures I may find it necessary to adopt. You will still look to me for further instructions as to the carrying any such measures into effect.

On September 11th Sir Edward Codrington, with the *Genoa* and *Albion*, arrived off Navarino, and beheld the whole of the expedition from Alexandria at anchor in the harbour, where it had arrived two days previously. The English squadron hovered off this place for above a week, awaiting the coming of the allies. On the 19th September Sir Edward Codrington notified the admiral commanding the Ottoman force in the port of Navarino that he would be prevented—by extreme measures, if necessary—from attacking the Greeks. Notwithstanding, on the 21st a division of the Turkish expedition got under way, and came out of the harbour. Their intentions were clear, and the British ships cleared for action. What the issue of this incident might have been it is difficult to say, had not the sails of a strange squadron appeared upon the horizon to windward whilst the English and Turks were still manoeuvring near the land. The vessels turned out to be the French fleet, under Admiral de Rigny, and whatever might have been the intentions of the commander of the Ottoman expedition, it retired back into the harbour immediately the strangers were near enough for the French colours to be visible.

By the arrival of Admiral de Rigny at Navarino, not only was Sir Edward Codrington's force largely augmented, but he was relieved of his isolated and critical responsibility by the certainty of a joint action in whatever steps might now be taken. The Russian squadron had not yet appeared; but the British and French admirals at once commenced proceedings by interviewing Ibrahim Pacha, the commander of the Turkish forces at Navarino, and clearly impressing upon him the determination of the allied Courts to carry out the spirit of the treaty, and the necessity imposed on them (the admirals) to enforce the armistice referred to in their instructions. The interview was a long one. Ibrahim said that the admirals must be aware he was a soldier like themselves, and that it was as imperative for him to obey orders as for them; that his instructions were to attack Hydra, and that he must put them into execution, it being for him merely to act and not to negotiate.

The admirals replied that they quite sympathised with the feelings of a brave man under such circumstances, and that they congratulated him upon having a force opposed to him which it was impossible to resist. They reminded him that if he put to sea in defiance of their amicable warning they must carry their instructions into execution, and that if he resisted by force the total destruction of his fleet must follow, which, they added archly and significantly, was an act of madness the Grand Seignior could not applaud. Amidst a profusion of Oriental compliments, French politeness, and British bluntness was this interview between the warlike Turk and the allied admirals carried on; and, although in conclusion Ibrahim pledged his word of honour to observe the armistice, yet the actual result of the long palaver was to leave things very much in the same situation in which they had been before.

Admiral Codrington's description of Ibrahim, contained in a letter written by him to his sister Jane shortly after the interview referred to, is particularly interesting. After a very graphic description of the Turkish camp and of Ibrahim's tent, he proceeds:—

> They first began with the ceremony of introduction, which, as there were a good many of us on either side, was proportionally long. . . . At length, however, I got settled, and began to look around me again. . . . This tent also was open, and from his sofa he looked down over the whole harbour, and really the sight was beautiful, covered as it was by the ships and boats of all sorts continually passing to and fro. His tent was *outside* the walls of Navarin; and, indeed, what force he had with him appeared to be outside of the town. Altogether, I thought he had chosen the coolest and most convenient place to pitch his tent in that could be found.
>
> But to return thither. He is a man of about forty years old, not at all good-looking, but with heavy features, very much marked with the smallpox, and as fat as a porpoise. Though I had no opportunity of seeing his height—as he was on his sofa, lying down or sitting the whole time—I should not think him more than five feet seven inches. He was, *for a pacha,* plainly dressed, I think, particularly as his followers and officers were covered with gold and embroidery; and, for a Turk, I think his manners were very good indeed. The conversation first began about the weather, and such common-place things; for I learnt (from the interpreter) he does not talk of business till *after coffee.*

Zante

Ibrahim proved treacherous. He disregarded his own word of honour to accept the armistice, and there followed a long series of negotiations, in which the attitude of the allied admirals gradually grew more threatening and that of the Ottoman leader proportionately defiant. On the 2nd of October, in the midst of a heavy thunderstorm, the Turkish fleet boldly put to sea. This was a direct breach of the parole which had been passed, and the Honourable Captain Spencer, in the *Talbot*, was instructed to inform the Turkish admiral that he would not be permitted to proceed, and that if he allowed a single gun to be fired at the English flag the whole of his fleet would be destroyed.

This message speedily caused the Turks to bring their ships to the wind, and the second in command, Halhil Bey, came on board the *Asia*. He admitted that he had been present at Sir Edward Codrington's interview with Ibrahim Pacha, when the latter bound himself in honour not to send any of his fleet out of the port, but pretended to believe that it had been sanctioned for a Turkish squadron to go to Patras. The British admiral bluntly informed Halhil that, having broken their faith with him, he would not trust them henceforth, and that if they did not put about and return to Navarino he would make them. This message was accompanied by the *Asia* firing a gun and filling her main-topsail; on which the Turkish fleet, by a signal from their admiral, swung their yards afresh and stood back towards the harbour.

This little incident confirmed Sir Edward Codrington in his intention of summarily enforcing the treaty he had been despatched to uphold. Admiral de Rigny, on his part, showed no less a degree of determination to maintain the pledge which his nation had conjointly given to the Greeks. Down to this period, however, the Russians had not appeared upon the scene; but on the 15th of October their squadron, under Count Heiden, joined the French and British fleets off Zante. Sir Edward Codrington, from seniority of rank, was commander-in-chief of the combined fleet. On the 18th of October the three admirals held a conference for the purpose of concerting the measures of effecting the object specified in the Treaty of London—namely, an armistice *de facto* between the Turks and Greeks. They considered that:

> Ibrahim Pacha having violated the engagement he entered into with the admirals on September 25th for a provisional suspension of arms, by causing his fleet to come out and proceed towards another point in the Morea; that since the return of the fleet, owing to meeting Admiral Codrington near Patras,

the *pacha's* troops had carried on a warfare more destructive and exterminating than before, killing women and children, burning habitations, etc., for completing the devastation of the country; and that all endeavours to put a stop to these atrocities by persuasion and conciliation, by representations to the Turkish chiefs, and advice given to Mehemet Ali have been treated as mockeries, though they could have been stopped by a word: Therefore the admirals found that there remained to them only three modes of action :—

1st. The continuing throughout the whole of the winter a blockade—difficult, expensive, and perhaps useless, since a storm might disperse the squadrons, and afford to Ibrahim the facility of conveying his destroying army to different parts of the Morea and the islands;

2nd. The uniting the allied squadrons in Navarin itself, and securing by this permanent presence the inaction of the Ottoman fleets, but which mode alone leads to no termination, since the Porte persists in not changing its system;

3rd. The proceeding to take a position with the squadrons in Navarin, in order to renew to Ibrahim propositions which, entering into the spirit of the Treaty, were evidently to the advantage of the Porte itself.

Having taken these three modes into consideration, the admirals unanimously agreed that the last method was best calculated, without bloodshed, but simply by the imposing presence of the squadrons, to produce the desired end. Sir Edward Codrington had a considerable difficulty to contend with in the jealousy which existed between the Russian and French admirals, and it called for no small exercise of tact on his part to maintain harmony in the combined fleet. The allied force was as follows:—

English: Three line-of-battle ships, four frigates, four brigs, one cutter.

French: Three line-of-battle ships, one double-banked frigate, one frigate, two cutters.

Russian: Four line-of-battle ships, four frigates.

In all twenty-four ships of war. The Ottoman force was as follows:

Three line-of-battle ships, four double-banked frigates, thirteen frigates, thirty corvettes, twenty-eight brigs, six fire brigs, five schooners, forty-one transports.

In all, one hundred and thirty sail of vessels. The Turks had in addition to this imposing force an army of 35,000 Egyptian troops in the Morea, of whom 4,000 were on board the transports.

On the 19th of October Admiral Codrington issued his instructions to his colleagues as to the manner in which the combined fleet was to be disposed on entering the port of Navarino. The order runs:

> It appears, that the Egyptian ships in which the French officers are embarked are those most to the south-east. It is, therefore, my wish that his excellency Rear-Admiral Chevalier de Rigny should place his squadron abreast of them. As the next in succession appears to be a ship of the line with a flag at the main, I propose placing the *Asia* abreast of her, with the *Genoa* and *Albion* next to the *Asia*; and I wish that His Excellency Rear-Admiral Count Heiden will have the goodness to place his squadron next in succession to the British ships of the line.
>
> The Russian frigates in this case can occupy the Turkish ship next in succession to the Russian ships of the line; the English frigates forming alongside such Turkish vessels as may be on the western side of the harbour abreast of the British ships of the line; and the French frigates forming in the same manner, so as to occupy the Turkish frigates, etc. abreast of the French ships of the line. If time permits, before any hostility is committed by the Turkish fleet, the ships are to moor with springs on the ring of each anchor. No gun is to be fired from the combined fleet without a signal being made for that purpose, unless shot be fired from any of the Turkish ships, in which case the ships so firing are to be destroyed immediately.
>
> The corvettes and brigs are, under the direction of Captain Fellows, of the *Dartmouth*, to remove the fire vessels into such a position as will prevent their being able to injure any of the combined fleet. In case of a regular battle ensuing, and creating any of that confusion which must necessarily arise out of it, it is to be observed that, in the words of Lord Nelson, '*no captain can do very wrong who places his ship alongside that of an enemy.*'—Edward Codrington, Vice-Admiral."

✶✶✶✶✶✶

Note:—It was known that a number of French officers were in the enemy's ships, and to these Admiral de Rigny addressed a letter of warning.

******

The combined fleet made an attempt to stand into Navarino on the 19th of October, but the wind was too light and the current too strong to enable them to effect their purpose. On the following day, however, at about two o'clock in the afternoon, the allied squadrons passed the batteries at the entrance to the harbour to take up their anchorage. The Turkish ships lay moored in the form of a great crescent, with springs upon their cables, the large ones presenting their broadsides towards the centre, and the smaller craft filling up the intervals between them. The allied fleet was formed in the order of sailing in two columns, the British and French forming the starboard or weather line, and the Russian the lee column.

Sir Edward Codrington, in the *Asia*, led in, closely followed by the *Genoa* and *Albion*, and anchored in succession close alongside a line-of-battle ship flying the flag of the *Capitana Bey*, another ship of the line, and one of the large double-banked frigates, each thus having her proper opponent in the front line of the enemy's fleet. The four ships to windward, which formed a portion of the Egyptian squadron, were allotted to Admiral de Rigny's vessels; and those to leeward, in the bight or hollow of the crescent, were to mark the stations of the whole Russian squadron, the ships of their line covering those of the English line, and being followed by the frigates of their division.

Admiral Codrington had been very express in his instructions that no gun should be fired until some act of open hostility was committed by the Turks, and this order was strictly carried out. The three English ships were permitted to pass the batteries, and proceeded to moor in their respective stations with great celerity. But upon the *Dartmouth* sending a boat to one of the six fire vessels lying near the entrance to the harbour. Lieutenant Fitzroy and several seamen in her were killed by a volley of musketry. This immediately produced a responsive fire of musketry from the *Dartmouth* and likewise from *La Syrène*, the flagship of the French admiral, followed almost at once by the discharge of a broadside gun from one of the Egyptian ships, and in a breath almost the action became general.

The *Asia* was ranged alongside the ship of the *Capitana Bey*, and equally close to that of Moharem Bey, the commander of the Egyptian squadron. As neither of these ships opened upon the British flagship, notwithstanding the action was raging briskly to windward, Sir Edward Codrington withheld his fire. No interchange of hostilities between the vessels took place, therefore, for a considerable while after the *Asia* had returned the first volley of the *Capitana*; and, indeed, it was evidently the intention of the enemy to try and avoid a regular battle, for Moharem sent a message that he would not fire at all. Sir Edward Codrington, equally willing to avert bloodshed, sent the British pilot, Peter Mitchell, who also acted as interpreter, to Moharem with a message to the effect that it was no desire of his to proceed to extreme measures. As the boat went alongside, a discharge of musketry from the Egyptian ship killed Mitchell, and at the same time she opened fire upon the *Asia*. Upon this Admiral Codrington opened his broadside in real earnest, and so furious was this fire from his ship that in a very little while the ship of the *Capitana Bey* and that of Moharem were reduced to total wrecks, and went drifting away to leeward.

The French and Russian squadrons played their part gallantly and well. Sir Edward wrote to the Duke of Clarence:

> The conduct of my brother admirals, Count Heiden and the Chevalier de Rigny, throughout was admirable and highly exemplary.

In the British division the *Genoa* and *Albion* took their stations with magnificent precision, and maintained a most destructive fire throughout the contest. The *Glasgow*, *Cambrian*, and *Talbot* followed the example set by the intrepid Frenchman who commanded the *Armide*, which effectually destroyed the leading frigate of the enemy's line and silenced the batteries ashore. Captain Fellows, in the *Dartmouth*, succeeded in frustrating the designs of the fireships stationed near the mouth of the harbour, and preserved the *Syrène* from being burnt. The battle was maintained with unabated fury for above four hours, and owing to the crowded formation of the Ottoman fleet, and the close quarters at which the allied ships engaged them, the havoc and bloodshed were prodigious.

As the Turkish vessels were one after another disabled, their crews set them on fire and deserted them, and the lurid scene was rendered infinitely more terrible and weird by the flaming ships and incessant explosions among the huddled and shattered craft. The resistance of the enemy then began to sensibly slacken. By the time that night had closed down upon the scene, the Turkish fleet was so crippled as to cease any longer to be a menace to the violation of the Treaty.

Sir Edward. Codrington wrote:

> When I found that the boasted Ottoman's word of honour was

made a sacrifice to wanton, savage destruction, and that a base advantage was taken or our reliance upon Ibrahim's good faith, I own I felt a desire to punish the offenders.

And most terribly punished they were. Never did British arms bear part in a more complete and decisive victory. When the dusk of the Oriental evening, obscured into a pall-like gloom by the dense banks of smoke, descended over the terrific spectacle, the enemy's cannonade had grown feeble and scattered, and presently ceased altogether. Their vessels continued to blaze and to explode. Out of the proud fleet which in the noontide of that day had floated serenely upon the blue waters of Navarin harbour sixty ships were totally destroyed, and the remainder driven ashore in a shattered condition, with the exception of the *Leone*, four corvettes, six brigs, and four schooners, which remained afloat after the battle.

The carnage was frightful. According to the statistics furnished by Monsieur Letellier, the French instructor to the Egyptian Navy, to Commander Richards, of the *Pelorus*. the enemy's losses amounted to 3,000 killed and 1,109 wounded. The defeat, indeed, practically amounted to annihilation. At ten o'clock on the night of the battle, Sir Edward Codrington was writing an account of the victory to his wife:

> Well, my dear, the Turks have fought, and fought well too, and we have annihilated their fleet. We have lost poor Smith, Captain Bell, R.M., and many good men.... I am entirely unhurt, but the *Asia* is quite a wreck, having had her full allowance of the work.

The admiral, however, had a succession of marvellous escapes, and, indeed, almost seems to have borne a charmed life throughout the battle. Mr. Lewis, the boatswain of the *Asia,* while speaking to him early in the action, was struck dead. Mr. Smith, the master, was also shot down whilst talking with him. Sir Edward was a tall man, and in his uniform must have made a conspicuous figure upon the *Asia's* deck. Instead of his cocked hat he wore a round hat, which afforded better shade to his eyes; this was pierced in two places by bullet-holes. His coat-sleeve, which chanced to be rather loose, had two bullet-holes in it just above the wrist. A ball struck the watch in his fob and shivered it, but left him uninjured.

Tahir Pacha afterwards admitted to Mr. Kerigan, on board the *Blonde,* that he himself posted a company of riflemen to aim at the British admiral and shoot him if they could.

THE BATTLE WAS MAINTAINED WITH UNABATED FURY FOR ABOVE FOUR HOURS

The combined fleets quitted the harbour of Navarino on the 25th of October, having tarried awhile, unmolested, to repair damages. They were suffered to depart by the Turks without the firing of a single shot, although it had been quite expected that the batteries would open upon them as they passed the harbour mouth. On the 3rd of November they arrived at Malta. Here they spent some considerable time in refitting. For his services Sir Edward Codrington received the Grand Cross of the Bath; the King of France conferred upon him the Grand Cross of the Military Order of St. Louis; and the Emperor Nicholas of Russia, in an autograph letter, bestowed upon him the rare honour of wearing the second class of the Military Order of St. George.

Navarino was fought without any declaration of war, and the news of hostilities created great surprise in England. Many questions were asked in Parliament as to whether the British commander-in-chief had done wisely to treat the Turks as enemies, and there was much vacillation displayed by the weak government—Lord Goderich's—then in power. In the following June Sir Edward Codrington received a letter of recall from Lord Aberdeen, dated at the Foreign Office, London, May, 1828. It was a most elaborate document of twenty paragraphs, embodying a number of charges of misconception and actual disobedience of his instructions, and concluded:

> His Majesty's Government have found themselves under the necessity of requesting the Lord High Admiral to relieve you in the command of the squadron in the Mediterranean.

He left Malta for England on September 11th, amid the hearty regret of his companions-in-arms, and arrived home in the *Warspite* on the 7th of October, 1828. A revulsion of public feeling had meanwhile taken place during the interval—indignation at his recall and general reprobation of the injustice with which he had been treated. The Duke of Wellington's ministry was now in office. His Grace summoned Sir Edward to an interview, but seems to have behaved in a very cavilling manner. The pride and sense of honour of the fine old naval officer were deeply injured by the treatment he was receiving from a country to whose annals he had just added fresh laurels. His resentment of the injustice done him is well illustrated by the following anecdote:—

About a year after he had been recalled, Sir Edward Codrington was present at a party given by Prince Leopold, when the Duke of Wellington came up to him and said: "I have made arrangements by which I am enabled to offer you a pension of £800 for your life."

The admiral's answer was ready, and immediate:

> I am obliged to your Grace, but I do not feel myself in a position to accept it. . . . I cannot receive such a thing myself while my poor fellows who fought under me at Navarin have had no head-money, and have not even been repaid for their clothes which were destroyed in the battle.

The duke remonstrated, said there was no precedent for head-money, and insisted that, as the pension was bestowed by the king. Sir Edward could not refuse it. But refuse it he did, stoutly and resolutely.

Shortly afterwards one of the duke's political friends inquired: "What are you going to do with Codrington?"

"Do with him!" answered the duke, "what are you to do with a man who won't take a pension?"

But time rights most things; and Sir Edward Codrington lived to see full honour accorded to him. and those who had fought under him at the Battle of Navarino.

THE BELGIAN WAR OF INDEPENDENCE
1830-31

Brussels, August-September 1830

By John Augustus O'Shea

It is told of Charles X. of France that he took the composer Auber aside early in 1830, and complimented him on his work *La Muette di Portici*, which had been recently produced. It vividly represented the revolt of the *lazzaroni* at Naples, and their mad attempt at freedom under the leadership of Masaniello. There was genius in it, and His Majesty felt that he must do the great little Norman some service—probably make him director of his court concerts—but he told him confidentially, "From this day forth I shall expect you to bring out the *Muette* very seldom." He was wise in his premonition. The tirades of Masaniello were too warm. They hastened the riot which led Brussels into a successful rising a few months afterwards. Perhaps the Bourbon monarch thought that the music of the Neapolitan fisherman might bring his reign in Paris to a like violent ending.

They say that everything in France ends with a song, as sometimes it begins. "The *Marseillaise*" heralds most insurrections, and surely a masterly opera might drive a king out of the country, as Lord Wharton's rhyme of "Lillibulero" hurried on the revolution of 1688 in England.

After the fall of Napoleon, Belgium was attached to Holland as a dyke against future encroachments by France, and the two countries got the name of the Kingdom of the Netherlands. The union was ill-assorted. There was a difference of race, of religion, and of temperament. An amalgamation of the nations was attempted and voted by a pretended majority, which declared that Belgium had adopted the fundamental law of the kingdom. But there were many flaws in this agreement. The Dutch language was exclusively adopted, and public careers shut out against two-thirds of the Belgians. Judicial reforms were adjourned, exorbitant imposts were exacted, subsidies granted to Belgian industry were lavished on intriguers from abroad. There was nothing alleged against the Dutch king, who was not an unjust man, and the Belgians, writhing against inequality, bore themselves with patience for fifteen years, and would longer had not an outbreak in the border State of France disturbed their composure.

Newspapers were silenced, and commented on French and Spanish affairs, leaving those at home for private interpretation. The minister, Van Maanen, introduced an obnoxious penal code, which was rejected, but its author remained in office. To the credit of the Belgians, not a single native was found to support the arbitrary conduct of the Government, but a Florentine and a forger, who had been sentenced at Lyons, Count Libry Bagnano, was the main auxiliary of Van Maanen at the press. A M. de Potter, who was conspicuous in his assertion of the rights of Belgium, was tried and sentenced to fine and subsequently to banishment, and this caused a profound dissatisfaction. The partisans of the "good king," nevertheless, announced the anniversary of his *fête*, and said it should be celebrated with the liveliest affection and enthusiasm.

The royal birthday was nearing. The events which threw the Belgian capital into such a ferment in August of that year were foretold by placards with red letters, secretly posted on the street corners and defining the following programme: "Monday, fireworks; Tuesday, illumination; Wednesday, revolution." The city was seething with political discontent, cries of "*Vive le Roi!*" were smothered in frequent hisses, and on the indicated Wednesday, August 22nd, the bill announcing the *Muette* was up, although warning had been given that the authorities had wished to forbid it through dread of disorders. The scene was memorable.

The young folk assembled as if they looked upon the representation as a triumph gained over the police and their supporters, and were prepared to applaud all the passages in favour of liberty and to hinder the fifth act from being played, as their desire was that the piece should close with the people in the ascendant, from the very opening of the doors the house was crowded by an eager audience, and those who had been unable to obtain tickets hung around the neighbourhood, awaiting what might happen if the fifth act were interrupted. That was their sole preoccupation at the time. The piece was admirably performed: the artists never declaimed with more animation. Shouts of "Bravo!" and elated salutes welcomed the spectacle of the

It was the Revolution—the smouldering embers which were soon to be roused into flame

revolt and the appeal to arms, every allusion was seized with quickness, and at the conclusion of the fourth act a portion of those present burst into the streets with cries of "Liberty!" These cries were repeated outside, and mingled with them were calls from groups of "Hurrah for Potter!" "Down with Van Maanen!" "Justice!"

Meanwhile, the fifth act was carried on peacefully until the close. While those in the Place de la Monnaie were filtering away through the adjoining streets, some youngsters gathered before the house of the *National*, the journal of Libry Bagnano, and began hooting the owners and editors by name. From outcries, they soon warmed to violence, paving-stones were wrenched from the ground, and the windows were shivered into fragments. Suddenly a voice was overheard advising them not to heed walls but go for Libry himself.

In an instant the street was deserted, amid yells for Libry the Rue de la Madeleine was rushed for, and his dwelling was tumultuously entered, but the bird had taken flight. It was high time, for the temper of the mob was visible by a broom with a running noose looped from it hanging from the second storey. Furniture of all kinds, clocks, mirrors, and bedding were sent flying through the windows and trodden under foot. One frantic fellow seized a dressing-gown of the fugitive Libry, and another a kettle.

Out of them they at once improvised a flag and a drum. Books and papers were shredded, and the streets covered as with a thick carpet by the wreck, and the cellar was penetrated, the wine handed out, and the liquor tossed off amid a rousing chorus. Then armed men began to show themselves in the assembly. It was the revolution—the smouldering embers which were soon to be roused into flame. Gun-makers' shops had been pillaged, pistols, poniards, and costly sabres were to be seen scattered about amidst the midnight rabble, and the armorial bearings and other marks of loyalty to the reigning family were torn from the warehouses of the royal tradesmen.

The civil and military authorities were aroused by the uproar. A detachment of grenadiers were marched into the street, when the less disorderly betook themselves homewards; but the more resolute and those worked to fits of madness by wine remained, and a struggle began at the top of the street. Two of the rioters were shot dead, and for the first time Belgian blood empurpled the roadway. Shortly before, the bulk of the rabble had gone towards the hotel of Van Maanen in the Sablon, and set about renewing their frenzied orgie. When the *gendarmerie* appeared, the crowd cried to them to remain neuter and no harm would be done to them. The *gendarmerie* obeyed, perhaps frightened by the sight of pikes and bayonets. But meanwhile trees were cut down in the Petit Sablon, barricades thrown up, and a mansion wantonly set fire to and damaged by the multitude, who only let the firemen approach to hinder the flames from spreading. The houses of General Vauthier, *commandant* of the place, of the director of the police, and of the king's *procureur* were attacked and ravaged almost simultaneously. The detested words of *roi* and *royal* were stripped from the walls or whitewashed over by those who were shortly before so vain of them.

At the sack of Libry's house a child picked up an ear-pendant, but a badly-dressed rioter saw him, and seized it and trampled it under foot without saying a word. Hatred, rather than plunder, was the motive of the masses. By degrees the young folk, as if sated with vengeance on property, diminished, but the number of the lower classes increased. They broke into the hotel of the provincial government, mistaking it for the seat of central government, smashed the furniture, burned the governor's carriage, and cast the archives into the sewers. Sundry citizens armed themselves and went to the posts held by the military, as the sole means to stop the effusion of blood.

The troops drew up in line of battle on the Grand Sablon, and in front of the palaces of the king and the princes. At the Cafe Suisse, in the Place de la Monnaie, a press of armed men entered to refresh themselves. Liquors were served to them in abundance. When a boy of fifteen asked for *faro*—a cheap, common beer—but was told it was not sold in the establishment, he lost his temper, clambered on a table, broke a chandelier, and discharged a musket at a mirror, splintering it into atoms. His example was followed by some companions, and the whole place would have been sacked but for the arrival of the *bourgeois* guard.

In other quarters the presence of the military exasperated the people. Numbers collected on the Grand Sablon, where the grenadiers and the *chasseurs* were ranged, and at six in the morning an officer ordered platoon firing, which soon led to bloodshed. Volleys were repeated at each instant, wounded began to be carried along the streets, the houses were shut and the windows packed with women and the inquisitive; faces grew wrathful, and cries of vengeance were fierce and common.

In the midst of the fever of the populace proclamations by the Regency were posted at corners promising reform, and appealing to the

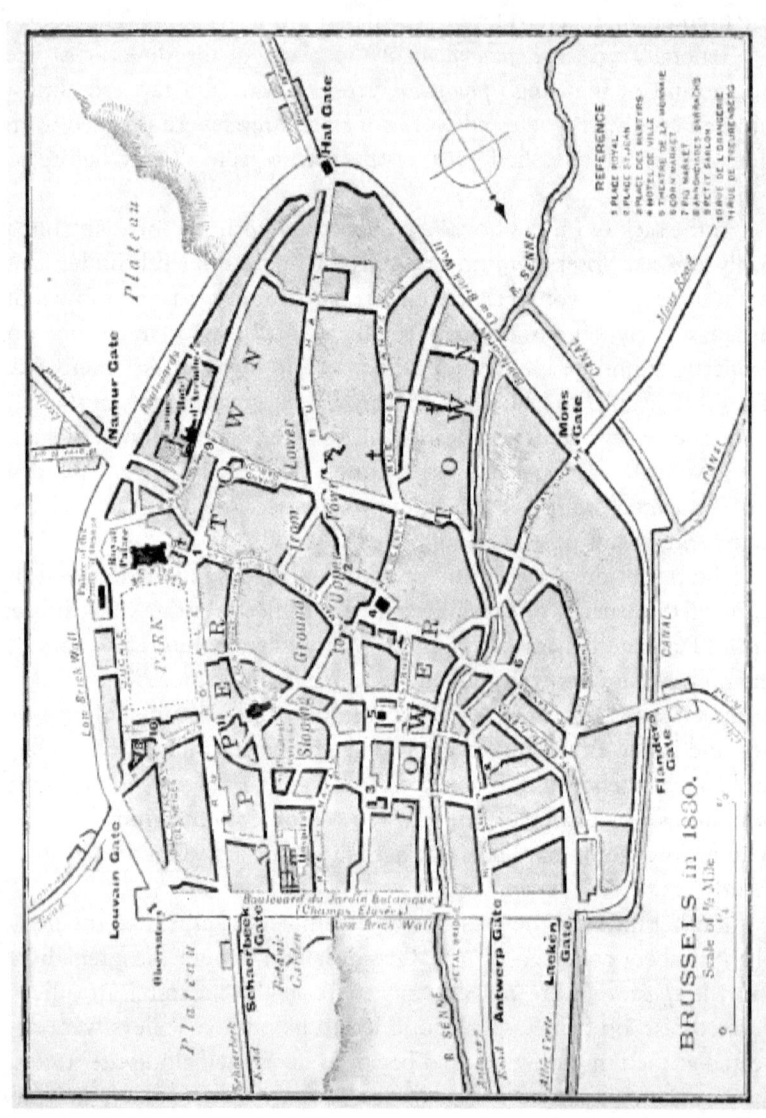

community to arm for the maintenance of order. About noon firing ceased. The troops fell back on the Place de Palais, and hostilities were interrupted. Groups furnished with all species of weapons paraded the thoroughfares. A French tricolour was visible for a few moments, but to avoid disturbances the ancient Brabant flag of red, yellow, and black was unfurled as the rallying signal, and these were adopted as the national colours. By a singular hazard an eclipse occurred about this period, and the reflection of the earth on the planet brought into relief a black disc edged with red on a yellow base. This was taken as a providential omen for the cause, and welcomed with universal acclamation as an auspicious token. Baron d'Hoogvorst accepted the command of the *bourgeois* guard, and forthwith began its organisation, which was barely got through in time to save from ruin the magnificent promenade intended for the illuminations.

Events were progressing rapidly throughout the country. The alarm had extended to various towns, where the population had formed civic guards. At Liege and Louvain, the citizens had seized the posts held by the troops; at Mons and Namur brute force was employed to subdue the alarm of the people. Ghent and Antwerp were the only places which disapproved of the agitators: it was thought they were seeking to plunge the country into misery and mourning.

At Ghent, the government distributed gold amongst the workmen, who thus got the hint to offer themselves to the highest bidder. The nation divided into two parties, the Liberals and the Ministerialists—the Belgians, or those for the southern provinces, and the Dutch, or the northerns. The dismissal of Van Maanen was loudly demanded, and the abolition of the taxes on grinding corn and slaughter of cattle. These were the points insisted on, or else there would be no submission.

Generals Abason, Vauthier, and De Bylandt were stationed with troops before the palaces, and kept aloft the Dutch flag, which resembles the French tricolour arranged horizontally. It was reported that the Dutch forces were advancing on Brussels and relieving the *bourgeois* from their care of the posts on the way. Reaction was feared by the Belgians, to whose mind the "three glorious days" of July at Paris were ever present. The Regency was reduced to a nullity. A deputation was sent to The Hague to ask for redress, and pending its return the troops on their road to the capital were countermanded. Two regiments of infantry with eight pieces of cannon were already at Malines, and a hussar regiment at Ghent, when they received orders to halt.

A VIEW IN BRUSSELS.

HÔTEL DE VILLE, BRUSSELS

The deputation consisting of several notables, such as Baron J. d'Hoogvorst, Count Felix de Merode (that restless family from whom our word "marauders" is derived), and Felix de Séeus, had their passports signed by General de Bylandt, and left with their proposal that the States-General should be at once convoked. But the troops kept tramping onwards from all parts of Holland, and the king's sons, the Prince of Orange and Prince Frederick, advanced by the cordon, ranged ladder-wise, as far as Vilvorde, at the gates of Brussels. The Prince of Orange from the palace of Laeken invited the *bourgeois* general, Baron d'Hoogvorst, with his friends, to come and confer with him. When they arrived the prince, clasping the buttonhole of M. Rouppe in his hand, said—

"Doubtless you know the penal code? You introduce to my headquarters illegal colours." (The black, red, and yellow of Brabant.)

"Prince," replied M. Rouppe, "those are the colours of the *bourgeoisie* whom I have the honour to represent; this badge is the mark of patriotism and not of rebellion."

Here that topic was dropped, and conference began.

Meantime the rumour had reached the capital that the princes had granted nothing and insisted that the flag and ribbons of Brabant should be laid aside. Immediately a multitude streamed towards the gates, trees were cut down, waggons requisitioned, water-vessels collected, streets unpaved, and barricades raised in all corners.

At ten that night, the 31st of August, a proclamation was posted on the Hotel de Ville intimating the princes' desire to enter at the head of the troops; but this was refused, and at last they were forced to accept the condition that they would come with their staff only and without troops, the Brussels delegates guaranteeing their personal safety.

On the morning of the entry, another fruitless attempt to have the Brabant colours removed was made. The civic guard, to the number of ten thousand, with the adopted rebel flags and guidons, marched to the bridge of Laeken. The Prince of Orange, with four of his officers, appeared. Not a cry was heard as arms were presented. His Royal Highness was much struck at the multiplicity of the barricades, and at the *phalanx* of butchers' boys, axe on shoulder, that preceded him as pioneers. A shout was raised of "*Vive le Prince! Vive la liberté!*" He lifted his hat and said, "Yes, my friends, live liberty; but why not say with me 'live the king'?" The call was saluted with a universal "'Sh!" Along the passage of the prince silence reigned. He regained his palace, stupefied at his cold reception. The deputation to The Hague returned that

The commandant fell dead with a bullet through his brain

evening with their report: it was so unfavourable that copies of it were snatched and cindered at the bayonet's point. The fermentation was growing, but no proper measure was taken to calm it.

The garrison was hunted from Louvain, and deputations of youth arrived at Brussels, and also from Liege, with five cases of arms. A proposal to separate north and south without other contact than dynasty was now made, and the Prince of Orange promised to convey it to his father, at The Hague. The troops, confined for ten days in the palaces, now left the city. At his arrival at Vilvorde, the prince heard that dragoons had left for Louvain. He issued countermands, but the people of Louvain had sallied out and repelled them, slaying their officer.

The king at length issued a tedious proclamation, full of the hackneyed sentiments which only vexed still more the Belgians, who resolved to establish a provisional government, and to declare frankly for secession. Brussels resumed its ordinary appearance; the "Brabançonne" was roared at the top of their voices by revellers in the taverns. The entire Walloon county, inhabited by the black-haired, French-speaking portion of the people, was awakening to a passionate yearning for liberty. The manifestoes of the king were derided. Still the Dutch troops were continuously moving. Namur was declared in a state of siege; Brussels was perpetually on the alert, and the advent of de Potter was invoked; skirmishers watched the environs for the approaching Dutch.

The Hotel de Ville was broken into by a disorderly crowd, and a store of Orange cockades discovered there; whereat there was an outcry of "Treason!" and the streets were paraded all night to the tuck of drum, and yells of "Down with the Hollanders!" News next day that the Liegeois had stormed the Chartreuse fortress which dominated their city, roused their courage. Brussels gave itself up to the people, who enrolled themselves, and talked of going out against the enemy. Companies of ill-dressed men, armed with pikes, forks, and knives, preceded by a herald armed with the rusty old sword of Saint Michel, were marshalled for the fray. Deserters from the Dutch Army, still in their uniforms, joined the ranks of their own countrymen.

By this hour, the troops had occupied ground at Dieghem and Ever to the causeway of Schaerbeek, at three-quarters of a league from Brussels. The tocsin was sounded, deep ditches were dug by the city gates, and pieces of cannon placed there, and the citizens mounted barricades and lined the entrenchments. Some of the volunteers went out to meet the troops, and near Dieghem there was an affair of outposts: several soldiers and two volunteers were killed. Prince Frederick was definitely drawing near and the entire population—men, women, and children—were in a state of defence. Vigilance was exercised to bar every reconnaissance of the enemy; and on Wednesday, the 23rd, a proclamation from the king, dated from Antwerp, was known at Brussels, stigmatising the "little number of the factious" who were striving at disorder, and stating at wearisome detail what he was going to do.

Two young men who left the Hotel de Ville to remonstrate with the terms of this proclamation were arrested at headquarters, and taken prisoners on the spot to Antwerp. There were desultory conflicts during the day, but it was plain that the time of palavering was over and the hour of stern action was at hand. Brussels was not fortified, its surrounding brick wall being low, and entrance was obtained there by eight gates. It was divided into two towns, the lower and the upper, or aristocratic, which contained the park, a spread of seventeen acres separated into three well-wooded alleys. The princes reckoned without the malcontents. They fancied they were a pack of silly fanatics, whose vapouring would be blown out with the first whiff of powder, like a guttering wick; and they made the mistake of going against this network of streets, sown with obstructions, with cavalry.

At day-dawn on the 23rd September, the alarm was given at the gates of Schaerbeek and of Flanders, that the Dutch troops were advancing in serried columns. At seven the tocsin rang out from the church steeples, and kept up their clangour until the fire had ceased in the evening. Before eight o'clock Colonel Boekorven presented himself at the Flanders gate at the head of 800 infantry, 300 hussars, and 4 pieces of cannon. A score of defenders of the post fired and drew back behind the barricades, which soon proved insufficient to cover them, and were speedily levelled by the enemy's pioneers. Rushing to about one hundred and fifty paces from the Pork Market, the Dutch troops had to halt in front of a stronger and more obstinately contested barrier.

Dr. Tremper, followed by some other *bourgeois* of the town, came forward, and, as *parlementaire*, called upon the military to retire. Threatening language was exchanged, and a discharge from the barricade flung into confusion the foremost ranks of the cavalry, whose commandant fell dead with a bullet through his brain. The infantry replied with volleys from platoons, which did no injury as they were aimed too high, in order to avoid the hussars in front, who were still in their saddles. But the conflict thickened into a regular din, the enraged population laving hold of everything they could procure to turn into weapons of offence. From the windows and the roofs, paving-stones, furniture, logs of timber, iron bars, stoves, and even quicklime, hailed on the soldiers. Horses and men were crushed; the enemy's ranks were flung into disorder, and the Belgian skirmishers, after a lively fusillade, charged with the bayonet, and pursued the enemy beyond Molenbeek.

At the gate of Laeken, which was garrisoned by forty *bourgeois*, the first cannon-shot was fired by the enemy. The high and strong barricades were exposed to cannon, and enfiladed from the Botanical Garden. The *bourgeois* retired to the Champs Elysées, and lost three of theirs in the BelleVue Hotel. But the enemy did not deem it advisable to try to enter the city, and withdrew without attempting a serious attack, and set off to rejoin the army of Prince Frederick, behind the Botanical Garden.

The Schaerbeek Gate was considered favourable to the decisive onslaught. The army corps which was put in motion numbered more than seven thousand combatants. At the instant of attack there were but sixty citizens at the position, the lost sentinels comprised, and these had no recognised chief. By degrees their effective was doubled, and the gallant Stildorf chosen captain. The three advanced barricades, too feeble and unarmed with guns, offered no resistance.

Sixteen pieces of artillery swept the Rue Royale for its whole length. About nine o'clock the grenadiers and the *chasseurs*, estimated at a strength of 1,800, under the orders of General Bylandt, doubled forward into the street, but they were brought to a short stop by the sustained discharge by the patriots at the two barricades of Treurenberg, and doggedly responded. Fire not less violent poured out from the Rue de Louvain, and two companies of grenadiers were detached to storm that thoroughfare and make a junction with the troops who had entered by the gate of Louvain. Arrived at the corner of the Rue de l'Orangerie, they were caught by a murderous fire, and made an effort to retrace their steps. But it was too late. The ground was swarmed over by the *bourgeois*, and, coming on to the noon hour, 150 grenadiers, realising that they ran the risk of being shot to the last private, lay down their arms and surrendered. They were led off prisoners to the barracks of the firemen.

Pretty well a similar scene passed at the Rue Notre Dame des Neiges. Attacked on the Place d'Orange, the Dutch detachment, after having sustained serious losses, arrived at the park and established itself there, occupying the streets in the neighbourhood and the palaces.

The attack of the gate of Louvain was simultaneous with those of Flanders, Laeken, and Schaerbeek. At the opening cannon-shot the very weak post of *bourgeois* retired by the Rue de Louvain, knocking over a number of the enemy by a desultory but destructive fire. The gate was forced by *cuirassiers* and lancers under General Tripe, who, joyous at his entry into the city, brandished his sabre as he shouted "Forward, my children, at the gallop to the Grand' Place!" The 700 horsemen hurried into the Rue de Louvain, but formidable barricades barred their rush, and, instead of continuing to the Grand' Place, the entire corps turned harum-scarum for the Namur Gate without having succeeded in disengaging the grenadiers, who were cornered and hustled in the prolongation of the Rue de Louvain.

By the interior of the city the Dutch arrived towards the Namur Gate. Seeing that its defenders retired upon Ixelles, they re-entered by the gate of Hal, and started to occupy the gate of Namur. The Dutch several times advanced to the *Athénée* (the military school), but the bullets and paving-stones forced them to move backward with loss.

At this crisis, the aspect of Brussels was woeful. All seemed lost. No defenders were seen but a few isolated knots, and these without concerted action or determined leaders. The grape-shot whistled through the city, the bullets positively spattered, the quick-repeated volleys of the sections filled the air with dismay. From four points of attack—the Hal Gate, the Place de Louvain, near Saint Gudule (the well-known cathedral church on the slope of a declivity), the Mountain of the park, and the Place Royale—all held by artillery, successive and sustained deafening reports thundered. The peals, lugubrious and redoubled, of the tocsin swelled over the brattle of the drums beating the *générale*. The rumour circulated that the gates of Laeken and Flanders were forced, and that the enemy was advancing by the lower town. About half-past eleven shopkeeper and artisan no longer believed resistance impossible. The bravery of the men placed at the gate of Louvain, the centre of the enemy's communications, decided the impression of confidence.

The ninth division of the Dutch forces, following at a distance the drums of the royal guard, which was directing its passage to the park, was cut and compelled to go back and try the route by the Schaerbeek Gate and the *boulevards*. This manoeuvre forced the detachment in the Rue de Louvain to capitulate. The post of Treurenberg was now rendered impregnable. Afar off the fusillade at the Observatory, held by fifty *bourgeois*, could be heard, still vigorous in its defence. Stildorf was grievously wounded in the leg before the Botanical Garden. The cry "To arms!" was heard on every side, and volunteers entrenched themselves in the houses of the Place Royale. The main barricade between the hotels Belle Vue and the Amitié was manned by the volunteers from Namur, the company from Tournai led by Renard and the best-armed of the Bruxellois, as well as the stone balustrade which extended beside the head of the Rue Royale. The citizens planted a piece of ordnance at this point, which commanded the palace.

Towards the Metal Bridge a crippled hero distinguished himself. This was a notable figure, one whose name is destined to go down linked with the imperishable renown of those crucial days. Charlier of Liège, surnamed "The Wooden-legged," was more active and skilful than most whose limbs were perfect. His zeal and address were only equalled by his cool and resolute bearing. On all points, he seemed to multiply himself, inspiring his comrades with his courage and carrying panic amidst the ranks of the enemy. Where his gun was needed, there sprang the *"Jambe de Bois"* as if by instinct. This limping warrior hobbled on the road to glory, thoughtless of risk and spurning fatigue, as if he were charmed and revelled in the tempest of lead, brushing through the fumes of pungent vapour as if they were his natural element. At the entrance of the park he stood with his trusty gun, crammed to the muzzle with grape, and blazed away at all opponents.

At midday, the Dutch were checked and paralysed, the successes gained at the gates of Laeken and Flanders ran from mouth to mouth, and the first shout of victory was heard in Brussels. The scene of the city at the climax of the stress of the struggle was a genuine pandemonium, recalling some of the terrible pictures fixed on canvas by the weird brush of Weirtz, who painted the local gallery, mad and ghastly. Old men and youths, rich and men of the plebs, broadcloth and blouse, panted and perspired at the carnage; women tended the wounded or picked lint, children shrieked at the novel excitement of the elders, blood was heated with the rapture of combat, and the groans of the stricken were forced out of hearing by the noise of curses or transport, the screams of wrath and the dull overpowering report of bursting gunpowder or the angry bang of brass field-pieces rising over the racket of falling masonry, the rataplan of echoing drum, and the oft-recurring jangle of the tocsin.

At half-past three the Dutch set alight the barrack of the *Annonciades*, and at sight of the rising smoke the alarm was raised that powder was stored there, and that they would all be blown up. Look alive! The fury of the citizens redoubled. The aged, the feeble, females, and even the very urchins rushed upon the incendiaries, who fell back and were repulsed towards the Place of Orange. The fire was got under. Three-fourths of the barrack was saved, and the barrels of gunpowder carried back almost within reach of the licking flames. In the interior of the town by this time all the barricades and windows were frowning with gun-barrels. It was as if every house was a fortress and every fortress lined with loopholes spouting death. At half-past six the inviolate *"Jambe de Bois"* had his cannon rolled towards the Place Royale. The Liège captain, the dauntless Pourbaix, hoisted a flag in the middle of the square, and held it erect and scatheless amid a storm of solid balls, large and small.

After the night's interval, a dry fine morning arose on the 24th in comparative peace. The tocsin no longer smote the upper spaces. There was a sort of dangerous tranquillity in the town, where streets were besieged and defended house by house. The three barricades of attack were strengthened against the risks of new assault. Reinforcements of Walloons arrived during the night by the gates of Hal and Anderlecht. And in the morning posters signed by M. d'Hoogvorst were visible making known that the inhabitants of Louvain and of Tirlemont had beaten back and compelled to flight the regular troops of Holland, sent against them by the Prince Frederick the previous evening.

The tidings of this double victory added to the ardour and confidence of the Bruxellois. There were irregular fights all day, and numerous casualties occurred here and there through the town, in spite of every care that was exercised. An unhappy mother passing in the Rue d'Isabelle, bundling her two infants in her arms, was mortally wounded with them, struck by shivering splinters. Of course, this was unintentional; but such incidents happen in every conflict of the kind, and the innocent are marked down for death as relentlessly as those with uplifted weapons.

Amongst the combatants there was a fair proportion of killed—upwards of sixty, and thrice the number wounded. The losses of the enemy were set down at 200. The inhabitants were prompt in their succour: lint, medicaments, and food were supplied in abundance. The apothecaries cheerfully gave up their drugs. There was no thought of charge. Comfort came forward to those among the defenders who were mutilated or expiring. Many brave young fellows, pale and

Where his gun was needed, there sprang the "jambe de bois"

blood-streaked, were carried to their doors on mattresses or hastily-made stretchers. And yet in addition to the ordinary hospitals which were already beginning to be overrun with cases, there were eighteen provisional ambulances established in various public buildings or private residences. Still there was high hope, and, in answer to M. Engelspach, who made inquiries, it was reported by the bakers and flour-merchants that there were enough provisions in the city for ten days to come.

On the second day, the bombardment of the capital was resolved on. At four in the afternoon Prince Frederick, from his camp at the gate of Schaerbeek, placed on a height behind the palace of the Prince of Orange a battery of shell-guns (mortars and howitzers) in a position to batter the town. The shells, launched to about two hundred, luckily did not create much damage. Nevertheless, the sinister rumour circulated that from the Dutch camp fire-balls were sent and Congreve rockets, and naturally panic seized certain quarters. At the set of the sun both parties occupied much the same positions as on the evening before. At night, when dusk should have been succeeded by darkness, various conflagrations lit up the town, and the noise of cannon and crackling musketry, and the jerky clash of the tocsin swirled in echo from every point (if the compass.

The people were kept busy helping to bandage the wounded and save the furniture from the burning houses. But there were others, not so weary of the work, who were strenuous to pile up barricades in every quarter where there was any possibility of their being attacked in turn. The *estaminets* and drinking-shops were thronged—the "*Aigle*," for example—and the exploits of the day recounted, and precautions taken that the terrain so valiantly disputed should not be yielded a second time to the surprise of the foe without defence.

After the cessation of fire—that is to say, between ten and midnight—a proclamation was read at the Hotel de Ville to the roll of the drum, which contained a passage counselling the *bourgeois* to redouble their vigilance and to augment barricade by barricade: "Stones thrown from the windows achieved half the revolution of Paris." This gave the cue to the patriots. In several districts water was boiling at once; gallons of quicklime were laid in; the wives of the workmen, mechanics, and day-labourers gathered their husbands' biggest and weightiest tools, picks and crowbars, sledges and hammers; wheels, ladders, hogsheads, tables, barrels, and barrows were raised to garrets and high rooms. M. Juan van Halen—one of the Belgian family emigrated to

Spain—was appointed General-in-Chief, and it was determined that the assault on the park should be delivered on the following day, the close of the week.

At sunrise, it was remarked that the Dutch troops guarded their positions intact, but had made some insignificant steps forward on the side of the streets of Namur, the Orangerie and Louvain. Prince Frederick's cavalry were patrolling along the line of inner *boulevards*, ready to go to the assistance of the threatened points. At four o'clock, just as the first signs of dawn were pencilling the sky, a few musket-shots were heard. Some grenadiers, crawling out from the park and the palace, attempted to get possession of the Belle Vue Hotel, whose defenders they imagined to be asleep. But Pellabon and Vereecken, with three men only, were on the alert and repulsed the enemy, forcing him to retreat after a loss of several. At six the fusillade recommenced to tuck of drum and the call of the alarm-bell to all men free, willing, and able to take up arms.

At the Town House an offer of armistice was made on the part of Prince Frederick, but rejected, as it did not seem distinct. There was a want of frankness about it, and accordingly it was received with suspicion. At ten two pieces of cannon arrived at a gallop in the Rue Ducale, unlimbered, and swept the ground with several discharges to the right and left of Wauxhall. At half-past ten the firing was redoubled, and the park, the Rue Ducale, and the *boulevards* were wrapped in curtains of smoke. The houses trembled with the vibration, and the reports of the cannon drowned the clanging of the bells. The mortars behind the Prince of Orange's palace were silent as if in a lethargy during the day; but a flying battery of the Hollanders, composed of six light pieces posted in the park, revealed itself at the entrance of the alleys and vomited grape on the Belgian skirmishers, amid ferocious outcries.

Soon the men of Liège raised impatient shouts that the park should be attacked with the bayonet—that it mattered not how many were the enemies: it would be time enough to count them when they were dead. Their enthusiasm inflamed some who heard them, and a stripling from Waterloo, bearing the Brabant flag, penetrated the park. A body of twenty brave fellows followed at his heels. But shortly they were decimated by cannon-shots and obliged to fall back; but the flag was planted anew on the barricade of Treurenberg. A large body of lancers—some say twelve squadrons—trotted about mid-day into the Rue Ducale, dismounted, and flung themselves into the palace of the States-General, occupied by the Dutch infantry, who stood in the most urgent need of reinforcement.

The fight was now maintained with obstinacy by the patriots. They were getting into the spirit of the thing, and vengeance sparkled in their eyes and flushed from their cheeks. The Dutch wounded sought refuge under every roof where they could obtain a shelter, and in their utter state of demoralisation themselves exaggerated their own casualties. Officers affirmed that half of the army had perished; that they had been shot from the windows of the Rue Royale without being able to see to reply; that, not having it in their power to carry away their dead, they had to cast their corpses into the wells in the park; that the dressings were applied to the wounded in the three palaces, or they were transported to Vilvorde when that was possible; and that already since the opening of this fateful day forty waggons packed with poor wretches had left. The order to "Cease fire" was rung out by the Dutch buglers at three, in the Rue Ducale.

Down on the *boulevards*, towards the gate of Namur, there was a fierce combat about noon. The volunteers had succeeded in mounting a piece of ordnance there, which was taken by an irruption of Dutch lancers but recaptured in turn by its own gunners, who lost two men before they could wrest it from the enterprising foe. In all the dwellings in this locality the fighting was bitter. The troops were driven by the skirmishing insurgents from every spot where they thought to ensure safety. This determined pursuit—the most implacable sort of warfare—was carried on, above all, on the *boulevard* of Waterloo, at the exterior walls of the Petits Carmes, at the Hotel d'Aremberg, and by the whole length of the Rue aux Carmes. Everywhere that the soldiers pushed in they smashed, looted, and tried to set fire to the houses. The truth was these regulars were having their heads turned in their rage, and were loosening and forgetting the bonds of discipline.

At the Place Royale, the conflict was well sustained. Sharpshooters were stationed on the eaves of the houses commanding the Rue Royale. The volunteers from Liège, from the cover of ambuscades, kept up a fire on the palace and the park with their artillery, while the enemy's cannon did not cease to direct its assaults on the Hotel Belle Vue, from which Pellabon and Vereecken retorted on their ranks with well-aimed gun-shots. The travellers who had sought safety in the vaults of the hotel began to apprehend that the ceiling would crumble on them, or that it might take fire. Under the conduct of Pellabon they quitted their asylum, and traversed the Place Royale to find a refuge elsewhere. Midway a lady found herself ill, but the ready Vereecken lifted her on his broad shoulders, and bore her along in safety to the Palais de l'Industrie. Juan van Halen decided to form a column of attack on the Montagne de la Cour, and supported by the battery of Charlier, of the wooden leg—who was still here, there, and everywhere that his aid was most required—to attempt an entrance into the park. This attack did not succeed, although tried as one o'clock was nearing; but Charlier, acting under the orders of his superior, advanced his piece opposite the Amitié Coffee House, and pestered the enemy with such a pestilent shower of grape that he did not show his nose out of the fosses of the park.

A heavy and drenching rain falling, and some inevitable disorders occurring, hindered the execution of a real bayonet attack. About two a battalion of grenadiers attempted to come out, but met by a well-nourished fire, was driven back without having been able to do more than reinforce its comrades, who held the staircase of the Library and some houses of the Rue Isabelle. One hundred and twenty of the Belgians were put *hors de combat* on this day, while the casualties of the Dutch were estimated at far more—it was reckoned that they lost nigh three hundred. Over sixty carts conveying wounded passed the gates of Louvain and Schaerbeek. The great hospitals of St. Pierre, St. Jean, and the Minimes were full at the close of the day's engagements. Those set up at the Chapels of Sainte Anne, of the Madeleine, and the Salasar had to close their doors against further inmates, their accommodation being strained to excess. Before night fell twenty-seven provisional ambulances were working.

Reinforcements began arriving from country' towns in the evening; each contingent had a flag at its head, and each volunteer wore the initials of his commune on his cap. Volunteers from Nivelles recounted that the Communal Guard had fired upon their townsmen, slaying three, and wounding seventeen.

The Sabbath rose with the 26th, and from the morning the church bells rang for mass. The park, which was the battle-ground, as if arranged, had a placid appearance after all the turbulence. Not a person was to be seen there. The Dutch skirmishers were immobile in the Rue Ducale. There was no change in the situation from previous days. Between eight and nine the enemy concentrated his reserves and brought together his artillery, as if about to undertake a twofold attack on the Place and the Rue Royale. His lines were marked by a screen of *tirailleurs*, to catch the notice of the patriots who were holding themselves in preparation to check the enemy, at the entrance to the Rue Royale.

Their volunteers were hidden in the houses or hotels opposite the park, and were not to fire until they had received a signal. They were strongly posted at the Belle Vue Hotel, the Amitié Coffee House, and Benard's establishment. Pellabon and Vereecken, of Brussels, took up their station there, while the volunteers from Wavre and Gosselies lay in ambush near, their muskets at the ready. One of them—M. de Lescaille, of Wavre, a very keen sportsman, who had acquired quite a local renown as a dead shot—placed himself in the gutters of the Belle Vue, and laid low to his own trigger more than twenty Dutch grenadiers as they popped their heads out of the ravine of the park. Three of his friends kept him supplied with loaded muskets as they were wanted: this fortunate fellow escaped with a slight wound. At ten the fracas became terrible in the Rue Royale. The skirmishers with the cannon posted in the Rue Ducale kept up a constant crepitation across the park, and particularly in the lateral alleys.

About mid-day M. Pletinckx, chief-of-the-staff, who held his own stubbornly with a single gun in the barracks of the *Annonciades*, advanced alone as a *parlementaire*, in the Rue de Louvain. He was arrested and led prisoner to the headquarters of the prince, and sent thence to Antwerp. At the elbow where the Rue de l'Orangerie intersects the Rue de Louvain a barricade was raised, which by an artful device held the soldiers in check. The *bourgeois*, aided by women, mostly wives of workmen, managed to make two puppets of straw, after the fashion of the effigy of Guy Fawkes on the 5th of November in London: these they stuck up, dressed like scarecrows, on the edge of the barricade, and each time the enemy fired, the head of the figure was lowered with a cord. These combatants of straw, who were the butt of the enemy's discharges, kept the soldiers diverted by the belief that they had knocked over an antagonist each time that the make-believe head was pulled out of range.

As the shades of evening descended the barricade was deserted, but the Hollanders cautiously approached it, and incontinently ran as they descried the mannequins on the watch. In the Rue du Marais, and elsewhere, the same ruse was employed, and with a similar success. In the morning, the skirmishers, pursued by a battalion, descended the boulevard of Schaerbeek, and were obliged to set fire to the bridge of the Senne to defend and maintain themselves at the two barricades of the Rue St. Pierre. The Dutch soldiers enkindled the houses at

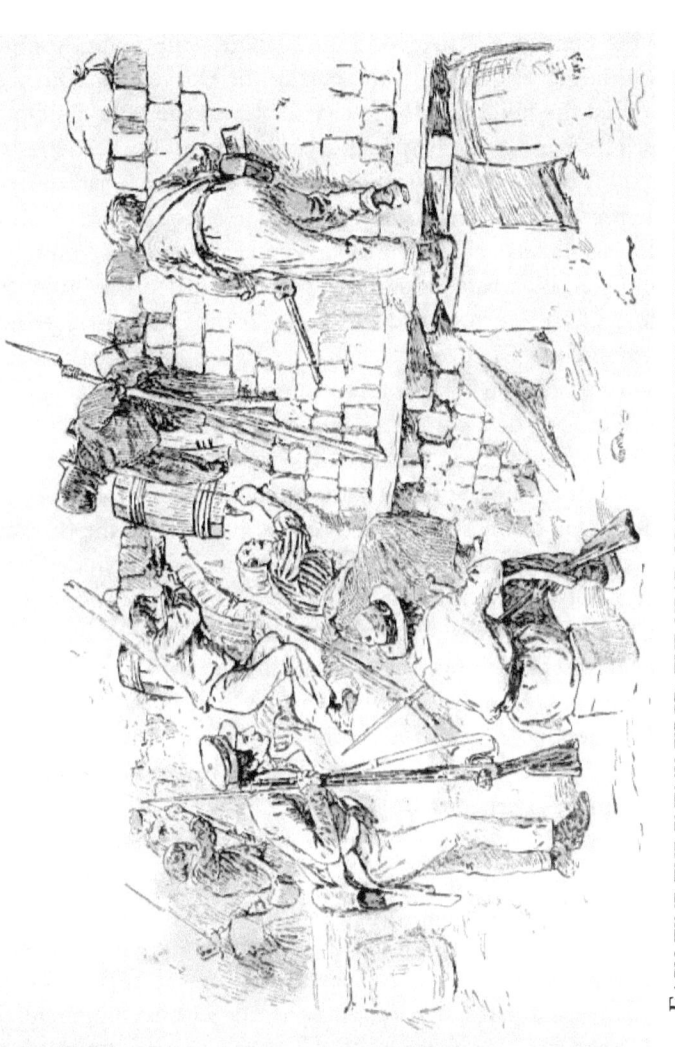

EACH TIME THE ENEMY FIRED, THE HEAD OF THE FIGURE WAS LOWERED WITH A CORD.

the corner of the Schaerbeek street and the *boulevard*, and about two o'clock, as the flames did not spread rapidly enough to their taste, they carried torches to them separately; then, posted in the Botanical Garden, they kept up a continual fusillade to prevent aid from being carried to the victims of the fire.

Eighteen new houses were a prey to the flames, and sixteen were completely burned: the fire continued far into the night. About six in the evening the shells from the rear of the palace of the Prince of Orange fired the buildings of the city stables, in the Rue des Douze-Apôtres. The conflagration spread with great rapidity, as there were 7,000 trusses of hay or straw stocked there: the halters had to be cut from the horses, who forthwith started out in terror from their heated and flame-encircled stables. The Belle Vue Hotel and the Amitié Café were occupied by a battery of guns which enfiladed the outlet from the park, and a piece was held in reserve at the Metal Bridge. Three of the volunteers of Leuze presented themselves as messengers at the foremost of the enemy's barricades, the officer telling them they need have no fear. One of them then summoned the Dutch troops to surrender. The officer refused; and as the *parlementaires* retired, a round of grape was sent at them at thirty yards without effect.

Firing began again in the Rue Royale, and at nine the discharges on both sides were thin, as if the powder was being husbanded. At ten the cannon of the Hollanders made its voice heard, and the left set itself in motion, and the skirmishers advanced in front of the park, but the general discharge from the Belgian lines compelled them to retreat; at the same time the volunteers at the Belle Vue Hotel hindered the deployment by a quick fire on the first under-works of the park.

Lurid masses of smoke appeared towards the left, the Hotel de Torringthon was burned to dislodge the Dutch, their grenadiers were chased, and the Rue Royale was in the power of the Revolution. The battery of *obusiers* at the palace of the Prince of Orange resumed the bombardment at noon, but without result. It was a terrible spectacle in the park: blood streamed in the alleys, corpses were prone here and there, hardly covered with a few leaves; branches of trees, statues, and railings hampered paths; here was a barricade of benches, there a redoubt, heaped from half a dozen dead horses. The houses were riddled with shot and bullets, and everywhere floated the flag of Brabant—pledge of success and liberty.

This was the most murderous day's work yet—there was more desperation and contempt for death. Two hundred patriots fell, and were interred in the Place St. Michel, which took the name of the Place of Martyrs; the losses of the enemy were counted at thrice the number. Seeing themselves in peril of being surrounded, the Hollanders stole away at four in the morning of Monday, abandoning the walls. The fight in the capital was over; the victory of Belgian Independence was assured.

The Polish-Russian War
1830-31

The Battle of Warsaw
6-7 September 1831
By A. S. Krause

Throughout the summer of 1831 the city of Warsaw lay like a city of the dead. Its magnificent palaces appeared as though deserted; its streets were lonesome, and the few who ventured from within their dwellings moved about as though smitten.

Although not declared, Warsaw lay in a state of siege. The struggle for liberty, long maintained by the brave nation of Poles, was drawing to a close, and all felt that though hitherto victorious in the field, they must fall before the countless hordes of Russia in the end.

There had been a rising in the previous year. Undeterred by the knowledge that they were a handful against millions, and encouraged by the recent examples of France and Belgium, the Poles of Warsaw had risen in revolt against the despotism of Russia, as personified by Constantine, the ferocious governor of their city.

The direct cause of the outbreak was, as is usual in such cases, slight—a bogus trial on a popular officer for an imaginary offence. A verdict contrary to the weight of evidence, a street row among the military students, a dozen of whom were promptly flogged with the knout, while others were imprisoned, and the mischief was done. The young Poles rose in November, and without ceremony broke into the prison and freed their comrades. The gates of the palace were forced, and the 'governor sought; but without success, he having escaped. But while Constantine evaded the vengeance of his victims, his lieutenants fared otherwise, and many of them fell into the hands of their relentless enemies. For the moment, the Polish capital was in the hands of the Poles.

The Russian aristocracy disappeared, and at every street corner meetings were held at which the proceedings were constantly interrupted by cries of "*Niech zyie Polska*"—Poland for ever! This state of things continued throughout the winter of 1830. The ice-bound *steppes* forbade the Russians taking action. But the *Czar* vowed vengeance, and he kept his vow. In the first days of spring a large army was despatched against the rebel Poles under General Chlopicki, who, while in command of the thirteenth and fourteenth Army Corps, had earned for his troops the nickname of the Lions of Varna. The war was waged to the death. The Russian troops, well drilled and ably commanded, elated with the successes of the past, met the untutored Polish soldiers with a confidence bred of conceit.

The Poles, imbued with a sense of patriotism, and recognising that it was to do or to die, fought each man for his own hand, neither giving nor expecting quarter, and the slaughter was frightful. Even at Ostralenka, where the Poles left seven thousand dead on the field, the Russian loss was over fifteen thousand; and at Waror the Poles took ten thousand Russian prisoners, besides a number of cannon, which were exhibited in the streets of Warsaw, amid the enthusiastic applause of the inhabitants.

After being beaten all along the line the Russian Army withdrew, leaving the flower of its surviving officers imprisoned in Warsaw, and for a while the Poles had rest. But only for a while. In the early summer, another army marched on the capital, and at the end of June General Paskewitsch, who had been specially chosen by the *Czar*, took the command. This officer enjoyed the personal friendship of the ruler of Russia, and he took the field with the express instruction from his master to teach the rebels a lesson which they would not forget. He lost no time in resuming operations, but changed his predecessor's plans. Hitherto, all attempts on Warsaw had been made from the right bank of the Vistula. With the exception of the Praga suburb the city lies on the left or south bank, so that to capture it from the north the Russians would have to fight their way across the Vistula either through the streets and across the bridges of Praga, or under the fire of the guns in the Polish works.

Paskewitsch decided upon making a flank march down the right bank of the river, crossing it near the Prussian frontier, where he had secretly arranged to obtain supplies and bridging material from the Prussian fortress of Thorn, and then marching up the south bank of the Vistula he could attack Warsaw on the side on which it was not protected by the broad river which had hitherto barred the Russian advance. The Polish Government was at this period presided over by

Old Town, Warsaw

The Jews' Market, Warsaw.

General Skryznecki, a patriot of good family and education, and a man of the highest principle. Skryznecki recognised the danger too late. He hurriedly occupied a strong position on the line of the Bzura River with 30,000 men, in the hope of barring the Russian advance; but on August 15th the Russians, in overwhelming force, drove the Poles from the river bank and forced them back upon Warsaw. Their city was now threatened by 60,000 troops, who cut them off from the country to the south of the Vistula, from which they had hitherto drawn supplies and reinforcements. While Paskewitsch thus hemmed in the Poles on the south, another Russian Army watched Praga; and thus, by the end of August, while the roads for miles round were guarded by Russian legions, the Poles found themselves shut in like rats in a trap.

And now for the first time the Poles realised their position. Surrounded by a relentless horde, their supplies cut off, they realised the futility of the claims of a just cause against the exigencies of necessity. The whole of the resources of Russia were against them; and while the sympathies of France and England went far to cheer the desperate band of patriots who yet fought for freedom, the fact that Prussia, though nominally a neutral state, was aiding the common enemy, was not reassuring. So far back as June this fact had been known, and General Skryznecki had written to the King of Prussia enumerating the various acts indulged in by his ministers, and demanding that they should cease. In this historic document the general proved that the Prussians were supplying the Russians with food from the storehouses at Thorn, that they had lent their skilled artillery to the Russians, that they had supplied ammunition and uniforms made in Prussia, and that most of the engineering works required by the Russians—including the bridge over the Vistula—had been executed by German engineers.

This letter was never answered, and Prussia continued in her breach of the laws of war, while the outlook in Warsaw became blacker every day. Nor were the dangers only from without. The Polish mob began to become turbulent, and necessitated the watching of soldiers who would have been better employed negotiating the enemy. But even these measures were insufficient to keep the rough element down. The irresistible descent of the Russian army was the excuse for an outcry against the noble Skyznecki; and in the hope of uniting the besieged he resigned his command of the Polish army, General Dembinski being appointed in his place.

But even this step did not succeed in quieting the rabble. On the night of the 15th August the mob rose and marched to the State prison, where Russian officers who had been taken prisoners in the war had been incarcerated. The excitement of the mob was intense. Their blood was up, and this is the only excuse that can be urged for the foulest deed that blemishes the history of Poland. The gates of the prison were forced, and the prisoners led out and shamefully ill-treated. The crowd behaved like wild beasts, chasing and attacking the unfortunate Russians; and after being tortured in every way that occurred to the imagination of their captors, the miserable beings were butchered in the streets, the gutters literally running in blood. Among the victims of this tragedy were four Russian generals and several ladies of high birth, who had been suspected of sympathising with the enemy. All were brutally murdered, the atrocities being continued for two days. At length order was restored by the military, who were withdrawn from the defence of the city for this purpose.

While these events were taking place within the city General Paskewitsch was pressing on in pursuit of the Polish Army, which he had compelled to retreat from the Bzura. But even here the defenders were unable to hold their ground, and on the 1st of September they retired behind the entrenchments which had been thrown up immediately before Warsaw. Here the final stand had to be made. The headquarters of the Russians was only three miles away from the city walls, and the capital was threatened on every side. The position was, in short, so acute that it is a matter of some surprise that the Poles did not retire within the city and stand a siege. This question has been ably discussed by a trustworthy historian, M. Brozozowski, who writes as follows:—

> It would have been very easy, for the army to defend itself within the walls and from house to house. It had already performed more difficult feats, and Europe doubtless would have rung with its heroism if, after the example of Saragossa, it had buried itself under the ruins of Warsaw. But the Poles could not, for the sake of a mere empty renown, consent to the destruction of a city which is the hearth-stone of their patriotism and the centre of their nationality—a city which in future struggles is yet destined to play an important part, for the Poles are far from succumbing under their present misfortunes—very far from abandoning the hope of again becoming a nation. (*La Guerre de la Pologne*)

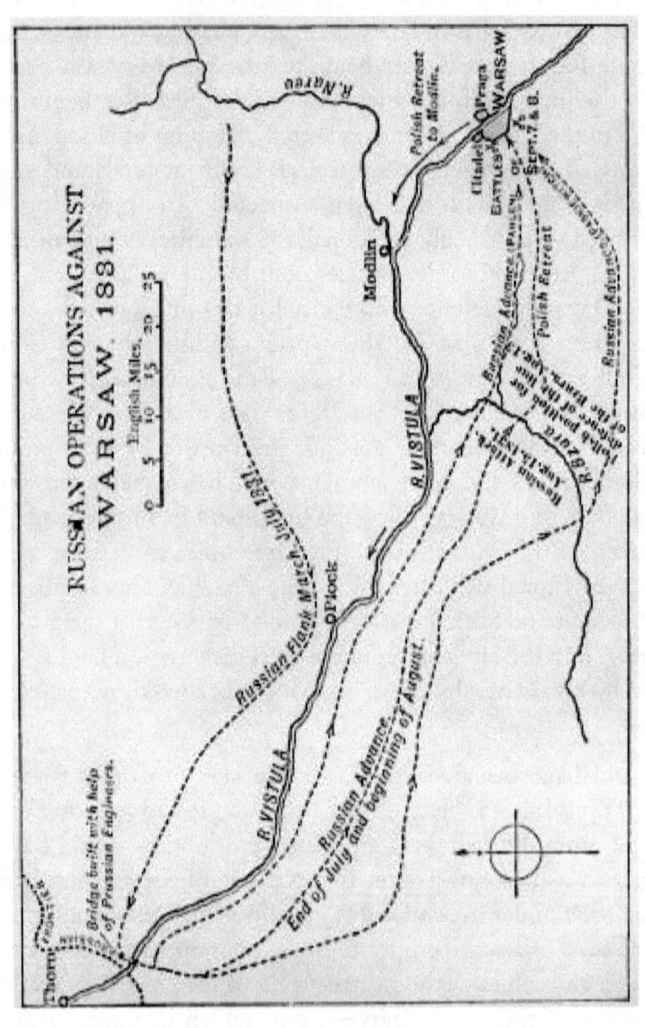

Russian operations against Warsaw. 1831.

But still, the attacking army waited before striking the final blow. Reinforcements from the south were expected. Several days were wasted pending their arrival, and when they arrived their pontoons stuck in the mud. But Paskewitsch did not mind the delay. He is reported to have said to one of his staff, "I await the aid of two armies—the army of the south and the army of famine." Nor were these expectations vain. While beleaguered from without, the doomed city was ravaged within. Gaunt famine marched unchecked through the fine streets, and starvation claimed more victims than did shot or shell.

Then it was that, recognising all resistance as futile, the Poles attempted to open negotiations with the enemy; but the mob would not have it, and the overtures made were cancelled in order to prevent a revolution, while an offer of terms made by Paskewitsch was rejected for a similar reason.

These preliminaries over, the attack upon Warsaw began in earnest on the morning of the 6th September. The fighting on this day was mostly at long range, but the Russian attack was so strong and the firing so fierce that the Poles had to abandon their first line of entrenchment. The assault then ceased, and both sides rested during the night; but at daybreak on the 7th the attack was renewed, and the slaughter was terrible. The Poles—especially the battalions occupying the redoubt on the Wola side of the Vistula—made an heroic resistance. The Russians had on this day no fewer than 386 guns in position, and the fire from them was so fierce and so continuous that nothing could

EMPEROR NICHOLAS.

stand before it.

The Poles were ploughed down by the hail of projectiles, and those spared by the shells were despatched by small arms. After some hours of bombardment, when a mere handful of the garrison of the Wola redoubt remained, the Russians closed up in their strength and charged with their bayonets. The result was disastrous in the extreme. General Sowinski, who commanded the outpost, fell pierced through and through; and when the Russians finally occupied the redoubt only eleven men remained alive out of three thousand.

While this scene of carnage was being enacted outside, the city was itself the scene of intense excitement. The majority of the inhabitants foresaw that their fate was sealed. Their only chance of salvation—the interposition of England or France—had failed them. Were even that to come now it would be too late. The cannonade of the besiegers was continuous, and every now and again a stray shell would fall in the streets, scattering death and devastation. around. And all that could be done in response was to fire occasional charges from the few guns left to the garrison. Men there were in plenty in Warsaw, and women, too, willing to play the man's part in fighting for their country; but the guns were few, and it was no uncommon sight to see eager, able men tear the rifles from the hands of the wounded as they fell, in order that the most might be made of the slender sources at their disposal.

Amid all this scene of horror there was one item of news which caused rejoicing. Marshal Paskewitsch had been wounded. It was said that he was, indeed, disabled. This was the one cheering event of the 7th September.

The 8th opened still and fine, but it was destined to be a bitter day in the story of Poland.

The Russians had moved up to the very gates of the town in the night, and only the innermost line of trenches and the shaky walls stood between them and the inhabitants. The cannonade re-commenced soon after daybreak, and the attack was even more furious than on the previous day. At least, it seemed so to those within the doomed city. The men in the trenches were ploughed down like flies, but their bravery was indomitable, and as each man fell, another took his place, to be ploughed down in turn. The men finally stood upon the brink of their trenches, and used the dead bodies of their comrades as cover; but it was futile. On and on came the Russian host, back and back went the Poles, until only the gaunt walls of Warsaw stood between them and those they sought to save. The enemy fought

THE RUSSIANS CLOSED UP IN THEIR STRENGTH AND CHARGED WITH THEIR BAYONETS with irresistible fury, carrying everything before them, inch by inch, at the point of the bayonet, while their guns were busied in sending missiles within the city, which spread fire and rapine in their train. The day was still undone when the walls were gained. The inmost line of defence was captured, its last defender slain. The plain for a mile around was strewn with the mutilated remains of what had once been brave men, and the tyrants of the North held Warsaw in their hands.

The city capitulated as the sun sunk in the west, and its inhabitants realised too late that their doom was sealed. What that doom was to be even the most imaginative failed to realise.

Having taken Warsaw, Paskewitsch spoke fair. He would, he declared, not enter the city till the following day, and meanwhile the Polish Army, what was left of it, might retire to Plosk. The Marshal admitted to having 3,000 men and 63 officers killed, and 7,500 and 445 officers wounded, while the Polish loss was found to amount to 9,000 slain.

Defeated though they were, reduced in numbers, without the hope of succour, and exhausted by the events of the past few days, the Poles retained their heroism. The army, what was left of the 30,000 men of which the garrison had consisted, formed in order in the great place in the centre of the city, and marched towards the gate. But it did not march to Plosk. It went instead to the fortress of Modlin, and made preparations for a final stand—a forlorn hope—trusting to fortune to turn the Russians yet. But the scheme was foredoomed. Paskewitsch, whose wound was slighter than was supposed, heard of the move, and promptly despatched a brigade against the Polish remnant. The garrison of Modlin was promptly surrounded, all retreat cut off. Entrapped, defenceless, without guns or food, the band of heroes lay down their arms and sought refuge on neutral territory across the Prussian frontier.

It does not come within the province of this history to detail the events which followed the capture of Warsaw. So far as the military history of this, the last great struggle for Polish independence, is concerned, the battle of Warsaw brings the story to a close. The horrors that followed still linger in the memories of the very old. The fearful outbreak of Asiatic cholera which devastated Central Europe, the tragic fate of the thousands of Poles who, trusting in the charity of the King of Prussia, were hounded across the frontier into the hands of the Russians; the equally tragic fortunes of those who took the word of the *Czar* and gave themselves up to the authorities; and the bitter savageries committed by the Russians in compulsorily emigrating the bulk of the people of Warsaw, sending children away from parents and husbands from wives, even to the furthest parts of Eastern Russia, are all part of history. Of the civilising efforts of the Russians while in occupation of Warsaw, we have a sample in the fact that the conquerors took nearly a million volumes of books from the city—400,000 from the Zuluski Library alone.

FRENCH INVASION OF ALGERIA
1830-47

The Fall of Constantine 1837
By Major Arthur Griffiths

The French invaded Algeria in 1830 in order to overthrow a power which for many centuries had been the scourge of Christendom. It sounds like ancient history to talk of the Barbary corsairs, yet they existed, as a matter of fact, till quite lately, making constant war against all maritime nations, harrying their commerce, and carrying their people into captivity.

It was only in 1816 that Lord Exmouth with a British fleet bombarded Algiers. The treaty which he forced upon the Day insisted on the abolition of Christian slavery for ever: as the immediate result, no fewer than 3,000 slaves were liberated from Tripoli, Tunis, and Algiers. But the *Dey*—an incorrigible old Turk—would not reform. For fifteen years, more his pirate ships infested the Mediterranean, and he was insolent and unbearable to the last. He was in the habit of compelling the British consul to approach him bareheaded and on foot, obliging him to await an audience seated humbly on a stone bench outside his palace. On one occasion, he struck the French consul with his fan.

France resolved at length to suppress him, and sent out a combined force, naval and military, to invade Algeria. An army of 34,000 men landed without difficulty, fought two victorious engagements, and marched straight upon Algiers. The city soon fell, and the *Dey's* power crumbled into the dust.

But this did not end the French operations. The complete subjugation of Algeria was a long affair. In the early years of the conquest there was continuous fighting, either against the indomitable Arabs or someone or other of the *Dey's* former lieutenants who here and there still resisted the French. One of these held Constantine, in the eastward, and defied the French authority for just seven years after the fall of Algiers.

This was Hadj Ahmad—an old Turk who had been a chieftain under the *Dey*, but who had constituted himself *pacha* or supreme ruler under the authority of the Sultan of Turkey. It must be remembered that for centuries the Sublime Porte had exercised *suzerainty* over Algeria, and the Algerian Turks owed nominal allegiance to Constantinople. Hadj Ahmad was by reputation a cruel and rapacious tyrant. His mountain stronghold was a centre of resistance, whence he laughed at the French. They issued a proclamation deposing him from his power; he told them to come and drive him out, and as he commanded at this time a very considerable force, mostly hardy mountaineers and excellent troops, his position seemed fairly secure. He was well supported by a capable lieutenant—one Ben Aissa, a man of low origin—a Kabyle or mountaineer, one of the turbulent tribe which gave the French much trouble to the very last.

It was now felt by the French—no less as a matter of prestige than for the completion of the conquest of eastern Algeria—that Hadj Ahmad should be overthrown. This was fully realised by the French general-in-chief, Marshal Clausel, one of Wellington's opponents in Spain who had fought him at Salamanca—a veteran soldier who had made war on a large scale, and who no doubt counted upon easily overcoming the old Turk. The marshal was, moreover, in a hurry; he expected momentarily to be recalled to France, and the season was so late there was little time left to take Constantine before the winter—always arduous in the mountain regions of Algeria—set in. Then he was sanguine of success, even without fighting. He had been assured that Constantine would open its gates directly the French appeared before it. This was promised him by an Arab adventurer named Youssoff, who had come over, and who later on rose to high rank in the French service.

Accordingly, Marshal Clausel pushed forward his preparations, and started on a difficult campaign with an insufficient force, very inadequately supplied. His whole army numbered barely 7,000 men. The roads were so bad—uphill all the way—that he took with him no siege-train and only the most limited number of mountain-guns—fourteen in all. There were only 1,400 rounds of ammunition for the artillery. For the same reason, the troops themselves were but badly found: the force had but fifteen days' rations, and half of these the men carried in their own haversacks. As a mere military demonstration Clausel's expedition might have answered, but it was manifestly unequal to serious business—it could neither face a protracted siege nor a determined assault.

From the first, too, misfortune dogged his steps. The weather became frightfully bad; tempestuous winds, storms of semi-tropical rain, and, on reaching the higher levels, icy cold set in. Every mountain stream—and numbers had to be passed—was swollen into a raging torrent; the paths and mountain roads were broken down or carried away. Fuel was terribly scarce, so that most nights the troops bivouacked without fire; they could not even cook their food. But after thirteen days of most disastrous marching, Clausel arrived at Constantine.

This city has been famous for ages, not only as the key of Eastern Algeria and the natural capital of the surrounding country, but on account of the splendid position it occupies. Constantine has always been deemed one of the wonders of the world. Some French writer has compared it to a picture standing on an easel. It is planted high up on a square and rocky plateau, with its back against the hills. Deep, wide ravines encircle it on all sides but one; at their base, a thousand feet down, flows the rapid Hummel, easily converted by rain and snow into an impassable flood. The only natural communication is on the fourth side—the southern—where the rocky peninsula is joined by an isthmus to the mainland; but from time immemorial the ravine has been bridged on the western side. When the French came to Constantine the bridge of El Kantarah was an ancient and beautiful Moorish construction, hanging high in the air as it spanned the gloomy gorge.

Marshal Clausel invested Constantine on the two sides just mentioned, the southern and western. One brigade took post at Mansourah, an eminence opposite the El Kantarah bridge; the other worked round to another height—that of Condiat Ati, which commanded the city walls and gates on the landward side. The leader of this second brigade was directed to hoist the tricolour flag on the highest point of this ground, as a signal to friends inside. But here was a fresh disappointment. Clausel waited in vain for any overtures from within the city.

The enemy meant fighting, not voluntary submission. Hadj Ahmad was in the open country at the head of a large body of alert and enterprising cavalry. Ben Aissa, who commanded the garrison, showed a firm front in the fortress. There was no choice for Clausel—his only hope of success lay in an immediate attack. His want of battering-train

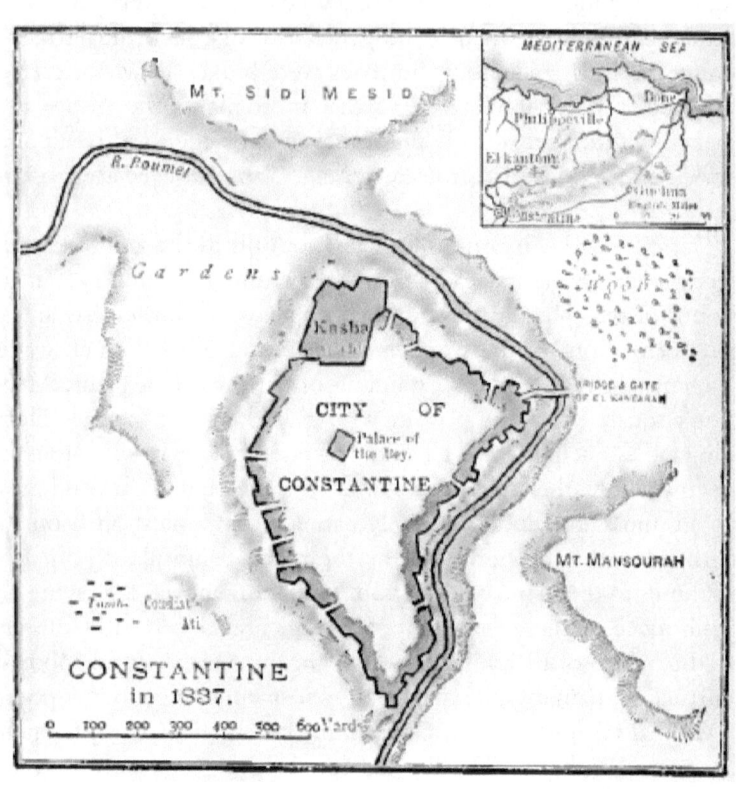

forbade the idea of siege; but worse than all, the French troops were growing demoralised from starvation and hardships, and it was obvious they could not hold their ground before the place for long.

There were to be two columns of attack, made simultaneously and at midnight—one at the land side from Condiat Ati, the other upon the El Kantarah bridge. Both were to be preceded by the demolition of the gates which barred the way. But now came a fresh mischance. Till now the nights had been overcast, with incessant rain. Just before the assault the clouds cleared off; a bright moon came out, and fully betrayed the movements of the assailants. All efforts to blow in the gates were checked by such a murderous fire that the French could make no progress, and the assault entirely failed.

About daylight Clausel was compelled to order a general retreat. Rigny's brigade at the bridge fell back first, and was presently joined by the other from Condiat Ati. Both were covered by the firm demeanour of a small rear-guard commanded by Changarnier—a major then, who afterwards became a famous general. He stimulated the courage of his little force by pointing out to them that, although the enemy numbered 6,000 and the French but 300, the proportion was equal: it was a fair match between them. Such devoted courage was amply rewarded. Clausel was extricated and retreated in good order unmolested by the Arabs, who, wearied with fighting, did not attempt to pursue. Six days later the shattered and unsuccessful French column re-entered Bone, having in a brief three weeks' campaign lost in killed, wounded, and sick nearly 2,000 men, or a third of the whole force engaged.

In this the first siege of Constantine, the luck had been entirely against the old marshal. Clausel was promptly recalled, and the French people, too proud to sit down under such a defeat, insisted upon a fresh expedition against the mountain fortress. The new force was organised on broader lines, and the chief command entrusted to General Damrémont, who had gained long experience in Algerian warfare. He was to be ably supported. There were to be four brigades of infantry, with a total of 10,000 men, and an imposing quantity of artillery, sixteen field-pieces, a siege-train of seventeen guns, and an ample ammunition-train. The artillery was under General Valée, who, although senior in rank to Damrémont, chivalrously offered to serve under him. Ten companies of sappers and engineers accompanied the army to assist in the siege.

The new expedition was composed in part or troops then newly raised, but destined to become famous in the annals of French warfare. These were the *Zouaves*, who made up mainly one brigade—that of the Duke de Nemours, a prince of the reigning house. In the early days of the French invasion a body of warlike mountaineers had been found among the Kabyle tribes who, like the Swiss in Europe, hired themselves out as mercenary soldiers to the native princes around. They were called "*Zouaouas*," and they wore a distinctive dress which foreshadowed the now famous *Zouave* uniform—the red *fez*, the short jacket, and wide red Turkish trousers.

The French willingly secured the services of these fighting-men, and embodied them in regiments which by degrees lost their native character and became filled with adventurous spirits—not always French born, but attracted from all European countries by the dashing nature of the service required from them. The *Zouaves* soon became remarkable for their brilliant exploits in the field, their impetuosity in attack, their boldness and self-reliance in the face of the most serious danger. Yet they required to be handled with discretion and forbearance. A lighter discipline was enforced in quarters, and this peculiar character led to their being commanded by the most rising and intelligent young officers in the French army. In addition to the *Zouaves*, General Damrémont's army included a foreign legion specially raised for this war, and, like the *Zouaves*, recruited from the more daring spirits of all countries.

The second expedition against Constantine started earlier than the first. It left Bone on October 1st, 1837, and, finding fewer obstacles, reached the Rummel on the 6th—six days' march against thirteen. But Constantine showed as bold a front as ever. According to an eyewitness, the French were received with vigorous demonstrations. Immense crimson flags were waved incessantly from the walls, Arab women from the roofs of the houses yelled shrill cries of defiance, which the Arab warriors hoarsely re-echoed. As the French appeared a brisk fire was opened upon them. Later on, when General Damrémont summoned the place to surrender, he received a most heroic refusal. The Arab emissary said:

> Constantine is well victualled and well-armed. It understands neither a breach nor a capitulation. We shall defend our town and our homes to the very last. The French shall not take the place till they have killed our last man.

General Damrémont acknowledged their courage, but declared

there would be all the more glory in beating them.

A more leisurely and more scientific plan of attack was now followed than in the first attempt. Batteries were established at points from which a breach might most easily be made, and which most favoured an assailant. This was at Condiat Ati, the height already mentioned, in front of which were a strongly fortified wall and gate, but with a comparatively level approach. The French fire was hot and continuous; within six days a practicable breach was made in the wall. On the morning of the 12th October General Damrémont came in person to reconnoitre, and was satisfied that the attack might now be made. Everybody was in high spirits; it was felt that the prestige of the French arms affected by the first failure was now about to be vindicated.

The luck, indeed, had changed, but it was still hostile, so far as the leader of the expedition was concerned. General Damrémont was destined to lose his life at the outset. He was so eager to inspect the breach that he ventured too near, and exposed himself rashly to the enemy's sharpshooters. Just as the Duc de Nemours was protesting, and the general had coolly replied "There is nothing to fear," a fatal shot struck him low. He fell lifeless on the very threshold of his triumph.

The command now devolved upon General Valée, who forthwith proceeded with the dispositions for attack. The bombardment was continued all day, and during the night the columns destined to enter by the breach silently took up their positions, there to await the signal to attack. There was no time to lose. Now, as at the first siege, adverse influences were beginning to work, and would soon have entailed another disaster. Sickness was increasing; the troops were ill-fed and much exposed; they were constantly drenched by heavy rains, and stood for hours knee-deep in mud and slush. Fever and dysentery were already making serious inroads in their ranks. The baggage animals—which might become of vital importance if retreat was ordered—were worn out with fatigue and shortness of rations. The French Army might be in a critical condition before long, and the knowledge of this, which was no secret, made all more determined to win a victory.

The attack was to be made in three columns, each to follow on and support the other. The first, led by Colonel La Moricière, afterwards a great general, consisted mainly of *Zouaves*; the second and third columns were commanded by Colonel Combes; the reserve, posted inside the Bardo Barracks, was under Colonel Corbin. Each column was 500 strong, the reserve 400. The remainder of the army lined the trenches or occupied posts of observation around Constantine, one brigade being held at Mansourah opposite the El Kantarah bridge.

The movement of attack was by successive companies of fifty men. About 7 a.m. the first company started at a run under the stentorian command of La Moricière—"Up, my *Zouaves!* forward at the double. March!" A hundred yards of open ground had to be crossed, and in the teeth of a death-dealing fire, but fifty by fifty, the gallant assailants with the headlong dash that ever characterises the French soldier in attack, entered the yawning breach. The second column was on the point of taking up the charge, when it was seen that the first assailants had met a serious check.

There was an inner line of defence—a wall, still unbreached, and commanded by a fierce converging fire. A call went up for scaling-ladders. The French sappers gallantly responded, but as they brought and placed them a whole section of the wall was thrown down by an unexpected explosion. Numbers were buried alive beneath the fragments, but the way was opened for the rest.

Now the second column was launched forward, and went gamely on. The Arabs plied them hotly with musketry, and just when a great mass of Frenchmen had got well past the breach and the second wall, there was a fresh catastrophe—a second murderous and terrific explosion scattered death and destruction around. The few survivors lost heart; they came streaming back with loud and frantic shouts of "Retire! retire! It is impossible. The whole ground is mined!"

It was a critical moment, but the prompt intrepidity of the leaders grappled with the danger and checked the retreat. A young captain of the Foreign Legion—St. Arnaud (better known afterwards in connection with the *coup d'état* and the command of the French Crimean army)—now came conspicuously to the front. Boldly advancing, he rallied his men, and led them on, crying "Forward! forward! Give them the bayonet. There is nothing to fear." The explosion had been caused by a powder magazine which had taken fire; the flames had spread rapidly, and had caught the powder bags carried by the French sappers—even the ammunition pouches of the infantry. Yet, in spite of the horrors of the situation, the assailants gathered fresh courage under the impulse of one man; the cry of "Forward!" was taken up on all sides, and the assault was gallantly resumed.

The difficulty was to get inside the town. Every house was held by small garrisons, and the resistance was very stout and unceasing. At last

IN THE TEETH OF A DEATH-DEALING FIRE

an engineer led St. Arnaud at the head of his company against a barricade formed across a narrow street, beyond which were some of the great thoroughfares of the city. St. Arnaud was lifted bodily over the obstacle, and found safety by falling on the ground inside. Of the hundred of shots aimed at him none hit him, although his scabbard was pierced and his cloak was burned by the powder. His imminent danger brought his men to his help, and all pressed on, entering a larger and the principal business street of Constantine. Here the roofs of the one-storeyed shops and the houses above were alive with Arabs, who kept up an incessant fire. There was no help for it but to take house after house, fighting ahead inch by inch, and in so fierce a struggle that the losses were cruel, and the French as they advanced waded among corpses knee-deep in blood.

But the progress made was always forward from street to street, the French leaders always encouraging their men, and assuring them that it was really safer to go on than to stand and be shot down. At last a small central square was reached, in which stood a mosque. Here three streets converged, and at last the firing slackened. By this time all the French columns had entered and were engaged within the town. General Ralhiéres had been sent forward to unite all in one general attack, and a concentrated determined effort was about to be made, when an Arab came running up, crying, "*Carta! Carta!*" He was carrying a paper in his hand—a letter addressed to the general in chief command, which contained a formal proposal to capitulate from some of the leading inhabitants.

But the wish to surrender was by no means unanimous. A stubborn spirit still animated many of the defenders, who preferred to risk the chances of escape with the alternative of a terrible death. Thousands lowered or threw themselves over the ravines around the town, and the dead or dying presently filled the rocky bed of the river below. The French victory was well earned, for the attack had been carried out with a courage that was not to be denied, and on the best principles of the military art. Only the vulnerable side had been assailed. No attempt had been made, as in the first siege, upon the El Kantarah bridge; and wisely, for St. Arnaud after the capture came upon this bridge at the inner side, and found it to be all but impregnable.

As but too often happens when fortified towns are taken by storm, terrible excesses followed this triumph. Constantine was barbarously pillaged and plundered by the French conquerors. For three days, the sack continued. But order was gradually restored, and with it came confidence, for the French general promised faithfully to respect the religion, property, and customs of the people. All the Arabs were invited to remain peacefully in Constantine. If they would lay down their arms and trust to the French authorities, they would be permitted to share in the government of their city. This proclamation gave general satisfaction, and quiet was soon established.

Nowadays Constantine, although still retaining something of its Arab character, is quite a French city, with its *boulevards* and squares, its *cafés*, its kiosks, and public gardens. But the memory of the great fight for its possession still survives in the names of its streets and in the statues of its conquerors. The Bardo barracks, Mansourah, the El Kantarah gate leading to the new iron bridge, are still extant, but the hill of Condiat Ati is being levelled, and the Place de la Brèche occupies the ground where the attacking column entered, and near at hand is a bronze statue to Marshal Valée. A stone pyramid just outside the city commemorates the death of General Damrémont, and streets are named after Colonels Combes and Peregaux, who were also killed at the assault.

The capture of Constantine marked an important epoch in the conquest of Algeria. But it by no means ended the struggle. There was fierce fighting for long afterwards, and all through this stormy period the colony has been to France what India is to England—a military training-ground. Nearly all the most notable French generals of the last generation won their spurs in Algeria. The names of Changarnier, Cavaignac, and La Moricière first became famous in Algerian military annals. The leaders of the French in the Crimea—St. Arnaud, Canrobert, Pélissier—were first distinguished in Algerian warfare.

Marshal MacMahon fought there, and Niel, Morris, Martimprey, and Le Bœuf Algeria is thought to be pacified now, but it is still held at the point of the sword; and as late as 1871, when the French power at home was imperilled by the German successes, a serious insurrection was set on foot, which for a time jeopardised the weakened forces in the colony. To this day, (1897), the most experienced French officers declare that the Arabs cannot be trusted, and that renewed fighting is always on the cards.

GALLERY IN THE PALACE AT CONSTANTINE.

The Second Turko-Egyptian War
1839-41

Moltke's First Battle: Nisib
June 23 1839
By A. Hilliard Atteridge

Nisib is one of the half-forgotten battles of the nineteenth century. Most readers will wonder where and when it was fought. Yet it was an event which had far reaching consequences, and might easily have changed the face of the East and the after-current of the century's history. And it is further notable as Von Moltke's first battle, for it was on the borderlands of Syria and Kurdistan and under the Ottoman crescent that the great strategist had his first experience of actual warfare.

Up to the end of the first quarter of the present century the curious military organisation of the *Janissaries* had been practically master of the Ottoman empire. In 1826 Mahmoud II. destroyed these too formidable guardsmen, who till then had formed the main force of the Turkish armies, and substituted for them regular troops organised on European principles. To quote a lively French account of the new force, "it was organised on a European model, with Russian tunics, French drill-books, Belgian muskets, Turkish caps, Hungarian saddles, and English cavalry sabres, and instructors of all nations." One of these instructors was young Hellmuth von Moltke, the future field-marshal of the new German empire.

Born at Lübeck in the first year of the century, the son of a German officer in the Danish service, Von Moltke was educated at the military school of Copenhagen, and received a commission in the Danish army. But in 1822 he transferred his allegiance to Prussia, and obtained a second lieutenant's commission in an infantry regiment then stationed at Frankfort-on-the-Oder. Next year he applied for and obtained admission to the staff college, and after three years of study returned to his regiment for a few months, and then for several years was employed only on staff duties, chiefly on military surveys in various parts of Prussia. In 1834, when he had risen to the rank of captain on the general staff, he obtained leave to travel, and after spending a short time in Italy, made his way to Constantinople, where, with the consent of his own government, he was officially attached to the staff of the newly-organised Turkish Army. His first important work in these new surroundings was to make a survey of the Bosphorus and the Dardanelles, and to improve the defences of these two approaches to the capital of the Ottoman empire.

But he had come to the East in the hope of seeing active service, and though he had to wait awhile, he was not disappointed. The *Sultan* and his advisers recognised the thorough grasp of his profession possessed by the Prussian captain, and kept him employed at the headquarters of the army in the capital, when personally he would have preferred to be in the field. But at last the situation on the borders of the empire became so serious that Von Moltke was sent to the front to assist with his advice the Pashas who commanded in Asia.

For fate, had declared against the Turkish armies. Since the destruction of the terrible Janissaries, the empire had lost province after province. Greece had been made into a kingdom; Servia, and what is now Roumania, were all but independent. The French were at Algiers. And finally, an Albanian soldier named Mehemet Ali, who had gone to Egypt in 1799 as one of the servants of Khosref Pasha, had made himself master of the country, and had overrun with his armies Arabia, Syria, and Crete. The Ottoman Government had been glad to avert further conquests by recognising him as the tributary ruler of this widely extended dominion; but Mehemet persisted in maintaining in Syria an army which was a constant threat to Asia Minor, and even to Constantinople.

It was commanded by his son Ibrahim, a skilful and daring soldier; and not only was Mehemet encouraged by the French Government to dream of a march to the shores of the Bosphorus, but French officers had been sent to assist and advise Ibrahim, in case he ventured on this enterprise. The *Sultan* knew that it was only a question of time when Ibrahim's well-trained army would march across the Syrian border, and he had little confidence in the military skill of the pashas who commanded the armies he had gathered for the defence of his Asiatic provinces. It was under these circumstances that in March, 1838, Captain Von Moltke was ordered to proceed to the headquarters of the Turkish Army of Anatolia, taking with him two other Prussian officers, his juniors in the service, who were to act under his directions.

Crossing the Black Sea, and making a rapid survey of several of the ports on its southern coast. Von Moltke and his companions finally disembarked at Samsun, and journeyed southwards by Amasia, Tokat, and Sivas, the point they were making for being the camp of Hafiz Pasha in the south of Kurdistan, on the upper course of the Euphrates. It was a long ride through a wild mountain country, with very primitive accommodation at the various halting-places. The crossing of the Anti-Taurus range was not the least difficult part of the journey.

The lofty plateau was a desert of snow, the track across which was just marked by the traces left by a small caravan which had preceded the party. The descent on the southern side was through a series of precipitous gorges. At last the adventurous travellers reached the banks of the Euphrates at Kieban Maidan, only a few miles below the point where the two streams that form its headwaters, the Murad and the Phrat, coming down from the mountains of Kurdistan, unite in a rapid river about 120 feet across. Another day's journey brought them to the camp of Hafiz Pasha at Kharput.

Hafiz was a Circassian soldier of fortune, who had distinguished himself greatly by his dashing conduct in several campaigns against the rebels in Albania. He was fairly well educated, and sharp-witted enough to recognise that the three Prussians could be of the greatest use to him, in case the threatened war began upon the frontier. He gave them a hearty welcome, made Von Moltke a present of a splendid Arab charger, and asked his advice as to what was to be done to improve the motley force which he commanded. His army was made up of a few regular battalions, an auxiliary force of local levies, some lumbering artillery served by half-trained gunners, and a mass of irregular cavalry.

The task assigned to him was to reduce to submission and keep in order the Kurdish tribes of the neighbourhood, many of whose chiefs were either in open rebellion or notoriously disaffected, and he was at the same time to be ready to meet an invasion of the Syro-Egyptian army which Ibrahim Pasha had got together at Aleppo. Nearer to Constantinople there were two other Turkish Armies in Asia Minor one at Kesarieh, under Isset Pasha, and another at Koniah, the ancient Iconium, commanded by Hadji Ali. These were to stop the Egyptians, in case they got past Hafiz Pasha. Von Moltke, of course, knew that divided from each other by 400 miles of difficult country these three *corps d'armée* were exposed to the danger of being destroyed in detail, in case Ibrahim crossed the border. But he was only a captain on the staff, sent to assist Hafiz. The time was not yet come when he had authority to combine the movements of armies. Had it been otherwise, Von Moltke might have changed the fate of the Ottoman Empire.

There were no trustworthy maps of the district, and as it seemed likely that, after all, the year would end without war being declared, Von Moltke proceeded to a survey of the Syrian frontier and the country round the head-waters of the Euphrates. Beyond the river, he pushed on as far as Orfa, the ancient Edessa, spending more than one night in old castles of the Norman type, the work of the Crusaders. He nearly reached the source of the Tigris, and then voyaged down it to Mosul, and regained the Upper Euphrates by crossing the desert with a caravan. But before he reached the *pasha's* camp he met a column of troops on the march. There were six battalions, eight guns, and a hundred horse, and they were moving northwards under the command of Mehemet Pasha, one of Hafiz's officers, the object of the expedition being to bring to terms a Kurd chief who had hoisted the flag of rebellion on a castle in the hills. Moltke, hearing that all was quiet at headquarters, attached himself to .the column.

The Kurd refused to surrender, and his castle was besieged. Von Moltke reconnoitred the place, planned the siege works, and superintended the batteries. The place soon capitulated, and the castle was blown up, for fear it should cost another expedition next year if it was left in a state of defence. It was Moltke's first siege. The capture of Paris, thirty-two years later, was to be the close of his active career of arms, as this was the beginning.

When he rejoined the headquarters of Hafiz Pasha, the Turkish general had just received news from Aleppo that Ibrahim had been largely reinforced with Syrian, Arab, and Egyptian levies, and was evidently preparing for an attack on the Turkish positions in Asia Minor. Separated, as he was, from the armies of Isset and Hadji Ali by hundreds of miles, Hafiz knew that the protection of the frontier depended on himself alone, and resolved to move closer to the border of Syria in order to make it impossible for Ibrahim to slip past him and gain the road to Constantinople without a battle. Accordingly, on April 1st, 1830, the camp at Malatia was broken up, and the Turks marched to the foot of the Taurus chain, encamping again near Samsat.

Here there was a delay while Moltke and a couple of Turkish staff-officers went forward to reconnoitre the country in front and select a defensive position barring the advance of the army of Syria. On April

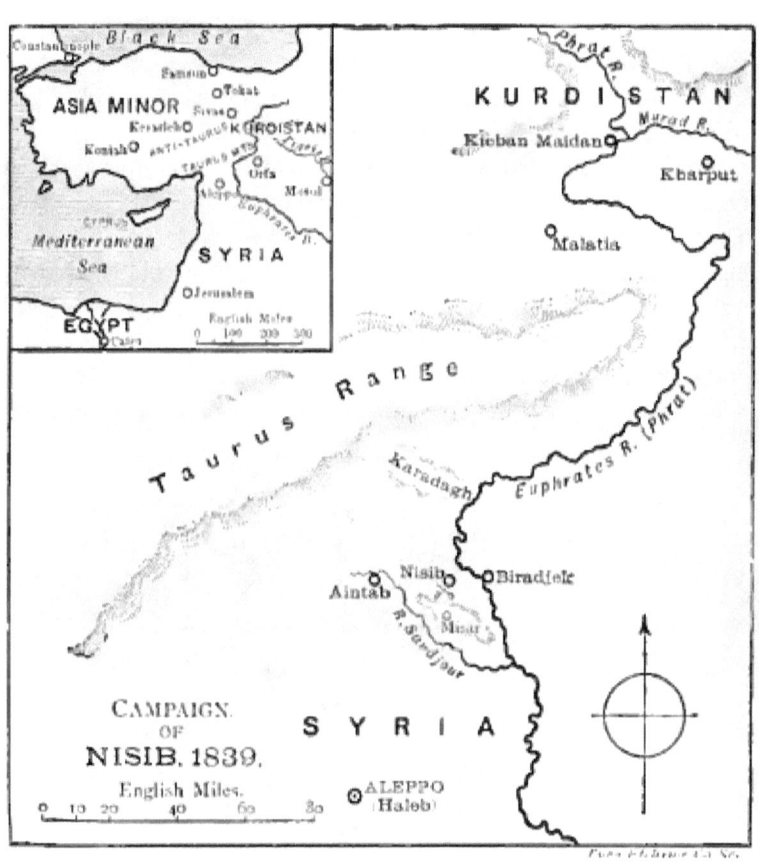

29th, after their return, the march was resumed and the Taurus range was passed, 2,000 men having been employed for a fortnight before in clearing the snow from the passes. The army marched in several columns, each moving by a different pass. Karakaik had been named as the point where they were to concentrate; but at the last moment Hafiz sent word that they were to unite much nearer the frontier, at Biradjek. It would have been a bad thing for him if Ibrahim had come across the border-line while his columns were thus separated, but the Egyptian *pasha* either was not ready to move, or, what is more likely, had no idea of the chance his Turkish opponent was giving him.

Moltke had selected the position at Biradjek. Close to the village of that name a low ridge ran across a bend of the Euphrates. The river covered both flanks, and the front between them was about two miles long. There was a gentle slope from the ridge of about 600 yards, with no shelter of any kind to protect an attacking force from the fire of the defenders. Behind the ridge, and between it and the river, there was a good camping ground, and shelter for the reserves from artillery fire.

The ridge was further strengthened by four earthwork redoubts,

A TURKISH BEY

thrown up just below its crest. The position was thus a natural fortress, improved by field-works. Its chief defect was that it would not have been at all an easy matter to get much of the army away from it across the river once the ridge was stormed.

But then Moltke, in choosing it, had made up his mind that the army of Hafiz Pasha could not be depended on to fight in the open against the superior forces of the Egyptians, and if defeated in a pitched battle he did not expect that in any case much of it would hold together in the retreat. He therefore advised that it should hold the entrenched camp at Biradjek until it was reinforced. Ibrahim would not dare to march into Asia Minor, leaving the army of Hafiz in his rear with Syria at its mercy; and if he attempted to storm the long ridge and its redoubts by a frontal attack, all the chances were that he would be defeated with serious loss, and that he would be unable to attempt anything more that year.

The cavalry had been sent forward to Nisib, a village close to the Syrian frontier. One of their horses escaped, and a few troopers rode across the border-line to look for it. They were attacked by the Egyptian cavalry, one of them killed, and the rest chased back to Nisib. This little incident upset all Von Moltke's plans, and changed the whole course of events in Syria; for Hafiz, when he heard of it, was indignant at what he described as an unpardonable outrage, and made up his mind to attack the Syrians and have his revenge, instead of remaining quietly camped behind his redoubts. Anxious to have the opinions of others to support his own, he called a council of war, and urged strongly that after what had happened nothing was left for them to do but to march against the Syrians. He had, he said, submitted the case to the *mollahs*, the Mohammedan doctors of the law, and they had replied that the act of the Egyptians fully justified an immediate declaration of war.

He asked Von Moltke what he thought, and the Prussian captain replied that the *mollahs* were no doubt excellent authorities on the question whether the war was just or not; but there was another question to be considered: Was it wise? And to answer this one had to know a great many things. What were the intentions of the *Sultan's* Government? What were the rival Great Powers of Europe going to do? What was exactly the enemy's strength, and on what resources of men and supplies could they depend to meet him? On several of these points he himself knew nothing, and the *mollahs* knew no more than he did. The responsibility of a choice rested on the *pasha* himself, and he ought to know, whether or not his sovereign, the *Sultan*, wished him to precipitate hostilities.

"But," concluded Von Moltke, "not having all the necessary information, I must decline to give an opinion."

Hafiz was disappointed. He had hoped for a unanimous vote for war, and he was especially anxious to escape responsibility' by having on his side the opinion of his Prussian military adviser. But Von Moltke wisely persisted in refusing to advise on any but strictly military questions. He would have nothing to do with politics. But the Circassian *pasha* was eager to avenge what he felt as a personal insult put upon him by the Egyptians, and at the same time he had persuaded himself that, whatever he might say openly, the *Sultan* wished for a war which might end in the reconquest of Syria, if not of Egypt. So, he decided to fight.

Marching out of the Biradjek position, he massed his forces about the village of Nisib, sending his Kurdish irregular cavalry to raid across the frontier, and detaching a column of infantry and artillery to summon the Egyptian garrison that held the frontier town of Aintab to surrender. The Egyptians refused his first summons, but no sooner had a few shots been fired against the place than they not only surrendered, but offered to take service under the Turkish standards. They were not the first troops that Hafiz had recruited in the same way. Many of his Kurdish regiments were composed of mountaineers who had taken his pay the day after they had surrendered to his fiving columns. But soldiers who transferred their allegiance so readily from one banner to another were not very reliable elements in an army.

Ibrahim and the Syro-Egyptian Army had all this time been camped quietly near Aleppo. There were only a few detached posts and some irregular cavalry watching the frontier, which was thus open to the raids of Turks and Kurds. But Ibrahim was preparing to move, and by a curious coincidence, while the Prussian Von Moltke was advising his enemy, he himself had for his chief military adviser an officer of the French Army, Captain Beaufort d'Hautpoul, a son of one of the Great Napoleon's generals. In the first week of June he broke up his camp at Aleppo. Ten days later his Arabs were driving the Kurdish horsemen back upon Nisib. On the 19th his vanguard cleared the pass of Misar, a defile in the hills to the south of Nisib, and next day his army bivouacked five miles in front of the Turkish position.

All that day and during a great part of the night the army of Hafiz was drawn up in battle array, expecting to be attacked. At nine o'clock

HURRYING TO THE SIDE OF HAFIZ,
HE URGED HIM TO AT ONCE MAKE A SHARP ATTACK.

on the 21st the Egyptians were at last seen to be advancing. Nine regiments of cavalry, Arab and Syrian horsemen in white burnooses, armed mostly with the lance and riding in a loose formation, moved towards the Turkish left. Behind them came some guns and a brigade of infantry. The gunners, directed by Beaufort d'Hautpoul in person, unlimbered and opened fire at long range against the Turkish centre and left. The Turkish batteries replied.

All the guns on both sides were smooth-bores, most of the shot fell short, and there were very few casualties. The firing might have gone on all day without much effect. But suddenly, at a signal from the artillery position, the Egyptian cavalry fell back, the guns limbered up and retired, and the infantry followed them. The Turks flattered themselves that they had the best of the day, and that the Egyptians were afraid to come to close quarters. The fact was that it was only a reconnaissance carried out by the French officer, who wanted to have a close look at the position of the Turks and to draw the fire of their artillery, in order to find out where their batteries were and what their guns could do.

All day Hafiz expected the attack to be renewed, and his troops were under arms. When night came, they lay down where they had stood all day, with their weapons ready to their hands. At dawn on the 22nd it was seen that the Egyptian army was breaking up its camp and retiring towards Misar. Great was the joy at the Turkish headquarters, but it did not last long. The scouts who hung on the rear of the retiring Egyptians were suddenly driven back by a cavalry charge, and then it was seen that the columns of Ibrahim's army were no longer moving on Misar, but, after edging away somewhat to the eastward of their first direction, were advancing on a line that would carry them past the Turkish left, and if they were not checked would place them in position between Nisib and Biradjek, so as to cut off Hafiz from what was at once his line of supply if he remained at Nisib, and his line of retreat if he abandoned the place. Ibrahim, with his army formed in three columns, was making a bold manoeuvre the success of which meant, not merely the defeat, but the destruction of the Turkish "Army of Kurdistan."

Moltke saw the full gravity of the situation. Hurrying to the side of Hafiz, he pointed out to him that an army which tries to outflank another necessarily exposes its own flank during the manoeuvre, and he urged him to at once make a sharp and well-sustained attack on the nearest of the three hostile columns. This would momentarily arrest the turning movement, and it might reasonably be hoped that the first column of the Egyptians would be seriously shaken, if not broken up, before the two others could come up to its assistance.

But Hafiz did not like the idea of moving down with his whole army from the rising ground which he had held so long, and all that he did was to launch against the column a few squadrons of his irregular cavalry, who were driven back by a few volleys and a charge of the Arab Horse. Then, seeing that it was hopeless to try to induce Hafiz to take the offensive, and that the opportunity for it would soon be gone, Moltke proposed another plan. The enemy had not yet interposed between Nisib and Biradjek; the best thing to do would be to retreat at once to that strong position, await an attack there, and resume the offensive after the expected reinforcements had arrived.

But Hafiz, with his staff grouped round him, met the suggestion with an unexpected objection. To go back to Biradjek would be to run away in the presence of the Syrians and Arabs and their Egyptian pasha. He was not afraid of them. He would not disgrace himself by flight.

Then Von Moltke, appealing to his two Prussian colleagues in support of his opinion, replied that what he proposed was not a flight, but a strategic retreat, an operation of war that the greatest conquerors had at times made use of as a prelude to their victories. There was nothing disgraceful in it, or he would not have suggested it. It was now a simple question of gaining time, and keeping up their communications with Asia Minor. If they remained where they were, the chances were all against them; if they once regained the lines of Biradjek, everything was in their favour.

There was a long discussion, on the one side Moltke and his colleagues urging instant retreat; on the other Hafiz, backed up by the *mollahs*, who declared that all the omens were in favour of fighting at Nisib, and also supported by many of his Turkish officers, who thought it more to their interest to side with the *pasha* than with the three "Franks" who had come to advise him. It ended in Hafiz Pasha declaring that nothing should induce him to abandon the position of Nisib; on which Moltke, worn out with fatigue, ill with a touch of fever, and discouraged at the stupid obstinacy of the Circassian *pasha*, went away to his tent, and tried to sleep through the day, declining all responsibility for what was being done.

What a contrast there is between Captain Von Moltke, stretched on his camp bed at Nisib in utter disgust at being unable to persuade a stupid *pasha* and his officers to extricate some 30,000 men from a false position in this campaign on the borders of Syria, and the same Moltke a few years later at the palace of Versailles, directing with all but absolute command the movements of nearly a million soldiers, with kings and princes waiting for his orders, and all Europe looking on in wonder at the brilliant strategy by which he was sealing the fate of France! But in the one instance he had to do with a *pasha* who would not listen to him, in the other with a soldier-king who had the insight to recognise and give free play to his marvellous genius for war.

All through that hot midsummer day the white cloaks and glittering lances of Ibrahim's cavalry spread like the foam of an advancing tide wave along the plain between Nisib and the Euphrates. Behind them came the three columns of Syrian and Egyptian infantry, with their lumbering artillery dragged along partly by horses, partly by long teams of bullocks. Towards evening the columns closed upon each other, and upon the left rear of the Nisib position. Then they camped in battle array, and the long line of their watch fires told Hafiz that they had taken up a position from which they were ready to attack him in the morning.

Late that evening the *pasha* sent for Von Moltke. Seated on a carpet in his tent, Hafiz asked the captain to sit beside him, gave him coffee and a pipe, and then entreated him to do what he could to help him in the defence of the Nisib position. Von Moltke replied that he still thought that a huge mistake had been made in accepting battle in such a place; but, while declining all responsibility for the choice of the position, he would do what he could to make the best of it. For the next few hours he was busy by the light of torches and watch-fires drawing up the Turkish Army, so as to meet the coming attack. All the troops, except a few cavalry scouts, were withdrawn from the plain. He chose a position on the high ground where the centre would be partly covered by a ravine. The right, which was nearest the Egyptians, was rapidly entrenched, and a battery of heavy guns were sent to strengthen the left. By 3 a.m. all were in position.

The long-expected battle began early on June 23rd. Ibrahim—or, rather, his French adviser, Beaufort d'Hautpoul—adopted a system of tactics which secured him an advantage from the very outset. He was strong in artillery, his guns being partly long field-pieces of Eastern design throwing solid round shot, partly French howitzers, short guns of comparatively large calibre, throwing shells. Keeping his infantry columns well out of range, he pushed forward all his artillery, escorted by his Arab and Syrian cavalry. The masses of horsemen to right and left and out of range, but within a short gallop in rear of the guns, made it a risky matter to try to rush them, even if Hafiz had had any other idea than doggedly clinging to the defensive.

Thus protected, the Egyptian artillery began to throw shot and shell into the position on which the Turks were crowded together. The Turkish artillery, provided only with solid shot for long range, and grape for close quarters, could do comparatively little damage to the enemy's batteries, and the Egyptian infantry was quite out of its reach. The artillery duel with which the battle began was thus a most unequal conflict.

Soon the bursting shells began to tell upon the Turks, many of the regiments that held the plateau of Nisib being composed of doubtful materials—such as the troops who had surrendered at Aintab and the Kurdish levies. Whole companies broke up as the shells burst over them, and at last a whole brigade on the left retired from the ground it was ordered to hold, in order to shelter on the reverse slope of the plateau. Some regiments of the reserve, seeing this movement in retreat, conformed to it, and it looked as if the whole line was beginning to give way. Moltke galloped to the left, and tried in vain to induce the brigade to resume its place in the front. Nothing he could say had the least influence on officers or men. They were in comparative safety, and they did not mean to march back again into the thick of the artillery fire. He gave up the hopeless task, and turning his horse, rode towards the centre.

As he approached it he saw a sight which might well dishearten him. Guns were straggling back one by one from the front, and, worse still, artillery drivers, who had cut the traces of their limbers, came galloping to the rear in flight, abandoning their guns. Several regiments had fallen on their knees in prayer—the prayer not of brave men asking help for coming battle, like the Scots who knelt at Bannockburn, but the frightened petition of men who had lost heart and head, and afraid to do anything for themselves, were begging for a miracle from Heaven. The Syro-Egyptian infantry massed in heavy columns, with their green banners waving in a long line in their front, were advancing, a forest of bayonets flashing in the sunlight, while their cavalry streamed out towards the flanks.

The crisis of the battle had come. On the left a brigade of Turkish regular cavalry, without having received any orders, rode forward to charge; but it had only reached the crest of the slope that led downwards towards the Egyptian right when a few shells, almost the last fired that day by Ibrahim's artillery, burst in their front ranks. Horses and men alike seemed to be panic-stricken. The mass of cavalry wheeled round and fled wildly to the rear, riding down and dispersing part of the Turkish reserves in their mad flight. Moltke was trying to keep the centre steady. Hafiz rushed to the right, where the Turks were firing their muskets at the advancing Egyptians at a range which meant a mere waste of powder and ball.

Seizing a standard, he put himself at the head of a battalion and called on them to charge the approaching Egyptians. It looked as if he was seeking for death in the midst of what he now recognised as a hopeless disaster. The men refused to advance. On came the Egyptians. But hardly anywhere were they met by anything more than an irresolute, ill-aimed fire from men who were calculating how long they could safely stay without risking having to cross bayonets with the enemy. As the line of green standards with the bright steel behind them came up the slope, most of the Turks and Kurds ceased firing and ran.

Here and there a handful, with levelled bayonets, stood back to back and sold their lives dearly. Some of the gunners stuck to their pieces to the last, and fired grape into the faces of the Egyptians; but for the most part it was headlong flight or abject surrender. Entire companies threw down their arms. Guns abandoned by their teams were captured in whole batteries. The mass of fugitives that streamed away over the back of the plateau fared the worst, for with a fierce yell the Arab horsemen rode after them, and for miles the plain was strewed with the corpses of the wretches who died at the points of their long spears.

As the line broke. Von Moltke had the good fortune to be near his two Prussian comrades. Thanks to their horses, the three Europeans extricated themselves from the mass of fugitives, avoided the pursuit, and after a ride of nine hours under the blazing Syrian sun reached Aintab in the evening.

Von Moltke had lost everything but the horse he rode and the clothes and arms he wore. He regretted most the loss of his journals and his surveys of Asia Minor and the Upper Euphrates, the result of many months of travel and exploration. But he was fortunate in having escaped with life. The course of European history might have been changed if the good horse that carried him so well had stumbled in the wild rush to escape the Arab spears.

Ibrahim seemed astounded at the completeness of his own success. There was a panic throughout Asia Minor, many of the new Turkish

THE MASS OF CAVALRY WHEELED ROUND AND FLED WILDLY TO THE REAR

levies disbanding on the news of Nisib. The Egyptians might have marched at once to the shores of the Bosphorus, but they hesitated to reap the fruits of their victory, and the intervention of England and Austria soon after forced them to give up all pretensions to rule in Western Asia.

Travelling across Asia Minor, Moltke and his companions saw everywhere signs that nothing could be done to help the Turks to hold their own. He was therefore eager to get back to Europe, and on August 3rd, when he saw the sea from the hills above Samsun, he felt the same joy with which the Greeks had greeted the same sight in their famous retreat from the Euphrates. Embarking at Samsun, he returned to Constantinople. His next experience of warfare was in the Prussian army.

By a curious turn of fate, he had among his opponents in his last campaign the same French officer who had so ably directed the Egyptian attack at Nisib. When the French Imperial army collapsed in 1870, and the new levies were being raised to meet the Prussian invasion, Beaufort d'Hautpoul, then living in retirement, offered his services to Gambetta, and was given the command of a division in Vinoy's army in the defence of Paris. The general took part in the great sortie that immediately preceded the surrender; and it so happened that as at Nisib, in far-off Syria, Von Moltke's first battle, so at Buzenval, under the walls of Paris, the last battle of the great Prussian strategist, Beaufort d'Hautpoul was among those who fought against him.

BIRADJEK

THE FIRST FRANCO-MOROCCAN WAR
1844

The Defeat of Abd-el-Kadr by the French, Isly August 14, 1844
By Major Arthur Griffiths

The scene was an improvised garden in North Africa, just across the frontier line between Algeria and Morocco, on the banks of the river Isly. The time—night: a cool breeze had succeeded the torrid heat of day, and the French camp was alive with gaiety, brilliantly illuminated by many coloured lanterns which blazed upon the pink blossoms of the oleanders and the tamarisks.

A military 'punch,' as it is called by the French Army, was in progress—a kind of festive entertainment given by the officers to some newly-arrived comrades.

The only thing wanting to complete success was the presence of the commander-in-chief.

Marshal Bugeaud—*le père* Bugeaud, as he was styled affectionately by his soldiers—had retired to his tent, and was already asleep on his truckle bed. He was worn out with fatigue. A momentous battle was imminent. The marshal had been busily engaged all day in preparing written instructions for all commanders of corps under his orders. Who would dare awaken him?

The only one bold enough for the task was a civilian—M. Léon Roche, the principal interpreter of the army and long the marshal's close associate and intimate friend. Even he was sharply received when performing this unpleasant duty. But when the old man heard the reason he got up; dressed, still grumbling, and started for the centre of the camp. Here he found himself surrounded by an animated concourse.

All the officers of rank crowded round him and welcomed him warmly. Then it was that he delivered himself of a famous little speech, which is said to have had no insignificant effect upon the fighting of next day. He said with much animation:

> It will be a great day, you may depend. We shall be terribly outnumbered. Our army has only 6,500 bayonets and 1,500 horse; the Moors, so I am told, are at least 60,000 strong—all horsemen. Yet I wish there were three or four times as many: the more numerous they are the greater will be their disorder, the worse the disaster when they are attacked.
>
> You see, ours is an army; the Moors have only a mob, and this is what, I think, will happen. I shall form my men, in the shape of a boar's head. The right tusk will be General Lamoricière, the left Bedeau, the muzzle will be Pelissier, and I shall be behind the ears. Who shall stop our penetrating force? My friends, we shall split the Moorish Army up as a hot knife cuts into butter. I have only one fear, and that is that the enemy will not wait for us.

This spirited speech evoked the wildest enthusiasm. A report of it, and of the words the old marshal had used, rapidly spread through the camp; it was repeated from mouth to mouth, and fired the troops with their leader's desperate but self-confident courage. All, like him, were only afraid the floors would escape out of their hands.

The Battle of Isly, then imminent, may be called the final stroke for supremacy in Algeria. Although not actually fought on Algerian soil nor against the Algerian Arabs, it yet stamped out their opposition by utterly destroying the power of Abd-el-Kadr, the great Arab chief who alone had successfully resisted the French for so long. These two men, Marshal Bugeaud and Abd-el-Kadr, the one a Frenchman, the other an Arab, are really the most prominent personages in the history of the Algerian conquest: both earned great distinction—the one as a soldier, the other as a patriot. Before dealing with the last great episode in this struggle, which had extended over fifteen years and is not definitely ended even now—for to this day, (1897), Arab submission cannot be called complete, and insurrection is always possible—some account should be given of the two remarkable men who were so closely connected with it. Isly may be said to have firmly established the fame of the one, Bugeaud, and to have practically closed the independent career of Abd-el-Kadr, the other.

Marshal Bugeaud was a product of the Napoleonic regime, one of the last of the great soldiers turned out by the *Grande Armée*. Born of

Algiers

a family but recently ennobled, he liked to call himself a man of the people: he always said he was prouder of his grandfather, the blacksmith, who had founded the family fortunes, than of his father, the aristocrat, who had dissipated them. Bugeaud was but badly educated, and at the age of twenty, when a big, burly, stalwart youth, he enlisted as a private soldier in the Imperial Guard, to find literally in his knapsack, the field marshal's baton which, the proverb declares, every' French conscript carries there. He won his epaulettes a couple of years later at Pultusk, in Poland, and he took active part in many of Napoleon's campaigns; but his promotion was not rapid, and he was only a colonel at Waterloo.

After his master's fall, he shared the emperor's disgrace, and retired into private life, only to return to the army and gain the rank of general after the revolution of 1830. He took then to political life, and as an outspoken deputy with the courage of his opinions he had to fight several duels in defence of them. In 1836 he entered once more upon his natural sphere, and was sent to Algeria as a general of brigade. At this time, Thomas Bugeaud was a hale man of fifty, tall, muscular, and broadly built, every inch a soldier, with the imperious manner and decided air of one practised to command; he had an iron constitution, was 'greedy of fatigue and inaccessible to the infirmities of age.' Bugeaud was the idol of his men: his first and last thought was for them; their comfort, wellbeing, and instruction were his most constant and unremitting care.

A dozen stories are preserved of him proving this. He was known to dismount from his horse to help a muleteer to replace the bundles which had fallen from a pack saddle. An eyewitness reports:

> I have seen him take the trouble to shift the sentries' posts after nightfall so as to deceive the keen-sighted Arabs and keep his men out of fire.

He would fall back to the rear-guard to admonish and encourage his soldiers, talking to them one by one in the kindest and most friendly way. Sometimes he would halt a column on the march and order the men to undress. Woe then to the commanding officer if any soldier was found to be without the regulation flannel belt!

The best story told is, perhaps, that which earned him the sobriquet of the Père Casquette (Father Flat-cap). On one occasion his camp was surprised: through the carelessness of the outposts the Arabs broke in and opened a heavy fire. All was dire confusion at first, but the marshal rushed out of his tent and restored order: indeed, with his own strong hands he struck down two of the assailants. But when all was over and the Arabs driven back, the marshal, as he stood in the strong light of the camp fires, saw that all eyes were directed to his headgear, and that everyone was laughing. Putting his hand to his head, he found that it was still covered with his night-cap; so he called someone to bring him his *kepi* or *casquette*, and the cry was set by some soldier-composer to music that very night. Next morning, when the bugles sounded the rouse, a battalion of *Zouaves* accompanied the music with a chorus about the cap—

> As-tu vu
> La Casquette,
> La Casquette?
> As-tu vu
> La Casquette
> Du Père Bugeaud?

The impromptu air pleased the old marshal mightily. Ever afterwards the first bugle-call at dawn was called the '*casquette*,' and the marshal himself was often heard telling a bugler to sound the *casquette*. Sometimes, when the troops were wearied and footsore, he would order the favourite tune to be played; the men, taking heart, would strike up the chorus, in which the general himself would join.

What especially endeared Bugeaud to his soldiers was his unfailing readiness to share their privations. Nothing annoyed him more than to see infantry officers riding saddle-horses. He issued a peremptory order once on the subject:

> This abuse must be immediately stopped. Infantry officers must not lose sight of the fact that the surest method of obtaining from their soldiers the self-denial and energy required to endure toilsome marches under a burning sun is to set the example of going on foot as the men do.

Upon one occasion the marshal was roaming through his camp alone and unobserved when he heard a dispute between an old and a young *Zouave*. The latter was bemoaning his fate: for three days, he had been wet to the skin, and not a chance of drying himself; not a bit of bread nor a glass of brandy was to be bought at the canteen. 'Conscript,' cried the other, taking him sharply to task, 'if you had been on sentry at the Père Casquette's tent as I was yesterday, you would give up grumbling. He is a duke and a marshal of France, but he was gnawing at a bit of biscuit like the rest of us, and drinking a mug of water.' There was a loud shout of applause from all around, and the marshal, when he afterwards told the story, said he had never felt so proud in his life before.

A leader of this sort was certain to be worshipped by his men, but old Bugeaud was equally humane and considerate to the Arabs. It is on record that when governor-general of the province he looked out of the window one morning as he was shaving, and saw a Maltese strike an Arab brutally. Without a second's thought the marshal ran out in his shirt-sleeves just as he was, with the soapsuds on his face, turned out his guard, and had the Maltese arrested and given in charge of the police.

When Bugeaud first reached Algeria, he was very much dissatisfied with the plan on which the war had been waged: he was certain that the Arabs would be best tackled by light movable columns unencumbered with baggage or artillery. In spite of the marked disapproval of his lieutenants he persisted in carrying out this system. At this time, Abd-el-Kadr was the most formidable antagonist the French had in Algeria, and it was with him that Bugeaud was now to try conclusions. He did so victoriously at the Battle of the Sickack, when at small cost he all but broke up and dispersed Abd-el-Kadr's forces.

But the Arab chief was still a danger, and Bugeaud was desired, if possible, to bring him to terms. The moment was rather critical, for Clausel had just failed in the siege of Constantine, and the French hold on Algeria was growing precarious. It was said that Bugeaud was to renew the war against Abd-el-Kadr if he could not induce him to make peace, but in this he presently succeeded, and the celebrated Treaty of Tafna was the result. By this the French recognised the emir as an independent ruler over the western part of Algeria and the mountainous interior, in return for which Abd-el-Kadr acknowledged the sovereignty of France. The Arabs on each side were to be free to come and go, and those within the French limits were to have full religious toleration.

It was hoped that this treaty would be the first step to a pacific settlement of Algeria, and as soon as it was signed the high contracting parties met to make each other's acquaintance. General Bugeaud (he was not yet a marshal) was very eager to meet the Arab chieftain who had so long defied the power of France. It was now seven years since Abd-el-Kadr had set himself up in opposition to the French by heading the Arabs of Tlemcen in a holy war against the *infidel* invader. When the French first invaded Algeria he was a remarkable youth, barely four-and-twenty, the son of a *marabout*, or priest, of great sanctity whom the tribes had invited to take the lead. This *marabout*, by name Mahiddin, refused, but passed on the offer to his son. Great things had been prophesied of Abd-el-Kadr: he had accompanied his father to Mecca, and there had been hailed by a holy *fakir* as a future *sultan* of the Arabs; and he undoubtedly proved the most remarkable man who had appeared among the western Mohammedans for more than a century. Towards the end of his career, in 1843, Marshal Soult classed him among the only three men then alive—all Mussulmans—"who could legitimately be called great." These were Schamyl the Circassian, Mehemet Ali the Egyptian Pasha, and Abd-el-Kadr.

The son of Mahiddin, as he was called, first took up arms against the French in 1833 by attacking Oran. Although repulsed, he gradually consolidated his power by his indomitable energy and the personal influence he exercised over the Arab tribes. Thousands of them flocked to his standard, and for four years he proved a most redoubtable antagonist. The person of Abd-el-Kadr at the time when Bugeaud met him was prepossessing, and gave outward proof of his inward remarkable character.

A prisoner who spent some time in his camp describes him as very small in stature, with a long deadly pale face and large black languishing eyes, an aquiline nose, small delicate mouth, thin dark chestnut beard, and slight moustache. He had exquisitely-formed hands and feet, which he was continually washing and trimming with a small knife. In dress, he studied the utmost simplicity, wearing fine white linen without a vestige of gold or embroidery. Bugeaud thought his appearance quite that of a devotee, but he was skilled at all martial exercises, was a fine horseman, and always beautifully mounted in the field.

The contrast between the stalwart old Frenchman and slightly-formed Arab must have been very great. Both were anxious to maintain their dignity; neither at first would give way. When Bugeaud dismounted, Abd-el-Kadr hesitated, but at length did the same; they sat side by side on the grass and talked for forty minutes. Then Bugeaud rose to go, but Abd-el-Kadr did not move from his seat. This might have been intentional disrespect, and was not to be borne, so old Bugeaud protested. As he afterwards told the French Chamber:

I fancied I saw in it a certain claim to superiority, and so I made my interpreter tell him 'when a French general rises, you should also rise'. While my interpreter was translating the words, I took Abd-el-Kadr by the hands and lifted him up. He was not very heavy.

A special interest attaches to the meeting of these two men, for they were again to be pitted against each other in the coming years. The Treaty of Tafna was only a truce. Abd-el-Kadr accepted the terms in order to get time for fresh preparations and to consolidate his power. He was now at the zenith, holding authority over a large territory, feared and obeyed by thousands of adherents. In France, the treaty was viewed with extreme disfavour, and after the fall of Constantine it was clear that a fresh appeal to arms would be gladly entertained at home.

When Abd-el-Kadr protested against a demonstration made by Marshal Vallee into the mountain country through the celebrated Iron Gates or *portes de fer*, the French Government decided to resume offensive operations. They were, however, forestalled by Abd-el-Kadr, who again raised the standard of a holy war, and much fighting with many massacres followed. Desultory operations, by no means favourable to the French, dragged on for three years, during which they lost hold on the interior and were more and more restricted to the ports and strong places on the coast. At last General Bugeaud, who was once more in France actively engaged in politics, was offered the supreme command in Algeria, and went back as governor-general to the scene of his old successes.

Bugeaud was a soldier of broad views and abounding commonsense. He saw that he had now to deal not with an army, but with a nation in arms. He knew that it was useless to operate with large bodies of troops against wild tribes constantly on the move; that he must catch them on the run, defeat them wherever he found them, compel them to lay down arms, then overawe them into peaceful submission. It was the further development of the lesson he had learnt in 1836. He organised his forces in small compact columns: a few battalions of infantry, a couple of squadrons of cavalry, two mountain-howitzers, a small transport train on mule- and camel-back; as speed was the first consideration, he employed only picked men, those inured to the climate and to fatigue.

They moved in the lightest marching order, carrying only muskets, ammunition, and a little food. A strip of canvas served as haversack, but

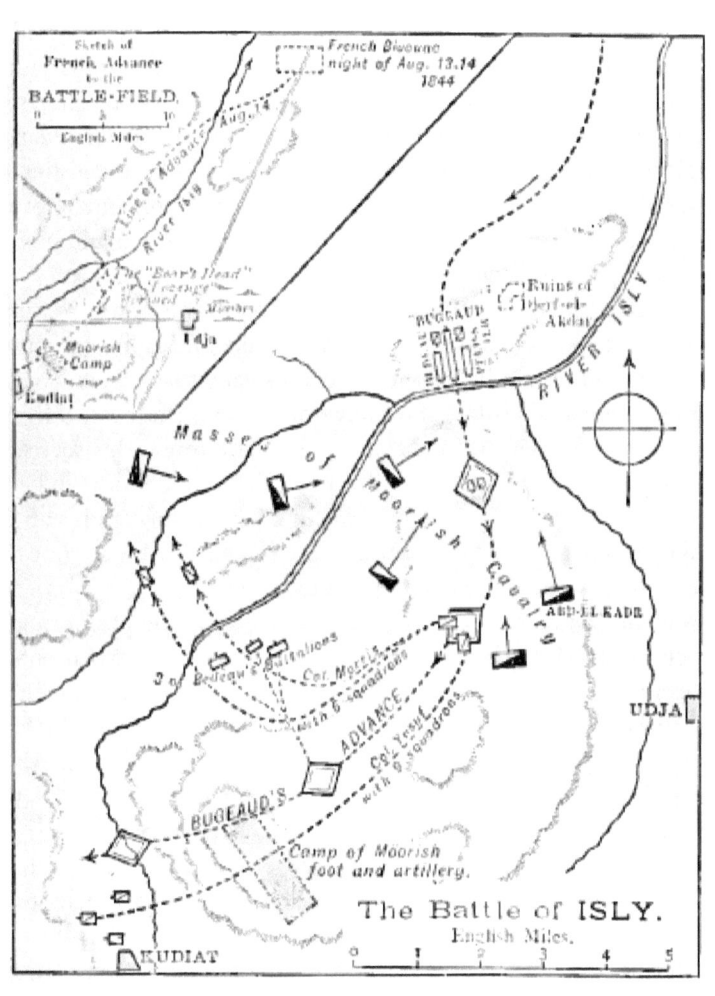

was unsewn; three of these could be joined together, and thus form a shelter for three men. This was the origin of the famous *tente d'abri*, the only form of encampment for a large portion of the French Army in the Crimea.

The command of those movable columns was entrusted to the smartest of the young officers Bugeaud found around him. He had no lack of choice. The campaign in Algeria had now lingered on for many years, and had served as an admirable military school, in which some of the most eminent soldiers, men to be hereafter more widely known, won early distinction. Among these were Changarnier, Cavaignac, Lamoricière, Bedeau, St. Arnaud, Canrobert, Pelissier, and the king's son, the Duc d'Aumale. The chief, ever active and enterprising, could count upon lieutenants eager to vie with him and give full effect to his views. Bugeaud set them a fine example.

The old general was indefatigable, ready to move at a moment's notice to any point that was threatened, to take the lead in any important operation. When he was at Algiers, a steamer lay in the bay with steam up prepared to take him anywhere along the coast. He slept very little, and when he woke at any hour he roused his secretaries and kept them busy with dictation for hours. Throughout it all he was full of gaiety and wit; he delighted in talking, in lecturing his staff, and telling amusing stories. Yet nothing was too small for his attention; he never missed or neglected an opportunity.

A couple of years saw a very marked change in the position of the French in Algeria. Marshal Bugeaud's method of warfare was entirely successful. He won combat after combat, driving Abdel-Kadr further and further into the hills. One by one he took the Arab chieftain's strongholds. The fort and citadel of Tackdempt, which was Abdel-Kadr's chief arsenal and stronghold, was captured and destroyed; then a second fortress among the hills fell into French hands; after that Boghar and Thaza were taken from Abd-el-Kadr, and he was driven back into the Atlas Mountains, while his power was much shaken throughout the province of Oran.

But he was not yet crushed, and while the French were engaged against the mountain tribes, Abd-el-Kadr made a descent upon the coast near Cherchell, which spread general alarm through the colony. Again, he was driven back and continually pressed by several corps, which, converging, sought to enclose him between them. One of these, commanded by the Duc d'Aumale, captured by a bold stroke Abd-el-Kadr's *smalah*, the great collection of tents with all his family,

Captured by a bold stroke Abd-el-Kadr's smalah

followers, and possessions, which he was in the habit of moving about with him wherever he went. Afterwards, when a prisoner in French hands, the *emir* declared that there were 60,000 people in his *smalah* when attacked by the Duc d'Aumale. This multitude consisted of tradesmen of all kinds, armourers, saddlers, tailors, smiths; an immense market was held within it weekly; all Abd-el-Kadr's treasure was there, his wives, his horses, all he owned.

The Duc d'Aumale, with a small force, had come upon the *smalah* after a long pursuit and a fatiguing march of thirty hours; his men had hardly slept, they had eaten with their bridles over their arms, and only chocolate or biscuit, for they were afraid to betray their presence by lighting fires. The great numerical strength of the enemy suggested prudence, but the duke was for immediate attack. "My ancestors never retreated," he said. "Gentlemen, I will not be the first to do so."

With a few brief words to charge both flanks and centre at once, he dashed on overbearing all resistance. Almost at a blow four thousand prisoners were captured, including the *emir's* wife and mother, much treasure, all the tents, standards, and stores. The rest fled. It was an instance where conspicuous daring tells—where six hundred intrepid men defeated five thousand. A military critic wrote afterwards:

> To attack such a superior force in this way, a leader must be five-and-twenty, like the Duc d'Aumale; he must hardly know what danger is, or have the very devil in him.

The French horsemen had covered ninety miles in thirty-six hours, and the supporting infantry were still eighteen miles to the rear.

'Yet the duke attacked without hesitation: it was good; it was brave; it was brilliant!' This was the verdict of General (afterwards Marshal) St. Arnaud.

The effect of this victory was disastrous to Abd-el-Kadr's cause. His adherents began to fall away from him; he was driven into the western corner of Algeria, and at last, despairing of other help, he crossed the Moorish frontier and threw himself upon the mercy of the Emperor of Morocco. This monarch, Abderrhaman by name, at that time the most powerful ruler in Northern Africa, a descendant of the Prophet, and a most devout Mussulman, at once promised his help. War against Abd-el-Kadr's new ally became inevitable, although the French Government were not disposed to enter upon it lightly. They first remonstrated with the emperor, insisting that he should neither receive nor succour the enemy of France. As the answer was a haughty negative.

Marshal Bugeaud did not wait for definite instructions from home (it was long before the days of the electric telegraph), but proceeded with all promptitude to take the initiative. Hostilities had already commenced on the frontier. There was sharp skirmishing at the outposts, but it was not till the middle of June that all hopes of an amicable settlement were at an end. By that date, Marshal Bugeaud had embarked at Algiers with reinforcements, and proceeded to the mouth of the Tafna. There he disembarked, and advanced to Lalla Maghrina in the direction of the Isly River and some fifty miles south-west of Tlemcen. He was backed up in this by another son of the French king, at that time commanding a French fleet off the coast of Morocco—the Prince de Joinville, who joined the marshal heartily in his desire for vigorous action. The prince without hesitation at once bombarded Tangier, and sent the news to the marshal, whose answer was characteristic. The message reached him the 12th of August; the reply ran as follows:

Prince, you have drawn a bill upon me; I engage to honour it. Tomorrow I shall execute a manoeuvre that will bring me within touch of the emperor's army before he is aware of it; the day after, I shall defeat it.

This bold prediction was fully verified. On the 14th of August, the Battle of Isly was fought and won.

Abderrhaman's son commanded the Moorish army, which was mainly composed of cavalry, estimated afterwards by Marshal Bugeaud at not less than 45,000 strong. It was posted on the western or further bank of the little river in a series of camps, seven in number, 'occupying,' said an eye-witness, 'a greater space than the circumference of Paris.' The French had reconnoitred the enemy's position with their foraging parties sent out daily some distance to the front to cut barley and grass for the cavalry and transport animals.

As a good plan to deceive the Moors, the foragers were despatched as usual on the 13th, with orders not to return at nightfall, when they would be reinforced in their forward position by the whole French army. By this stratagem, the entire force was got within easy reach of the enemy unobserved. Express orders were issued forbidding the men to light fires or even to smoke their pipes.

At daylight Marshal Bugeaud made a demonstration across the river, but encountered no enemy. His advanced line, however, verified the position of the Moorish camp; and now as he prepared to cross with his main body, the Moorish cavalry came down to dispute the passage of the river, but were driven off by the fire of the French skirmishers. The French attack was to be directed upon the highest point of the hills opposite where the Moorish prince had his headquarters surmounted by his standards and his parasol. The advance was made in the formation devised by the marshal when he called it a boar's head. The right and left tusks were represented by infantry in columns ready instantly to form square when threatened by the Moorish horsemen. These now swooped down in immense numbers and with determined courage upon the flanks or 'tusks,' and were received by the squares 'prepared to receive cavalry,' while the skirmishers ran in and lay down for shelter under the bristling bayonets.

The mounted men could not face the deadly fire now opened by the French infantry, and began to waver. Their charges were made in columns of great depth; the first line, being checked, threw the second into disorder, and both fell back upon the third, causing great confusion. The Moors, although good marksmen, could not return an effective fire, and their bullets went too high. Now the French artillery, no more than four light field-pieces, did great execution, and the enemy's onslaught had obviously failed.

Marshal Bugeaud saw that the critical moment had arrived, and proceeded to use his own cavalry with great promptitude and effect. It was in two portions, commanded respectively by Colonels Tartas and Morris. The first half of a total of nineteen squadrons was, with its right pivoted on the river, to circle round to the left and charge the camp; the second, under Colonel Morris, was to repel a threatened attack upon the French right flank by charging the enemy's left. The first of these movements, headed by Yusuf—an Italian by birth, who had once been an Arab slave, but who had joined the French on their first arrival and entered the *Spahis*—was entirely successful: his six squadrons of *Spahis*, supported by three of *Chasseurs*, carried all before them, and, in spite of a well-sustained artillery fire, entered the camp and captured it. Everything—guns, tents, the shops of the artisans, all stores, ammunition, and food—fell into the victor's hands.

At this time a body of still unbeaten cavalry menaced Bugeaud's right flank, and was met by Colonel Morris with six squadrons of *Chasseurs*. He encountered a stubborn resistance, but was presently supported by Bedeau's infantry, when the Moors gave way. Morris now pursued, but the enemy faced round again, and, rallying his forces, seemed inclined to try to retake the camp. There were some twenty thousand of them, and they only yielded to a fresh attack made by the three arms: the artillery went into action on the western bank, the infantry under cover of the guns, the whole of the cavalry followed, and the Moors were completely overthrown. The enemy now retreated in hot haste, and were pursued for several miles. There was one episode in this last phase of the fight which might have proved disastrous to the French. Colonel Morris adventured too far with his horsemen, and found himself surrounded and in danger of being cut off. But he succeeded in holding six thousand horsemen at bay with his five hundred *Chasseurs* until assistance could reach him.

The victory, gained at but small expenditure of life, was yet decisive. From twelve to fifteen hundred Moors were killed or taken prisoners; more than a thousand tents, many guns, a large quantity of small arms, and vast stores of war material were captured. At noon, the French marshal entered the Moorish prince's tent, and beneath its magnificent shelter was regaled upon the tea and cakes prepared in the morning for that unfortunate youth. He himself had fled many miles to Thaza, and orders were already issued to continue the pursuit, when the emperor sent two chieftains into the French camp with proposals for peace. The terms eventually agreed upon were a substantial war indemnity, a rectification of the frontier between Algeria and Morocco, and finally the expulsion of Abdel-Kadr from Moorish territory with an undertaking that he was never again to receive support or assistance.

But Abd-el-Kadr was still at large. He appears to have taken no part in the Battle of Isly, although he must have been in the immediate vicinity. The day after, he was reported to be only a day's march distant, and a bold attempt was made by General Yusuf to seize him. The chief of the *Spahis* disguised a hundred of his troopers in Moorish dresses taken from the spoils of victory, the pointed headgear, long gun, and black *burnouse*, and after a forced march of fifteen miles he came unexpectedly upon an outpost which he charged and captured. There was no Abd-el-Kadr, but his secretary was made prisoner, carrying the official seal and with papers on him indicating his chief's movements. To know where the *emir* was going did not mean his capture. For three years longer, he ranged the mountains or the desert of the interior, a proscribed fugitive without a vestige of his former power. At length in 1847 he came in voluntarily, and surrendered to the Duc d'Aumale, who was then governor-general of Algeria, and the conquest of the province was complete.

Abd-el-Kadr was sent to France and kept there in a sort of open captivity for a number of years. Eventually he was permitted to withdraw to Damascus, where he lived as a French pensioner until his death in 1853.

MARSHAL BUGEAUD

The Sonderbundkreig
1847

The Battle of Gislikon
November 23, 1847
By A J. Butler

"What battle is this?" we can conceive our readers asking; "and where is Gislikon?" The form of the name may put some on the right track. In one of the most frequented regions of Switzerland "-ikons "are as common as "-inghams" in England, and no one who has travelled over any of the railways about Zurich or Lucerne can have failed to notice some instance of the odd-looking termination. Switzerland is indeed the country to which we are going, and among those of our readers who have already visited that "playground of Europe," we will venture to say that at least one-half have been close to, if they have not actually passed over, the field on which the battle that we are going to describe was fought. For Gislikon lies not more than six miles from the top of the world-famous Rigi; it is a station on the not less famous St. Gotthard railway.

Having got so far, we are prepared for further inquiries, not unmixed with incredulity. It is hard for us to realise that a battle has been fought in Switzerland during the last fifty years. One can almost as easily imagine a battle in England as in that prosperous little country, which many of us look upon as almost an appendage to England, and associate with nothing more serious than holidays and hotels and mountain-rambles. The better-informed have heard of cantons, and probably think that they are something equivalent to English counties or French departments; while they suppose that the country called "Switzerland" has always been much where it is now, with the same frontier and the same territory.

How many, we wonder, realise when they cross the well-known

Gemmi Pass from Leukerbad to Kandersteg that they are passing from one sovereign State, with its own laws, into another, and that while the State into which they are going, Bern, has been part of the Confederation which is now called Switzerland for more than 500 years, the one which they are leaving, Valais, only became so at a date when Mr. Gladstone was already six years old?

So, it is, however, and men much younger than Mr. Gladstone can remember a time when Bern and Valais were actually at war with each other, just as, a few years later, Pennsylvania and Louisiana were at war. Happily, in the case or Switzerland the war was quickly finished, lasting hardly as many weeks as the greater conflict lasted years, and involving, as we shall see, a far smaller loss of life and property than many wars which have had far less important results. It is probably not too much to say that had the battle not been fought where it was, or had the issue been different, there would now be no Switzerland at all on the map of Europe.

Before describing the battle, we must give some account of the events which led to it. The years of peace which followed the Battle of Waterloo, were by no means years of domestic tranquillity for most of the Continental States. The various absolute governments had been thoroughly frightened by the events of the French Revolution, and ruled more absolutely than ever. The rearrangement of Europe also, which followed the fall of Napoleon, had, in many cases, produced much discontent; and, in one way or another, every country was going through a critical period. Kings were driven from their thrones; men were constantly punished for the mere expression of their opinions; secret societies were formed, and assassinations were frequent.

Switzerland, too, had its troubles, though as the form of government in every canton was already republican, these took the shape rather of fights between contending parties than of rebellion followed by repression. One great cause of difference was to be found in the various views as to a revision of the "Federal Pact," or treaty, which governed the relations of the States to the Confederation, the Liberals wishing to see these drawn closer, while the Conservatives favoured cantonal independence. Other differences were due to local causes. Thus, in Schwyz a serious quarrel arose over the use of the common pastures. The wealthier men who could keep cows were thought to have unfair privileges over those who had only sheep and goals. The former were known as "horn-men," the latter as "hoof-men." They represented the Clerical (or Conservative) and Liberal parties respec-

At Bern

tively, and the Federal Diet had, in 1838, to interfere to keep the peace between them.

The comparative strength of parties varied very much in the different States, and even in the same State sudden changes of feeling were not infrequent. Moreover, matters were complicated by religious differences. Some of the cantons were Catholic, some Protestant, while in others the population was more or less evenly divided between the two forms of faith. It by no means followed that the political divisions went on the same lines as the religious; and in almost every canton there were representatives of both parties. Lucerne was the most powerful of the Catholic cantons, and until 1841 had been on the Liberal side, and in favour of a revision of the Federal Pact. In that year, however, the government was utterly overthrown at the polls, and the Clerical party came into power, headed by Constantine Siegwart, an able and ambitious man. who had formerly been strong on the other side.

The neighbouring canton of Aargau, which was divided between Catholics and Protestants, and which had only joined the Confederation in 1803, had in the previous year found it necessary to suppress its monasteries, which had fomented opposition to the government. Lucerne made a strong effort to persuade the Federal Diet to treat this as a breach of the Constitution, according to which all religions were to be respected; and Aargau, although many of the Catholic inhabitants were in favour of the suppression, only escaped stronger measures by consenting to restore some of the monasteries. This business, which was not finally settled till 1843, embittered the feeling between the two cantons, and in Switzerland generally. Seven cantons—Lucerne, Uri, Schwyz, Unterwalden, Zug, Fribourg, and Valais—made a formal protest against the decision of the Diet to leave Aargau alone; and subsequently formed themselves into a separate league, "for the protection of the Catholic religion." This league was known as the *Sonderbund*.

Events now began to move rapidly. In May, 1844, fighting took place in Valais, not far from the spot where tourists now go to see the "Gorge of the Trient," and the Liberals, who had been in power until the previous year, were driven out, not without bloodshed; the leaders only escaping by swimming the Rhone. About the same time, Lucerne called in the Jesuits to direct education in the canton. There has always been in Switzerland a good deal of suspicion of this order, who have been, rightly or wrongly, believed to exercise a considerable underhand influence in politics; indeed; the recent conflict in Valais was thought to have been instigated by them; and though they already had a footing in some cantons, their introduction into what was at this time the leading State of the Federation was viewed with alarm, even by many Catholics and Conservatives; while it grievously offended all the cantons in which there was a Liberal majority.

Matters were not improved when the Lucerne Government seized and imprisoned its leading opponents. In the following winter and spring armed bands of irresponsible volunteers from Aargau, Bern, and other cantons, with some exiles from Lucerne, made attempts to invade that State. In the second and more serious of these 3,600 men, under Colonel Ochsenbein (who, a year or two later, was President of the Diet), succeeded, on March 31st, 1845, in getting within a few miles of the city of Lucerne, but were beaten back by the cantonal troops, with a loss of 140 killed and 1,800 prisoners.

Herein they got no more than they deserved; but the Lucerne Government put itself in the wrong by the extreme severity, amounting to a Reign of Terror, with which it now proceeded to treat its opponents, and by the undisguised manner in which it promoted the organisation of the separate league. The government also began to intrigue with foreign powers, especially France and Austria, obtaining arms from the former and money from the latter. Three thousand muskets with ammunition which the Austrians attempted to forward from Milan, were impounded by the authorities of Canton Ticino; and so audacious were the Lucerne Government grown, that they actually complained of this as a violation of State rights.

It was obvious that the remaining fifteen cantons, comprising nearly five-sixths of the whole population, could not long tolerate the presence of this hostile league in their midst. A glance at the map will show that of the seven cantons composing it, one, Fribourg, lies apart, while the others stretch continuously from the extreme south-west of Switzerland, near Chamonix, away to the Lake of Zurich. Not only do they divide the Confederation almost in two, but they hold three out of the five main roads which lead through Switzerland into Italy including the two which at that time were, and probably still are, by far the most frequented—the Simplon and the St. Gothard. Moreover, the attitude of the Great Powers showed plainly that the very existence of Switzerland as a separate and independent nation was at stake. None of the Continental Governments had any love for the little State, which, besides showing that men could live and thrive under

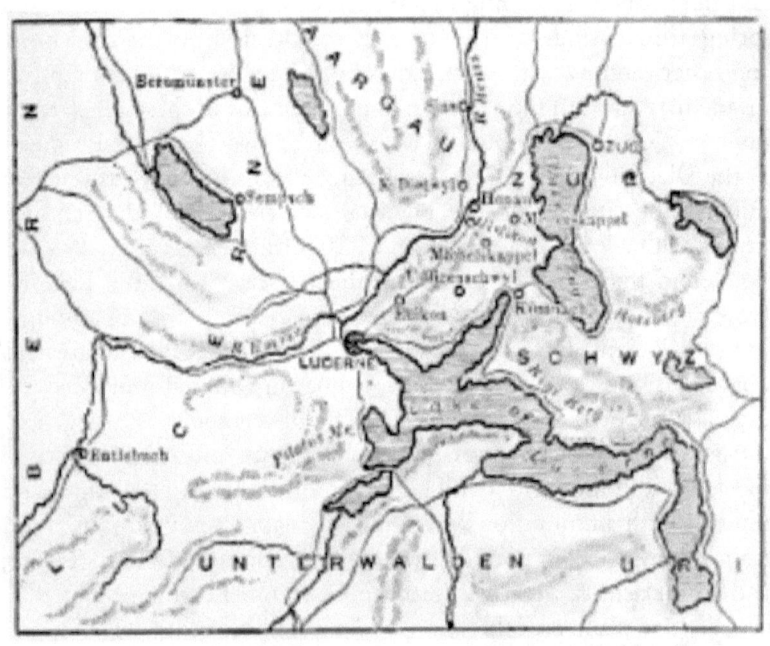

LUCERNE AND SURROUNDING DISTRICT.

a republican constitution, was always ready to offer shelter to those of their subjects whose political views made residence in their native countries unsafe.

Accordingly, we find the Protestant King of Prussia no less anxious than the Protestant M. Guizot, Minister of Louis Philippe, for the success of the Catholic *Sonderbund*; while Austria and Sardinia, who a few months later were to be at each other's throat, agreed at least in sending help to Lucerne. The task of the loyal cantons was not easy. In several of them parties were very evenly divided. The only central authority at this time consisted of the Federal Diet, in which every canton, no matter what its size, had an equal representation, while the members were only deputies, bound to vote as the majority of their State directed them. The important canton of St. Gallen, the fifth in numbers, and one of the wealthiest, was long in deciding. The Catholics form about three-fifths of the population there, and it was not till May, 1847, that the local elections resulted in a Liberal majority, and consequently the return of a Liberal member to the Diet.

On July 20th, the Diet was at last able to pass a resolution calling upon the Sonderbund to dissolve itself, as being in contravention of the Federal Constitution. The next three months were spent in efforts to bring this about peaceably, but the leaders had gone too far to retreat. They relied, also, not merely on the intervention of the Great Powers, but on their own favourable position in a district almost inaccessible from most sides, on the ancient reputation of the so-called "Forest Cantons"—Schwyz, Uri, Unterwalden, and Lucerne, which had been the original cradle of Swiss liberty.

On October 20th, the *Sonderbund* deputies offered to dissolve their league, but only on conditions which were equivalent to a concession by the other side of all the claims to assert which the league had been formed, and on the rejection of these terms by the majority, they left the Diet, Bernard Meyer, the deputy from Lucerne, calling upon God to decide between them. "You had better not speak of God," exclaimed the deputy from Catholic Solothurn; "this business is not His, but the Devil's work." On November 4, the Diet finally resolved that the *Sonderbund* be put down by force of arms, that the frontiers of the seceding cantons be occupied, and all intercourse with them be broken off.

The command of the Federal forces had been entrusted to Colonel William Henry Dufour, of Geneva. Switzerland possesses no standing army; but every able-bodied man goes through military training, and

FRIBURG

there is a permanent staff of superior officers, on which Dufour held the post of quartermaster-general. He was now sixty years old; and though in his youth he had served in the French army during all the time of Napoleon's great campaigns, and risen to the rank of captain, he had seen no active service, having passed those stirring years as an engineer-officer in the island of Corfu, which for most of the time was blockaded by the English fleet. When Geneva became part of Switzerland, in 1815, he transferred his services to the Confederation, and gained a considerable reputation as a student and teacher of military science.

He was also at the head of the Commission which from 1833 onwards was engaged in the production of the finest map of any country which up till then had existed—Ordnance Map of Switzerland. Only a few days before he had remarked to one of his officers that it was lucky for them both that their duties would prevent them from taking an active part in the conflict! As the result showed, no better man could have been chosen. On October 25th, he received the rank of general, and took the oath of office as commander-in-chief. In a few days, he had under his orders a force of nearly 100,000 men and 174 guns.

The *Sonderbund* leaders had been unable to find a commander among the citizens of the seceding cantons. Their choice finally fell upon Colonel Ulrich Salis-Soglio, of Chur in Graubünden. Like Dufour, he was an elderly man, but had had the advantage of actual military experience. He had served in the Bavarian Army during the Leipzig campaign, and had distinguished himself at the battle of Hanau. For twenty-five years, he had been an officer in the Swiss regiment in the Dutch service. He is described as a man of charming manners and chivalrous courage; but by no means Dufour's equal as a strategist. Curiously enough he was a Protestant. The *Sonderbund* forces amounted in all to about 78,000 men and 72 guns. He commanded only the forces of the "Forest Cantons" and Zug. General Maillardoz commanded in Fribourg, General Kalbermatten in Valais.

Dufour's first care was to secure himself from attack in the rear by subduing Fribourg, which, as we have said, is separated by the cantons of Bern and Vaud from the rest of those composing the *Sonderbund*. His strategy for this purpose was simple, but effective. The town of Fribourg is not more than sixteen or seventeen miles from Bern, in a westerly direction. It was strongly fortified, and defended by a force of from 12,000 to 15,000 men. The defenders naturally expected that the attack would come from the direction of the Federal capital, and they had made their arrangements to resist it on that side by throwing up batteries and blocking the roads with trees. Dufour caused his first division, under Colonel Rilliet, to advance in three brigades from Vevey, Moudon, and Payerne, in Canton Vaud, with instructions to reach Matran, some four miles south-west of Fribourg, on November 12th. This manoeuvre was executed punctually.

At the same time, Colonel Burckhardt's division, which had been stationed in Canton Bern, instead of advancing directly upon Fribourg, made a night-march to the right, and took up a position about the same distance north-west of the town. Lastly, Colonel Ochsenbein was directed to make a demonstration on the side of Bern, so as to draw off the attention of the defenders from the movements on the west and north, and at the same time to watch the approaches from the south. These dispositions were all so accurately carried out that on the morning or November 13th Dufour was able to send a missive to the mayor of Fribourg, pointing out that his city was surrounded by superior forces—they were from 25,000 to 30,000 men, with sixty guns—and that under the circumstances he could surrender without discredit.

The authorities of the city saw the force of his arguments, and agreed to an armistice for twenty-four hours; and on the following day a capitulation was signed, the first article of which bound Fribourg to leave the *Sonderbund* forthwith. This success was not quite bloodless, for on the afternoon of the 13th some of the outposts of the first division who were stationed in a wood on the west of a town, and had not heard of the armistice, made, under some misconception, an attack upon a redoubt which was close in front of them. The artillery on both sides came into action, and the Federal troops lost seven killed and fifty wounded.

The fall of Fribourg, says Dufour, fell like a thunderclap on the *Sonderbund*, and astonished the rest of Europe. His own task became much easier, owing to the spirit of cheerfulness and unanimity which now took the place of the indecision and even reluctance which had been felt in many quarters. He lost no time in grappling with the more arduous part of his work—the subjection of Lucerne. Hitherto he had given strict orders to his subordinate commanders that they were to act entirely on the defensive, and his orders had been obeyed, though to do so must have required some self-restraint on the part of those officers. For the *Sonderbund* forces were by no means inactive.

Major Scherrer seized the colours

The canton of Aargau runs down in a long tongue between Lucerne and Zug, forming the district known as the Freiamt. At the northern end of this tongue, where it widens out to the full breadth of the canton, is the village of Muri, where one of the suppressed monasteries had been situated. Perhaps the *Sonderbund* expected to find some sympathisers in that district. At all events, on November 12th a strong force, in two columns, under General Salis and his Chief of the Staff, Colonel Elgger, respectively, entered Aargau, with the intention of marching by different routes upon Muri. The general, starting from Gislikon, entered the Freiamt at its southernmost point; while Elgger, keeping within the territory of Lucerne, was to take a parallel line and approach Muri from the south-west. It was a foggy day, and the two columns, separated by a range of lofty hills, completely lost touch of each other. In the afternoon, Salis made an attempt to destroy a bridge which the Federal engineers had thrown over the River Reuss, to connect Zürich with Aargau. But he was met with a stout resistance, and compelled to retire.

Near Muri he again fell in with troops from St. Gallen and Appenzell, who received him with a vigorous fire, and he found nothing to do but return to his starting-point. Colonel Elgger was at first more fortunate, and drove the Aargau troops back with some loss. His own son, who was acting as his *aide-de-camp*, got a bullet in his head, but lived to edit the Swiss *Military Gazette* thirty years later. Presently an order to the artillery to retire in order to take up a better position, caused a panic among some troops from Valais, who probably did not understand the words, and only saw the movement. They fled, and Elgger, having lost a part of his force and hearing the sound of Salis' guns grow fainter and fainter, had nothing to do but to withdraw. A third column, which was to have invaded Aargau further to the westward, succeeded in surprising the Federal outposts and bombarding an unfortified village; but did not wait for the arrival of the Aargau battalions, which hastened up at the summons of the alarm-bells.

In the south, where the Federal strength was less, matters for a few days looked more promising for the *Sonderbund*. On November 17th, a body of 2000 men, with four guns, crossed the St. Gotthard Pass in a storm of wind and snow, and fell upon Airolo. The Ticino troops, who were holding that place, 2700 strong, hardly expected a visit in such weather, and allowed themselves to be surprised. Before they' knew what was happening, the village was surrounded by the riflemen of Uri, and cannon-balls were crashing through the snow-covered roofs.

They fled in disorder to Bellinzona, with a loss of six killed and thirty wounded, leaving weapons, ammunition, baggage, even their colonel's despatch-boxes and dressing-case, in the enemy's hands. This was the nearest approach to success which the *Sonderbund* had. It was hoped that Ticino, being a Catholic canton, at least a portion of the population might welcome the invaders; but they received no encouragement, and in a few days the approach of the Federal Army to Lucerne rendered their retreat necessary.

For Dufour did not let the grass grow under his feet. Two days after the capitulation of Fribourg had been signed, his headquarters were at Aarau, the capital of Aargau, and all his dispositions made for striking the decisive blow. Lucerne is very well situated for defence against an enemy approaching from the north. The stream of the Reuss, flowing out of the lake towards the north-west, presently sweeps round to the north-east. Just at the angle the smaller River Emme joins it from the south-west, so that a continuous obstacle is offered to an attacking force. Between the Reuss and the Kussnacht arm of the lake (which washes the foot of the Rigi) is a range of lofty wooded hills called the Rooterberg, which continue almost to the Lake of Zug; and in the other direction, a similar line of hills, cut by deep gorges, runs parallel to the Emme.

It was on this latter side that the ill-starred attempt of the Free Corps had been made in 1845. Dufour determined on this occasion to approach from the other direction, along the line of the Reuss, and between that river and the Rooterberg. It was a hazardous operation: in his own words, "*taking the bull by the horns.*" Gislikon, the point where the main road crosses the river, while that on the right bank comes close to it, was strongly fortified; and the Rooterberg afforded an admirable position for sharpshooters and artillery. But by advancing from this side he would, if successful, separate Lucerne and Schwyz, and would strike at the heart of the secession. Therefore, while ordering all the five divisions which he intended to employ, to converge by various roads on Lucerne, from east, north, and west, he resolved to make his main attack with the fourth and fifth, under Colonels Ziegler and Gmür. Of these, the former was at present quartered in Aarau, the latter between the Reuss and the Lake of Zurich.

The attack was fixed for November 23rd. Two days before, the little canton of Zug, which had entered the Sonderbund somewhat reluctantly, seeing that further resistance was useless, capitulated, thereby relieving Dufour of anxiety for his left flank. On the 22nd the General

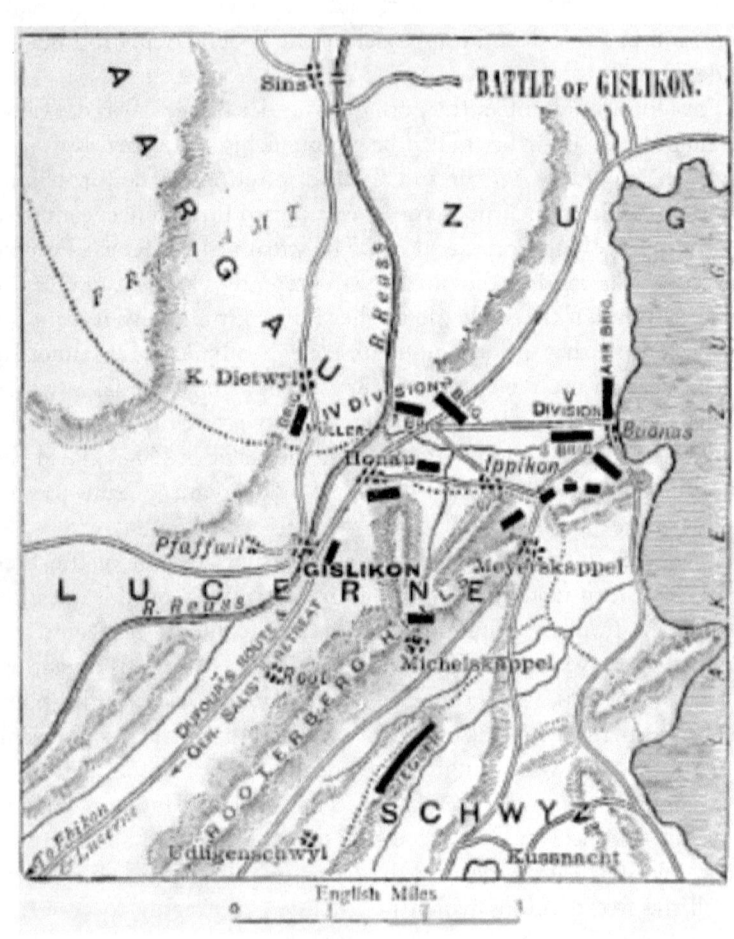

issued a proclamation to his troops, reminding them that they were performing a duty to their country, and bidding them lay aside all feeling of hostility as soon as the victory was won. They were specially enjoined to respect all churches and buildings used in the service of religion, and to see that no injury was done to non-combatants or to private property.

That evening Colonel Ziegler's division bivouacked in the "Freiamt," right up to the frontier of Lucerne. It was a clear night, and round the Lake of Zug they could see the watchfires of the fifth division, which was now occupying that canton. In the early morning of the 23rd the Aargau engineers threw a bridge of boats over the Reuss at Sins, another being placed a couple of miles higher up, at Oberrüti. Ziegler, with two brigades of his division, under Colonels Egloff and Kônig, crossed to the right bank, and came into touch with Colonel Gmür and the fifth division, advancing from the Lake of Zug. The third brigade, under Colonel Müller, was to remain on the left bank, and attack Gislikon from the direction of Klein Dietwyl. It should have acted in conjunction with the third division, under Donatz, which occupied the next place to the westward, but bad roads hindered that commander from arriving in time to take part in the main action.

About nine in the morning the batteries of Gislikon opened fire upon Müller's brigade, compelling it to retire for a time. One of the first shots killed Captain Buk, a refugee from Lucerne, who was marching with the column. Colonel Ziegler, meanwhile, was making progress on the other side of the Reuss. In spite of the fire from the Rooterberg, and from the Lucerne artillery in front of the village of Honau, he pressed on, and presently his guns coming into action caused the enemy's batteries to retire. They made a short stand in Honau, but were soon forced back upon Gislikon, where regular earthworks had been thrown up. Here they made a resolute defence, the battery under Captain Mazzola specially distinguishing itself.

On the other side, Rust's battery (from Solothurn) galloped through Honau, leaving the infantry behind, and took up its position in an orchard, five hundred paces—this was before the days of rifled cannon—from the earthworks. Its first shot killed and wounded five men in Hegi's company, which retired, leaving Mazzola's left flank uncovered. Mazzola, however, literally "stuck to his guns," though the artillery on the further side of the Reuss was now playing upon him, and presently compelled Rust to retire behind the fighting line, barely saving his guns from capture by the Lucerne *chasseurs*. A plucky action on the part of one of his subordinates is recorded. Just after the Solothurn guns had retired, a body of troops was seen in the spot they had occupied. In the smoke and haze of the November day, it was not certain whether they were friend or foe.

Corporal Pfiffer asked his captain's permission to go and ascertain, which Mazzola willingly gave. Pfiffer left the battery, and went forward till he could see the others clearly; then, waving his sword, cried: "Fire, Captain; it is the enemy!" and made his way back. General Salis, who had taken up his position in the battery, pressed a piece of gold into his hand; but the sturdy Swiss rejected it, saying: "No need for that, General; I only did my duty." The narrator of this story, himself a bitter partisan on the Catholic side, adds that Pfiffer was a well-known adherent of the Liberals. Here, as later in the American Civil War, when hostilities had once begun, men put the defence of their homes first, and let their private opinions wait for quieter times.

The troops whose identity Corporal Pfiffer had ascertained were some battalions of Egloff's and Kônig's brigades. These were Appenzellers under Benziger, and Aargauers under Häusler. The former could not face the storm of grape with which they were received, and took shelter in some gravel-pits. Häusler's men, with whom the Brigadier-Colonel Egloff was himself riding, began in their turn to waver. At this moment, Major Scherrer, whose own battalion was also unsteady, seized the colours, and fixing them into the ground, cried out: "Switzers, do you know what that means?" Thus encouraged, Häusler's men held their ground, and, presently, through the personal efforts of Egloff and his staff, the fugitives were rallied, and the line restored.

Meanwhile, the Lucerne and Unterwalden companies had pressed too far in the direction of the Rooterberg, allowing the Federal skirmishers to penetrate between them and the artillery, so that the earthworks were denuded of all covering infantry. Egloff at once ordered up three batteries, and under the fire of these, combined with that from others on the other bank, the intrepid Mazzola, after nearly an hour's duel between his one battery and five or six of the enemy's, was compelled to withdraw, and abandon Gislikon. General Salis, too, who had taken up his position in the battery, had been severely wounded in the temple by a grapeshot, though he made light of his wound, and refused to leave the fight.

König's brigade, meanwhile, to which had been assigned the duty of clearing the west slopes of the Rooterberg and sheltering Egloff's left flank, had met with a sudden resistance. Again, and again they had to fall back, until Ziegler himself, dismounting and leading the right wing, succeeded in pressing the enemy so far up the hill as to secure Egloff from a flank attack, and set part of his own main force to operate against Mazzola. König, with the left wing, attempted to force the position of Michelskappel, on the crest of the ridge, but could not succeed in dislodging the troops from Schwyz who held it. Gmür's division, meanwhile, had captured Meyerskappel, on the eastern side of the ridge, and was advancing upon Lucerne by the road between the hills and the lake.

But the retreat from Gislikon had decided the battle. At 3 p.m. General Salis gave the order to retire upon Ebikon, a village not more than three miles from Lucerne. In the city, itself, men had been listening all day long, with painful anxiety, to the thunder of the cannon, but no news of the fight had reached them. At four, arrived an orderly from the general, bringing a message couched in the form usual with defeated commanders, to the effect that he had been compelled to retire temporarily upon Ebikon, but hoped to maintain his ground there for a time. He added, however, that the loss of Gislikon had rendered the position of Lucerne very precarious. A steamer had been in readiness all day, and on the receipt of this news, the Council-of-War, with Siegwart and Meyer at its head, went on board, taking the military treasury and all documents, papers, etc., with them, and steamed up the lake to Flüelen, leaving orders to General Salis to arrange for an armistice.

The general himself arrived about 8 p.m., suffering from his wound, and after giving the requisite instructions, departed to Unterwalden. As an old soldier, he doubtless knew that further resistance meant useless bloodshed. Colonel Elgger, his Chief of the Staff, had been for two days maintaining a stout resistance in the Valley of Entlebuch, west of the city, to the seventh Federal division, under Colonel Ochsenbein—who had his former defeat on almost the same ground to avenge—and had hastened back to Lucerne, when night put an end to further fighting on the 23rd. He was at first in favour of defending the city; but was soon convinced of the hopelessness of the situation, and agreed to communicate with Dufour.

At 9 in the morning of the 24th came the reply that it was too late to countermand the advance, but that the Federal troops were allowed to enter peaceably, and the Federal flag was displayed, no warlike measures would be taken.

Rust's battery galloped through Honau

Accordingly, at midday on the 24th, the Federal forces marched into Lucerne by all the gates. Twenty days had finished the civil war. The total losses were, on the Federal side, 60 killed and 386 wounded; on that of the *Sonderbund*, 36 and 119. Dufour attributes the smallness of these figures to the fact that the fighting took place in a broken and thickly-wooded country, where cover was plentiful. Something was, no doubt, also due to the inexperience of the gunners.

Great care was taken to prevent any excesses on the part of the victors. The Bern division, between whom and Lucerne bitter feelings had existed ever since 1845, was not allowed to take part in the entry into the city, but had to remain, by Colonel Ochsenbein's orders, in the suburbs. Dufour ordered a joint "Church parade" to be held, the Catholic troops attending Mass in the chief church of Lucerne, while a service was held in the open-air for the Protestants. Subsequently he wrote:

> The troops on both sides showed by their conduct that every Swiss is a born soldier.

The Confederation had had a narrow escape. On the day when war had been declared, M. Guizot had, on behalf of France, proposed to the other Great Powers that a joint note should be sent to the Swiss Diet calling upon them to submit the questions at issue to foreign arbitration. As it was hardly doubtful that the proposal would be rejected, this meant armed intervention, with the certainty of an ultimate partition of Switzerland. The Continental Powers were ready enough, but Lord Palmerston, then English Foreign Secretary, who had. as he said, "no wish to see Switzerland made a Poland of," managed, by objections and suggestions, to postpone the delivery of the note till November 30th. By that time the Diet was able to reply that there was no longer any *Sonderbund*. In the course of the following year, Prussia, Austria, and France had matters enough of their own to attend to; and the Swiss were able to proceed unmolested with the revision of their Constitution into the form under which the country has prospered ever since. Formerly a Confederation of States, they have since 1848 been a Confederated State.

The conflict left—except, perhaps, among a few of the *Sonderbund* leaders—no ill-feeling behind. Some years later Dufour could write:

> The citizens of the old cantons (*i.e.* the Forest Cantons) nearly all have pipes with my picture on them, and call me 'Our little Dufour.'

His long and useful life ended in 1875.

LAKE ZUG

THE 'TEN DAYS OF BRESCIA' REVOLT
1849

The Storming of Brescia
March 31–April 1, 1849
By A. J. Butler

The year 1848 has been called the "Year of Revolution." All over the Continent of Europe thrones were tottering, in some cases falling; the old arbitrary and repressive systems of government which had prevailed since the downfall of Napoleon were drawing towards their end. In Italy, the movement was strongly felt. Over a great part of that country arbitrary government existed in its most hateful form, being administered by foreigners. The provinces of Lombardy and Venetia had to take their orders from Vienna; and though as individuals the Austrian-Germans are a kindly and genial race, their political system was marked by pedantic officialism, and their rule was consequently of a kind calculated to be especially offensive to a high-spirited and somewhat disorderly people, with traditions of hatred to Germans extending back over six or seven centuries.

The Lombard cities with Milan at their head, and glorious memories behind them of municipal liberties wrested at the sword's point from German emperors, chafed especially under the yoke; and the sight of the neighbouring State of Piedmont enjoying, as part of the Sardinian Kingdom, something like constitutional government under its old rulers, the house of Savoy, was not likely to make them more patient. In March, after five days of fighting, Milan drove out the Austrians, and almost simultaneously the Sardinian Army invaded Lombardy. Venice also rose in insurrection, and even in Vienna itself matters looked so threatening that the minister.

Prince Metternich, who had been the mainstay of reactionary and coercive policy, was forced to resign. Fortunately for the Austrians, their affairs in Italy were in the hands of a capable soldier. Marshal Radetzky was at this time little short of eighty years old, but he had lost nothing of his skill. Withdrawing behind the Mincio, he rallied his forces, and issuing forth again, before the end of the summer, he had inflicted a series of defeats on the Sardinian Army, driven it out of Lombardy, and retaken Milan.

Among the other Lombard cities none was so closely linked with the fortunes of Milan as the neighbouring city of Brescia. Lying at the very foot of the Alps, of which the last spurs descend in green vine-clad undulations to the Lombard plain, and clustered round the foot of the hill on which stands its ancient citadel, known in mediaeval times as "The Falcon of Italy," Brescia has had a chequered and turbulent existence almost since the beginning of history. Few cities, probably, have been more frequently in a state of revolt against something or somebody. It was hardly to be expected that the Brescians would sit quiet while their brethren of Milan were striking a blow for freedom; but their rising was soon suppressed, and all that they gained was the imposition by the Austrian general, Haynau, of a fine upon the city amounting to some £50,000.

During the winter, Brescia was seething with revolution, but no overt steps were taken. The Austrian commander seems to have thought that dissatisfaction could be removed by stopping all outward manifestations of it, even the most childish; and edicts were issued forbidding the wearing of red shoes, velvet coats, and hats of a particular shape. In March, 1849, the Sardinians renewed the war, and on the 16th all troops were withdrawn from Brescia for service in Piedmont, leaving only a garrison of 500 men with fourteen guns in the castle, a few gendarmes in the town, and a great many sick in the various military hospitals, where also arms seem to have been stored. Half the fine imposed by General Haynau had been paid, and the remainder fell due on the 20th of this month. Half of this balance had by the 23rd been received at the municipal treasury, but no more. All further payments were refused, and the officials of the corporation, whose duty it was to collect it, were maltreated, and ultimately sent out of the city in custody.

Throughout the proceedings, the deputy mayor (in the absence of the mayor himself) and the other regular municipal authorities, seeing the impossibility of a successful resistance, and foreseeing the terrible consequences which a fresh revolt would undoubtedly entail, did their best to counsel moderation and submission; but they were either not listened to or insulted as aristocrats and cowards. A "Committee of Public Defence" was formed, consisting of an engineer and a lawyer,

THEN BEGAN A MURDEROUS FIGHT

the latter being apparently the moving spirit. A man with a turn for devising inflammatory proclamations, and no practical knowledge of military affairs, is about the worst leader that an excitable populace can have at such a juncture; and such Signor Cassola, to judge from his own account of the transactions of these days, seems to have been.

A few troops, mostly deserters from Italian regiments in the Austrian service, were at the disposal of the insurgent leaders; but these, to the number of about 400, were kept outside of the city, on the slope of the hills known as the Ronchi, lying to the north of the road which leads eastward from Brescia to Verona. There were also in the city a certain number of retired officers who were willing to cast in their lot with their fellow-citizens; but their offers of service were declined, and every parish was told to elect its own chiefs.

The first actual attack on the Austrian garrison was made on the 23rd, when a piquet of soldiers, engaged in convoying provisions to the castle, was set upon and roughly used, being chased through the town, and a few men clubbed to death. The imperial eagles were also torn down from the public buildings. An attempt was then made to get arms from one of the hospitals; but the guard opened fire, and the insurgents retired. The *commandant* of the castle, however, thought it as well to withdraw into the castle such of the sick as could be moved, as well as the *gendarmes*, and further demanded of the town council that the officials who had, as we saw, been arrested earlier in the day, should be delivered up to him.

These had been placed in the custody of the troops on the Ronchi, so that the town council were unable to comply, whereupon a few shells were thrown into the town during the night; while from every tower the church-bells hurled back defiance in the old Italian fashion. On the following morning, at the request of the military doctors who remained in the hospitals, the bombardment was suspended, on condition that the sick should not be molested, as in the present temper of the people it was not unlikely that they might be.

Meanwhile, the fate of Italy was being decided, at any rate for some years to come, on another field. Radetzky had met the Sardinian army under its king, Charles Albert, and overthrown it utterly on the field of Novara. News travelled less rapidly then than now, and it was not for two or three days that the result of the battle was known at Brescia, and then the true intelligence was disastrously blended with falsehood. A Polish adventurer, named Chrzanowski, held high command in the Sardinian Army.

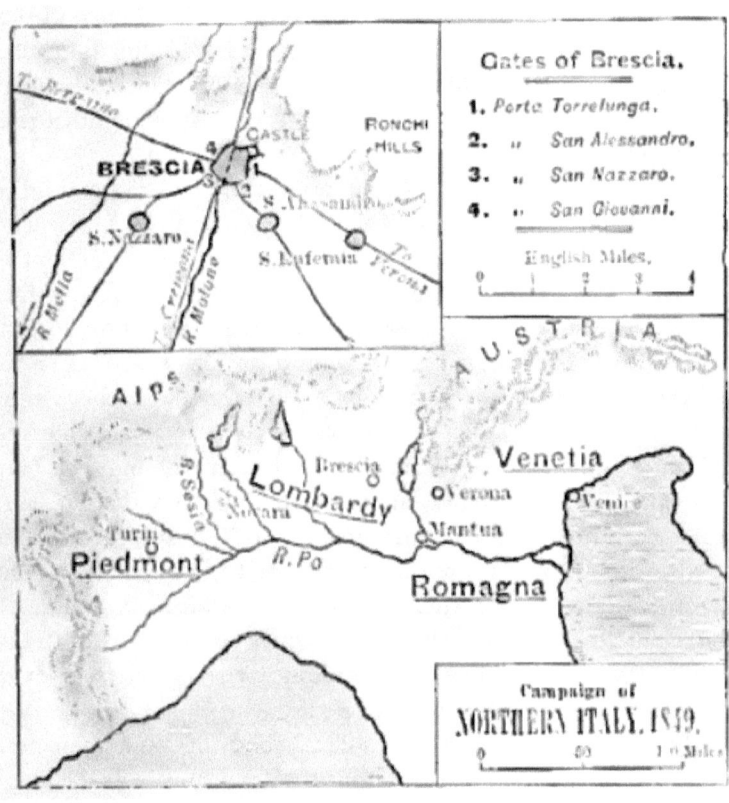

A bulletin, purporting to come from this man, was spread through Piedmont and Lombardy, to the effect that, repudiating the armistice signed after Novara, he had attacked the Austrian Army, and favoured by the breaking down of a bridge over the River Sesia, had succeeded in dividing it, and forcing the great part to lay down their arms, had in turn extorted from Radetzky an armistice binding him to evacuate Lombardy at once. This ridiculous story, though wholly unconfirmed, was placarded over the town by the Committee of Public Defence, who must be held responsible for the stubborn resistance to which it excited the people, and for the 'terrible retribution which that resistance incurred.'

On March 25th, General Nugent arrived before Brescia, from Verona, bringing with him a force of 1,000 men and two guns, which reinforcements, in the course of the next few days, more than doubled. He established himself in the village of Sant' Eufemia, about three miles to the east of Brescia, after dispersing the force on the Ronchi, and on the 26th summoned the citizens to surrender and take down the barricades which by this time had been erected. On their refusal, he assaulted the Torrelunga gate, by which the Verona road enters the city, but was repulsed after four hours of furious fighting. The bombardment from the castle was now renewed, and the Committee sent a message to the *commandant* threatening for every shell that fell into the town to put to death ten of the sick in the hospitals. It does not appear that this atrocious threat was ever carried into execution. But by this time there was very little government or discipline in Brescia. Sorties were undertaken without orders, just at the pleasure of the commanders of the armed bands.

Then, on the evening of March 28th, a body of young men, headed by Tito Speri, made a sortie from the Torrelunga gate. Falling in with a superior force of the enemy, Speri, who seems to have kept his head, proposed to retire. His followers, however, cried out upon his cowardice, and, waving his sword, he called upon them to follow him, and dashed at the enemy. As usually happens in such cases, not more than thirty had the courage of their tongues, and Speri, with his little band, were soon surrounded. After a short scuffle, most succeeded in cutting their way through; but the leader and five others were taken prisoners, and a few remained on the field. Speri presently managed to make his escape, but was in after-days recaptured and hanged at Mantua, one of the stupid pieces of cruelty which in these years too often disgraced the Austrian Government.

On the final liberation of Lombardy in 1850, his fellow-citizens erected a statue of him in a square of the town through which the visitor passes on his way to mount the steep Line which leads to the castle. After this adventure, sorties were forbidden, and hostilities were confined for a day or two to keeping up a fire of small-arms upon the castle from the neighbouring houses and barricades, by which a few gunners were killed. But the end was not far off. In the night of the 30th, General Haynau arrived and took the command. Including the troops in the corps, he had less than 4,000 men at his disposal, but his arrangements were quickly made. Throwing one battalion into the castle, to which at its north-eastern corner there is access without passing through the town, he divided the remainder into five bodies, sending one to block each of the roads by which the city is approached.

The main assault was to be delivered, as before, on the Porta Torrelunga. In the course of the forenoon he was approached by the municipal officials; and at their request he undertook to abstain from further action till two in the afternoon, on the chance of his terms being accepted. But by this time passion ran too high for any conciliation. The people hardly knew in what cause they were fighting: they had nothing to do with Piedmont—even the tricolour of United Italy was not displayed. For the present, they fought under the red flag; and even this to the majority probably had no particular signification. As of old, the citizen knew no country but his own city; and if Florence three hundred and fifty years before had overawed the hosts of France by the mere threat to ring her bells, why should not Brescia try her fortune against Austria? At two o'clock, then, the bells rang out once more, and the rattle of musketry gave the answer of the citizens to all proposals for surrender.

Still Haynau, ruthless as he is reputed to have been, seems to have shrunk from exposing either his men to a street fight or an undisciplined population to the fury of a storming army, and it was not till four o'clock that the guns of the castle opened upon the town. At the same time a detachment of troops was sent to make its way along the eastern rampart, and take in flank the barricade which defended Porta Torrelunga. This was effected, and Nugent's column fought their way in. The general himself fell mortally wounded, but the column pressed on. Haynau, in his report to Radetzky, says:

Then began a murderous fight, conducted on the part of the

insurgents, from barricade to barricade, from house to house, with the utmost obstinacy. I could never have believed, (adds the stolid German with some *naiveté*), that so bad a cause could have been so stubbornly defended.

The troops, however, fought no less stubbornly, and though losing heavily, had before nightfall established themselves in some of the first houses.

At daybreak on April 1st the bells of Brescia rang out for the last time. Haynau, on his side, ordered a vigorous bombardment, and renewed the assault. Fighting was resumed with more ferocity than ever. No quarter was given, and every house from which a shot came was mercilessly set on fire. Discipline was bound to tell at last. Foot by foot the soldiers advanced, under pouring rain, through the narrow, barricaded streets. Flank attacks gradually cleared the gates of San Alessandro on the south, and San Nazzaro at the south-east corner (where now is the railway station), and by evening that of San Giovanni on the west was in the hands of the Austrians. Meanwhile, a force from the castle had forced the barricades which had been raised at the head of all the streets leading to it, driving the defenders back to the lower ground.

The insurgents were now cooped up in the north-western angle of the city. Their ammunition was failing. The "Committee of Public Defence," as such bodies are too apt to do, had taken steps to secure its personal safety; the municipal authorities offered the capitulation which had been demanded a few hours before; and by six o'clock the struggle was over. On the Austrian side, a general, two colonels, six other officers, and 480 men had been killed, and at least as many wounded. That the conduct of the troops, after the capture of the city, was worse than usual under similar circumstances has hardly been proved; but many brutalities were undoubtedly committed.

Still, it hardly behoves us, with our memories of San Sebastian, to cast stones at others; and it must be admitted that their provocations were great. From the cowardly attack on a few soldiers and gendarmes, with which the rising began, to the murder of some alleged "police-agents" perpetrated when it became clear that the cause was lost, many acts were committed by the insurgents which could not fail to exasperate the victors. But the unhappy city had surely been punished enough, and the shootings, hangings, and floggings which earned for General Haynau the nickname of "the hyæna," were superfluous cruelties. They were not forgotten ten years later, and served to add a louder ring to the cheers with which Brescia welcomed the French and Sardinian armies within her walls in 1859.

THE FIRST ITALIAN WAR OF INDEPENDENCE
1848-49

The Battle of Novara
March 23, 1849
By Major G. Le M. Gretton

On the night of the 21st of March, 1849, the Piedmontese and the Austrians lay facing each other in the Lomelina, a fertile province of Piedmont which lies along the western bank of the Ticino. On the Piedmontese left there had been sharp fighting throughout the day, and the bivouac of the King of Piedmont was formed near the village of Sforzesca, on a plain covered with the bodies of the dead. The villages were filled with wounded men; the sky was red with the glare from burning farms and from the camp-fires, round which the troops waited for daylight to recommence the fray. As far as the king had been able to learn the result of the various scattered combats which had taken place during the day, his troops had been successful; his infantry had shown steadiness, his cavalry great dash.

A Savoyard regiment, though much harassed by the enemy's skirmishers, coolly reserved their fire until the main body of their enemy were within easy range. Then they poured in a storm of bullets, which they followed up with a charge so desperate that the Austrians fled, panic-stricken, before them. When the officers succeeded in halting the Savoyards, the men had angrily inquired why they were not allowed to pursue; and, in reply to the explanation that there were no regiments in support, they had retorted proudly:

"Do Savoyards ever need supports?"

Close to Sforzesca there had been a brilliant little *mêlée*. A battalion of Piedmontese, after routing a body of Croatian infantry with the bayonet, were caught in disorder by Hungarian hussars, who, charging like a whirlwind, compelled the Italians to take refuge behind a battery of artillery. So straight did the Hungarians ride that they were almost among the guns when, in their turn, they were defeated by a well-delivered counter-stroke. In the very nick of time two squadrons of heavy cavalry took them in flank, and, after emptying many saddles, drove the survivors headlong back.

But Charles Albert and his staff were racked with anxiety about their right. Early in the day two divisions had been ordered to seize the town of Mortara before the Austrians could occupy it; and although heavy firing in the afternoon and evening showed that his troops were hotly engaged with the enemy in the neighbourhood of this town, no news came to him of the result of the fighting. Determined to set a good example to his men, the king lay down on the bed of empty sacks which had been extemporised for him; and he even slept, though ill and fitfully. At his head stood two faithful servants, whose Court livery of crimson and gold looked strangely out of place amidst the horrors of the battlefield. An *aide-de-camp* sat by him to replace the rug which the king constantly threw off, as he tossed and muttered, and thrust his right arm out threateningly in the direction of the Austrian army. Around him lay the staff, encircled by a ring of sentries, who, leaning on their arms, watched the disordered slumbers of their monarch with superstitious awe.

In order to understand the short campaign which ended at Novara, it is necessary for a moment to glance at the state of Italy in 1848-9. Early in his career the Great Napoleon had overrun and conquered the peninsula. Much to the advantage of her people, he had replaced the miserable princelings who tyrannised over her various States, by a strong and energetic government, under which Italy became more prosperous and more contented than she had been for centuries. In 1815 the Congress of Vienna had undone the material good which Napoleon had accomplished. The temporal power of the Pope was restored; Lombardy and Venetia were placed under the Austrian yoke; and Modena, Piedmont, Naples, and Tuscany were returned to their former kings or dukes.

As these princes were all connected by blood or marriage with the house of Hapsburg, Austrian influence was predominant at their Courts, and Italy' became in all but name a province of the Austrian Empire. Like their Bourbon cousins, the Italian princes returned from exile "having learned nothing and forgotten nothing." Their only idea of government was a despotism. In their States, there were no parliaments or representative institutions, and as the press was gagged there was no means of calling attention to the injustice and the abuses which everywhere were rampant. Every possible difficulty was placed in the way of those who wished to visit other parts of Italy, as it was considered undesirable that men should upset their minds by travelling. In some States, it was made penal to pronounce the name of Napoleon! In Rome, it was proposed to give up lighting the streets at night because the custom owed its origin to the French, and the faces of the public clocks were altered because they marked what the populace termed "French time." Throughout the peninsula, the police and their spies were omnipotent, and sought to regulate men's thoughts and actions, from their political opinions down to the cut of their coats.

The Austrian officers of today, (1901), as we see them in their own country, are high-bred and courteous men of the world. But in the first part of the century their manners were by no means as agreeable as they are now, and their conduct towards the Italians, whom they chose to consider as a conquered race, was brutal, and greatly increased the hatred of the population towards the rulers who surrounded themselves with foreign bayonets in order to be able to oppress their native-born subjects with impunity. A shrewd English traveller thus describes a typical scene in one of the many towns garrisoned by Austrian troops:—

> Several white-coated Austrian officers came into the dining-room of the hotel clanking their swords and speaking in a loud overbearing tone. They were, fortunately, too far off for us to be annoyed by overhearing their conversation, except when they raised their voices to abuse the waiters, which they did in execrable Italian, but with a surprising volubility of expletives. These remarks were generally prefaced with 'You beast of an Italian,' or something equally remarkable for good taste and feeling. After a little time, their mirth grew louder, and reached an unwarrantable height when one of the party, loudly apostrophising the unfortunate waiter, asked him if he could tell him in what light he and all other Austrians regarded the Italians. The man's sallow cheek grew a shade paler, but he made no reply as he busied himself in changing their plates. 'Do you not know, you beast?' reiterated the officer, stamping as he spoke, 'then I will tell you: we all of us look upon you Italians as the dust beneath our feet as the little creeping beasts we crush at every moment of our lives, at every step we take. Ha! ha!'

The degradation of their position raised among the Italians a passionate desire for liberty and for national unity. To this yearning for freedom is due the long series of wars against Austria, which, though at first unsuccessful, finally achieved the complete independence of the Italian people, and changed a country formerly contemptuously termed "a mere geographical expression" into one of the Great Powers of Europe.

In 1847-8 Charles Albert, King of Piedmont, astonished the world by granting to his people a constitution modelled on that of England. By this act he at once placed himself at the head of the movement for national unity; and early in 1848 he proclaimed war against the Emperor of Austria, and invaded Lombardy with the avowed intention of expelling the Austrians from Italy. At first things went well with him, but after a few weeks the tide turned in favour of Radetzky, the war-worn veteran who commanded the emperor's troops in Italy. After a series of reverses, which culminated in a severe defeat at Custozza (name of ill-omen for the Italians, for the Austrians again defeated them there in 1866), Charles Albert was compelled to sue for an armistice, while the remnants of his army a mere mob of starved, demoralised, and ragged men—painfully regained the frontier of Piedmont.

By dint of immense exertions during the truce, which lasted for seven months, the King of Piedmont partially reorganised his troops and rendered them (in point of numerical strength) respectable for a little country of about five million inhabitants. In March, 1849, just before the commencement of the five days' campaign which ended at Novara, 148,000 men served under Charles Albert's colours; but though they presented a creditable appearance on parade, the composition or the infantry left much to be desired. A third of them were reservists, who, after about a year's service in the ranks, had been allowed to return to their homes.

Of these, 30,000 were married; and all most strongly objected to the idea of active service. Another third of the infantry were absolutely raw recruits. The remainder had been a year or eighteen months under arms, and had, no doubt, profited by the experience gained in the campaign of 1848; but they had not shaken off the feeling of disbelief in themselves and in their officers engendered by defeat.

The cavalry, artillery, and engineers were good, but the commissariat and transport services were indifferent, the medical corps was inadequately supplied with ambulances, and there was a deficiency of no less than 400 officers in the various branches of the service. Not only among a large number of the soldiers, but also among many of the higher ranks, the idea of recommencing the conflict was unpopular—with some on political grounds, with others because they recognised the impossibility of waging war single-handed against the Austrian Empire. The king recognised the difficulties of the military position; but he knew that if he did not renew the war with Austria the whole of Italy would consider he had betrayed their cause, and the majority of his own subjects would rise against him.

He, therefore, chose the lesser of the two evils—a war in Lombardy rather than a revolution in Piedmont; and although after deducting from his strength 18,000 men in hospital and 40,000 for garrison duty he could only count on some 85,000 troops for service in the field, he "denounced the armistice," and intimated to the Austrians that hostilities would recommence on the 20th of March, 1849.

The king's military capacity had been so much questioned since his defeats in the campaign of the previous year, that he decided to delegate the supreme command to some general of wider experience than his own. The choice fell not upon a Piedmontese, but upon a Polish adventurer, Chrzanowski, who had served with the Russians in their Turkish campaign in 1829, and against them in the Polish insurrection of 1831. Deeply did the Piedmontese generals resent their supersession by a foreigner, and grievous was the friction between the general-in-chief and the commanders of his divisions throughout this short and mismanaged campaign.

Although the Emperor of Austria possessed many provinces each as large and as populous as Piedmont, he was unable to send any reinforcements to Radetzky, for the rebellion in Hungary absorbed all the resources which the Court of Vienna could then command. Therefore, after providing for the investment of Venice, which had risen against her Austrian oppressors, and securing the safety of his lines of communication, Radetzky could only place in the field an army of the same strength as that of the Piedmontese. But though the numbers were equal, in morale the Austrians were greatly superior. Proud of their victories in 1848, they entered upon the campaign of Novara with thorough belief in themselves and with the utmost confidence in their old general, who, at the age of eighty-three, was still strong in body and vigorous in mind.

The knowledge of actual warfare which Field-Marshal Radetzky possessed was remarkable. Towards the end of the eighteenth century he first saw active service in a campaign against the Turks, and encountered Napoleon at Montenotte during the future emperor's Italian campaign of 1796. He was present at Marengo; he shared in the disaster of Hohenlinden; he commanded divisions at the battles of Eckmühl, Aspern, and Wagram, where the Austrians fought with their usual courage and their usual ill-success. At Kulm and Leipzig, he held important positions on the general staff; and he served in France in 1814, when Napoleon displayed such marvellous skill in his campaign against the overwhelming masses of the Allies.

As many of Radetzky's troops were Hungarians—men whose brothers were then at death-grips with the Austrians on the plains of Hungary—their fidelity would have been doubtful had the old general not been the idol of his soldiery. His personal influence kept them so true to their colours, that on the resumption of hostilities the Magyars sent him a deputation to ask to be allowed to go to the front at once, so that they might show their loyalty to the emperor by deeds and not by words!

When the armistice expired, the hostile armies were separated by the swift, deep current of the Ticino, a river which in its course from Lake Maggiore to the Po forms the frontier between Lombardy and Piedmont. As the objective of the Piedmontese army was Milan, the greater part of Charles Albert's forces were concentrated about Novara, a prosperous country town from which the white spires of Milan Cathedral can be seen glittering in the sun. A division of 8,000 men, under General Ramorino, had been detached to the south-west, with orders to watch the bridges near Pavia, the old university town which stands close to the junction of the Ticino and the Po. Pavia is about thirty miles from Novara, and about halfway between them a little town, Mortara, marks the point where most of the important roads in the district converge. Two or three considerable streams flow parallel with the Ticino, and feed the numerous canals which irrigate the country to the westward of this river.

Plantations of mulberry trees, with vines trained in festoons between their trunks, mark the boundaries of the soft deep rice-fields; and causeways, often raised above the level of the ground, connect the solidly-built towns and villages which dot the surface of the fertile plain. Radetzky's Intelligence Department was far superior to that of Charles Albert; for, while the Austrian staff was fully acquainted with all the movements of the Piedmontese, the king obtained no tidings of the rapid concentration which the old field-marshal had effected at Pavia. On the morning of the resumption of hostilities 60 battalions, 40 squadrons, and 186 guns arrived outside its gates, and streamed

THE UNIVERSITY PARVIA

through the dark and narrow streets which lead towards the Ticino. As the troops defiled past the balcony in which the old general had placed himself, German artillerymen, Polish lancers, Tyrolese riflemen, Hungarian hussars, and Croatian infantry vied with each other in the enthusiasm with which they cheered their octogenarian chief.

Greatly to their surprise, the Austrians passed the frontier without difficulty. They were not even seriously opposed at the strong position of La Cava, which Ramorino had been specially ordered to defend; for this general, who was either a traitor or a fool, had left his post and transported nearly all his division to the southern bank of the Po, where they were absolutely useless for the rest of the campaign. After the war was over, Ramorino was tried for disobedience of orders and shot; but his death in no way atoned for the injury he had inflicted upon the Piedmontese cause. Owing to his misconduct, the Austrians gained so great a start that by the afternoon of the 21st, Radetzky had been able to direct the main body of his army on Mortara, and thus seriously threaten Charles Albert's communications with Turin, his capital.

Chrzanowski sent off two divisions to hold Mortara, while with the rest of his troops he attempted to make his way southward, down the right bank of the Ticino, and thus menace the field-marshal's line of communication with Pavia. To paralyse this movement, Radetzky covered the roads between himself and the Ticino with detachments of all arms, with orders to drive back the Piedmontese wherever they encountered them. In several places along the line, as has already been stated, there was sharp fighting; and not only at Sforzesca, but in other points on Charles Albert's left, the troops of Piedmont distinctly held their enemies in check.

And now to resume the account of the five days' campaign. In the middle of the night of the 21st the Duke of Savoy—Charles Albert's eldest son, best known in history as Victor Emanuel, the first King of Italy—rode into his father's bivouac to break to him the disastrous news that Mortara had fallen into the hands of the enemy. Chrzanowski had entrusted to the young prince and to General Durando the defence of this town, an all-important spot on the series of roads between the army and the fortresses from which it drew supplies. The strength of their combined divisions was respectable. Twenty-nine battalions, 16 squadrons, and 48 guns should have sufficed to hold the Austrians in check until Chrzanowski could attack them in flank from his own left; but, owing to their neglect of proper military precautions,

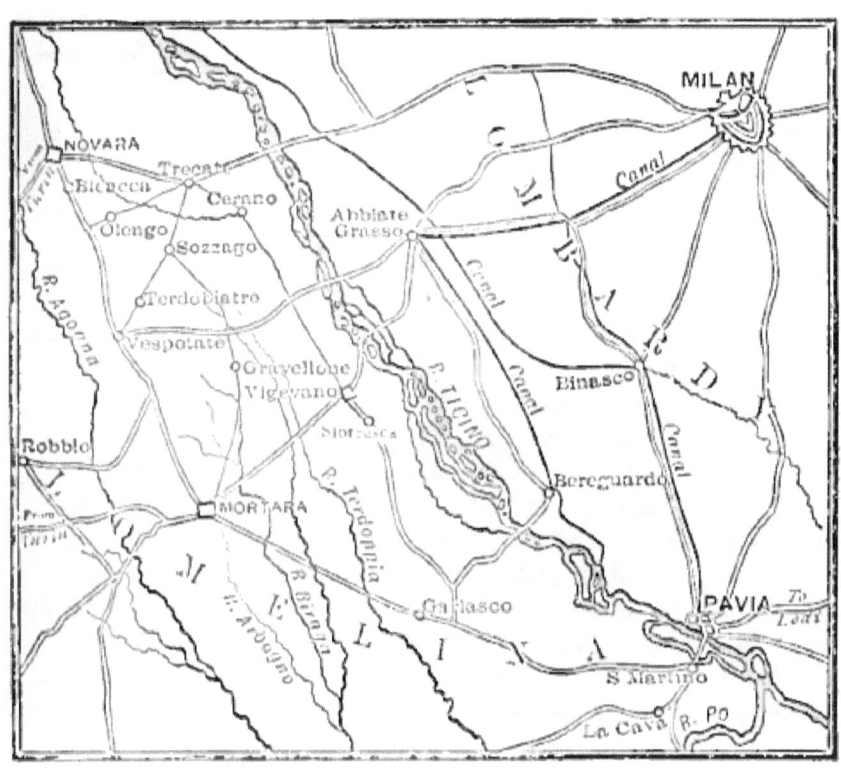

the Piedmontese lost the day.

Durando took up a position too close to the town, and intersected by canals which rendered it difficult for him to reinforce his fighting line or to move his reserves from one flank to another. The Duke of Savoy's division, in second line, was drawn up to the right of the town, where it could be of little use in the battle. The outposts were badly placed and badly handled. No adequate steps were taken to fortify Mortara—no loopholes pierced, no walls crenelated, no barricades prepared to defend its streets against a sudden rush. Invalids, stragglers, muleteers, camp followers, and all the non-combatants of the army were allowed to congregate in the little town, and to impede the movements of the troops through its narrow streets.

Although heavy firing had been! heard at intervals during the day on the Piedmontese left, by a curious infatuation the generals came to the conclusion that the Austrians would not attack Mortara till the morrow. Discipline became relaxed; many of the officers left their regiments to dine at the village inns; the men were foraging on their own account, when suddenly a picket of Nizzard cavalry galloped wildly into the camp, shouting that the Austrians were upon them. From the south and south-east heavy columns of white-coated infantry could be seen converging upon Mortara, and before the Piedmontese troops had all been collected, a heavy fire of artillery was poured into their disordered ranks. The Duke of Savoy and Durando were as completely surprised as were the French at Beaumont in 1870, and with the same result.

After several hours' fighting they were badly beaten, and the Austrians obtained possession of one of the most important strategic points in Lombardy. In this engagement, begun at dusk and continued till late at night, the generals soon lost all control over the troops, and each colonel fought entirely for his own hand in the combats which raged from field to field and from house to house. The stress of the fighting fell on Durando. A convent on which the right of his Une rented was stormed by the Austrians, retaken by the Piedmontese, and again recaptured by the Austrians. His infantry, demoralised by the fire of guns of which they could see nothing but the flashes, gave way, and in their retreat fired heavily upon the regiments which the Duke of Savoy was bringing to their aid, and then fled in panic to the town. They were closely pursued by two battalions of Hungarians, who had already penetrated some distance into its dark and winding streets before Benedek, who commanded them, discovered that six

MARSHAL RADETZKY AFTER THE BATTLE OF NOVARA.

fresh Piedmontese battalions were advancing upon him.

In the small Lombard towns, the houses are well adapted for defence, for they are strongly built, with small low doors and few windows set high upon the walls. Benedek instantly flung part of his men into the buildings which commanded the street, down which he slowly led the remainder to the attack, when suddenly a fresh danger burst upon him. Out of the murky darkness of the side streets appeared the gleam of bayonets, warning him that other columns of the enemy were threatening him in flank and rear. The position was desperate, but Benedek was equal to the occasion. The streets and lanes were encumbered with broken carts and with the bodies of dead horses, and with these materials his handy troops rapidly extemporised barricades, behind which they entrenched themselves, while with sublime audacity their chief sent an officer to summon his assailants to surrender, as "further resistance would be useless!"

This *ruse de guerre* was successful, and 1,700 men laid down their arms to Benedek at the very moment that they should have been making him and his brave men their prisoners. Two squadrons of the Nice regiment, however, scorned to surrender; and selecting the moment when the Austrian ranks had become disordered by victory, cut their way safely out of the town and joined the Duke of Savoy. Durando's division had melted grievously away in this engagement, but Victor Emanuel, by dint of immense exertions, succeeded in keeping in hand a large number of his troops.

In this affair, the Piedmontese lost 2,000 prisoners, 500 killed and wounded, and 5 guns; while the Austrians had only 300 soldiers placed *hors de combat*. The decisive character of the action, which greatly affected the morale of the Piedmontese two days later at Novara, was chiefly owing to Benedek's resolute conduct. It earned for him the Cross of Maria Theresa, the highest military decoration which an Emperor of Austria can bestow.

During the 22nd the whole of the Piedmontese Army fell back upon the town of Novara, where Chrzanowski decided to give battle to the Austrians. For a defensive action the ground to the south of the town presented considerable advantages. On the flanks the position was protected by canals and rivulets; while to the front was cultivated land, much cut up by wet ditches, strong stone walls, and long rows of mulberry trees, with farms and country houses, each capable of being converted into a little fortress, dotted over the surface of the plain, which sank gently towards Mortara. The main road, which connects

Novara with Mortara and along which the Austrians must of necessity advance, was commanded by rising ground near the hamlet of La Bicocca.

So rapidly had Charles Albert's army dwindled away under mismanagement and defeat, that not more than 50,000 men could be brought into the field on the morning of the 23rd. Three divisions were placed in the front line: Durando commanded on the right, Bes in the centre, and on the left the veteran Perrone was entrusted with the defence of La Bicocca and the Mortara-Novara road. Behind him in second line stood the Duke of Genoa, while the Duke of Savoy supported the divisions on the right and centre. Three battalions of sharpshooters (*bersaglieri*), extended as skirmishers, covered the front of the position. which was not much more than 3.000 yards in length. These dispositions were completed by nine o'clock, when, in drizzling rain, dispirited by their reverses and half-starved by the breakdown of their commissariat, the Piedmontese formed up to await the Austrian attack.

In less than two hours their outposts were in contact with the advance-guard of the three army corps, commanded by D'Aspre, who was marching along the Mortara-Novara road. At first D'Aspre imagined he had only to deal with a rear-guard, covering a retreat, but soon he discovered he was in presence of the whole of the Piedmontese Army. He instantly informed the generals who were moving on the roads to his right and left; and then, remembering the ease with which before he had conquered at Mortara, without waiting for reinforcements, he boldly attacked the army of Charles Albert.

On the Piedmontese right and centre, though there was desultory skirmishing all through the day, nothing of importance took place; for the battle was fought out on their left, round the villages which command the Mortara road. Chrzanowski's plan seems to have been to tire out the Austrians at La Bicocca. He forgot that mere passive resistance never gains a decisive victory, and that a general must be prepared to counter-attack his enemy with vigour. A brilliant opportunity for such a counter-stroke presented itself in the course of the engagement; but Chrzanowski, too slow of intellect to appreciate it, lost his chance and, with it, the battle for Charles Albert.

The engagement began with a vigorous assault upon Olengo, a hamlet on the road a few hundred yards to the south of La Bicocca. Perrone had strongly occupied it as a detached post, to bar the approach to the more important village in its rear. By a sudden dash, the Hungarian battalions of Prince Albrecht's advance-guard seized some of the outlying houses; then, turning fiercely upon a regiment of Piedmontese, they captured their colours and drove them in confusion out of the village. But before the Hungarian officers could restore order after this hand-to-hand combat, the tables were turned. A corps of sturdy mountaineers from Savoy fell upon them, and handled them so roughly that, to save his favourite Magyars from destruction, the archduke had to thrust the whole of his reserves into the fray.

For several hours, reinforcements reached D'Aspre very slowly, for the narrow roads were blocked by the baggage-waggons of his army corps. As fresh troops came up they were hurried into the fight, which eddied round the villages on the Novara road. Early in the afternoon the Austrians stormed La Bicocca. and so nearly took Charles Albert prisoner that his escort crossed bayonets with the Hungarian infantry. Soon the Duke of Genoa, with two fresh brigades from the second line, recaptured the hamlet at the point of the bayonet; and then, bringing up several batteries, he poured so fierce a fire upon Olengo, that the Austrians who occupied it became demoralised, and made but a feeble resistance to the bayonet attack with which he followed up his cannonade.

During the shelling of this village incidents occurred which show of how good material the Piedmontese officers were made. The captain of a battery fell, hard hit, with his arm carried away by a round shot. He did not leave post, he refused to be carried to the ambulance, and he steadily fought his battery as long as the action lasted. A young subaltern, fresh from the artillery school, was laying a gun on a rapidly-approaching infantry column, when he staggered and almost fell. His father, a general officer, called to his son to ask if he was hurt. The lad gave the order to fire with a steady voice, then, raising the bleeding stump of his arm above his head, he shouted, "*Viva il Re*" (God save the King), and fell senseless upon a heap of corpses.

The Duke of Genoa was arranging his troops for a further advance against the Austrians, who were much weakened by their losses and badly supported by their reserves, when Chrzanowski, far too stupid to realise that the crisis of the battle had arrived, peremptorily ordered him to retire to La Bicocca. Had the young general been allowed to continue his attack, he might have won the day; for Radetzky, himself, has stated that at this moment he had thrown his last available man into the fight, and had no further reserves at hand with which to meet the Piedmontese, "who fought like devils."

When Italian soldiers forty years ago, (as at 1901), were unsuccessful in war, or when they received an unexpected or unwelcome order, they instantly concluded that there was treachery at work among their ranks. The troops at Olengo saw that victory was within their grasp; they knew that not half the army had yet been under fire; they realised that a general advance along the line would have completely overwhelmed the Austrians. Therefore, this inexplicable retreat roused their suspicions against the foreigner who commanded them. From that moment, the men lost heart; and though many of the regiments fought on most gallantly, others cried "Treason," and, disbanding themselves, fled to the town. Charles Albert, seeing one of the doubtful regiments wavering on their march, rode up to them and, taking their standard in his hand, offered to lead them to the front—in vain!

"Sire, it is too late," muttered the colonel "half an hour earlier, they would have followed you anywhere!"

The officers—high and low, old and youngest a brilliant example to their men, and showed how soldiers should fight for the honour of their country. The aged General Perrone, the commander of the left wing of the army, while rallying his men for a charge fell mortally wounded. He ordered the men who supported him to lay him at the feet of the king, to whom he murmured: "Sire, I offered to you and to my country the last days of my life. My duty is accomplished."

About four o'clock in the afternoon, sometime after the pressure on the Austrians had been removed by the recall of the Duke of Genoa, Radetzky's reinforcements began to arrive from all directions; they relieved D'Aspre's overtasked troops, and formed up in heavy columns for the final assault upon La Bicocca, the luckless village which had changed hands already so often during the day. They carried it, but not without fierce fighting and heavy loss. The king and his sons were in the thick of the combat, urging their men to do their duty to the last. Near Charles Albert two gunners were shot dead, the head of one of his escort was carried away, three of his *aides-de-camp* were killed, and a soldier was pierced by a musket-ball close to his horse's head. In his despair at seeing the Austrians sweeping like a torrent through the left of his line, the king cried out: "Is there no cannonball left for me?"

The loss of La Bicocca and the rout of Perrone's division were fatal to the Piedmontese, for their centre and right were enfiladed from the heights on which the village stood; there was a general retreat, which the efforts of the Duke of Savoy were utterly unable to prevent. It is said that late in the evening he sat on his horse and faced the enemy

The parting of Charles Albert and Victor Emanuel after the Battle of Novara.

in dumb despair. The Austrian guns were briskly shelling his troops to hasten their flight, as they streamed past him, a hopelessly broken army; behind him was the little town of Novara, where Piedmontese stragglers, throwing discipline to the winds, had already begun the work of plunder. Suddenly he raised his sword above his head, and swore a mighty oath that Italy should yet become a free and united nation.

After experiences, more remarkable than those which usually fall to the lot of kings in the nineteenth century, he lived to see his oath fulfilled. His reign commenced in the most picturesque manner, for on the very night of the defeat Charles Albert summoned all his surviving generals to Novara, to announce to them that he had abdicated in favour of his eldest son, Victor Emanuel. Then bidding an eternal farewell to the young king, who knelt weeping before him, Charles Albert, accompanied by only one faithful *aide-de-camp*, quitted the army, and passing unrecognised through the Austrian outposts, reached the Mediterranean and took ship for Portugal, where in a few months he died of a broken heart. When his successor realised that he had inherited a demoralised army, an empty treasury, and a population ripe for revolution, he can have had but little hope of ever seeing the Italians freed from the Austrian yoke; but he did not despair, and, thanks to his own steadfast courage and the help of Cavour and of Garibaldi, twenty-one years later he was crowned at Rome, as Victor Emanuel, first King of Italy!

WAR IN THE CRIMEA
1853-56

Omar Pasha at Chetaté and Calafat, 1854

By William V. Herbert

In the years 1829 to 1834, when Hussein, the bloodstained exterminator of the *Janissaries*, of European notoriety, was Pasha of Widdin, there lived in the latter town an obscure personage, a fugitive foreigner from across the Croatian border, a deserter from the Austrian Army, a convert to Islam, who was known to the townspeople by the assumed name of Omar, and the additional courtesy-title of Effendi, his real name, known to none, being Michael Lattas. He earned a precarious living as clerk to the pasha aforesaid, with which despised office he combined the even humbler one of teacher to his master's children of the rudiments of history and geography, and of an elementary knowledge of Italian and German. He made a little "overtime" (not much, for the grim *pasha* was a hard taskmaster) by writing the letters of illiterate persons.

A strange person was this Omar Effendi—taciturn, coarse, unsociable, uncouth, shabby, and always in pecuniary difficulties; a young man (he was not twenty-three years yet when he first came to Widdin) with the demeanour of a sexagenarian. He was not married, and seemingly desired not to be; for never did he cast amorous eyes on any one of the many fair maidens of the town—the so-called "Spanish" Jewesses, the Bulgarians, the Roumanians—whose beauty was renowned throughout the country. He had no friends, and never tried to make any; he lived for himself and by himself, books being his only companions—records of wars and great deeds, which he begged or borrowed of the wealthy Greek and Armenian traders, if he could not obtain them in the public library of the town, the creation of Pasvan Oglu, the last of the great *Janissary* leaders.

To his master, he was useful in many ways: he spoke Turkish without the trace of an accept, knew the tongue of the despised *Rayahs* and several Western idioms, and, by means of a very fair education, was clerk, interpreter, secretary, translator, businessman, and steward all rolled into one. An intelligent observer—there were not many in Widdin—must have gained the impression that this mysterious young man was suppressing himself. Such was the case. He played a waiting game, and, being endowed with stupendous latent power, could rise grandly to the occasion when such a one proffered itself.

But before this occurred, some more years of degradation and adversity had to be gone through. In 1834 Omar left the town, in the middle of the night, to many clamouring creditors' disappointment, his only possessions in the wide world being a small bundle, a few silver coins, and a letter of recommendation from his master—who favoured his plans—to the Seraskier of Stamboul. He partly tramped, partly worked his way as a carter, to the capital, the El Dorado of many an adventurer whom the Occident had cast out.

Now there was at that time—and there is, in a smaller degree, now—no place in the world so paved with gold to a man of abundant energy and a conveniently small dose of scrupulousness as Constantinople. Granted that you possess a knowledge of two or three European languages, can read and write Turkish, possess latent power, strength of purpose, and an individuality of your own, employment by government and quick advancement are certain, if only you know how to make yourself agreeable, and understand the art of closing, your eyes and keeping your mouth shut when occasion requires it. In 1834 Omar was clerk in the *Seraskierat*; in 1835 teacher of writing to the *Sultan's* eldest son, with the honorary title of captain.

In 1837 he exchanged the reed for the sword and entered active service, having already had a few years' military training in the battalion of Austrian frontier-guards which he had left in disgrace. In 1839 he fought under the eyes of Moltke in the disastrous Battle of Nisib against the Egyptians; and later in the same year he, then a colonel, established his fame by his victory at Beksaya in Syria. Thenceforth his promotion was rapid, and his warlike experience manifold. There is no necessity to enumerate either; suffice it to say that when in October, 1853, the ninth Russo-Turkish war broke out, which was so soon to develop into a European struggle of hugest dimensions and unequalled horrors, known to history as the Crimean War, Omar, then forty-seven years old, was appointed commander-in-chief of the Ottoman forces in Europe, with the rank of *Mushir* or marshal, the highest military grade of the Empire.

Twenty years after the despised Omar Effendi, literary hack and absconding debtor, had sneaked out of the Plevna Gate of Widdin's fortifications like a thief by night, the far-famed soldier Omar Pasha, the hope of the Ottoman Nation in the impending struggle, made his state entry by the same gate, with pride, pomp, and circumstance, surrounded by a brilliant staff, escorted by a gallant cavalcade, acclaimed by the populace, greeted by the "*Selam dur*" ("Present arms!") of Turkey's best battalions. An hour after his arrival he went to pray, ostentatiously, at the grave of his former master and the founder of his fortune, Hussein Pasha, now dead six years; and towards dusk on the same day (17th October, 1853) a brigade with several batteries occupied the large island situated between Widdin and Calafat, roughly fortified it, and pitched camp there.

The die was cast, and it was Omar who had boldly thrown it. Russia had not complied with Turkey's reasonable and moderate demand for the evacuation of the Danube Principalities, at that time the hitter's undisputed property, and the high-handed *Mushir*, who had addressed a solicitation to that effect to Prince Gortschakoff, the Russian commander-in-chief, then in Bucharest, had anticipated by six days the grace which the young Sultan, Abdul Medjid, Omar's former pupil and actual patron, had accorded to the Czar Nicholas I.

The Turks had taken the precaution to concentrate a large corps (20,000 men with 40 guns, not counting the stationary ordnance, and 5,000 irregular horsemen) in and around Widdin during September and October. The Russian detachment destined to operate in this quarter was commanded by General Fischbach, consisted in the beginning of only one division, with its complement of cavalry and artillery, and was, at the commencement of hostilities, still quartered, with the bulk of the Russian forces, in and near Bucharest, whence it sallied forth on the 25th October towards Crayova.

At that time, Calafat was rather a strong place. It had a complete semicircle of redoubts, trenches, and ditches flooded with Danube water, many of which dated from the campaign of 1790, when the Austrians had stormed and captured them. A pontoon-bridge connected the place (then a village, but both more extended and more populous as a village than today, 1901, as a town, counting some 4,000 inhabitants) with the large Danube island; another, between the latter and Widdin, provided with a closable aperture for passing vessels, completed the communication. The total length of the two bridges was 2,200 yards; that of the communication from shore to shore was close on 3,000 yards. The Roumanian bridge-head was situate three miles south of the present site of the town, but well within the Calafat fortifications; the Turkish lay within Widdin's inner *enceinte*.

On the 23rd October, the respite elapsed, and the *Sultan's* decree of war became absolute. Four days later the general of division, Ismael Pasha—hitherto commander of Widdin, but now subject to Omar and to the latter's adjutant, friend, and factotum, Ahmed Pasha, a Vienna-trained man—crossed over to Calafat with twelve battalions and some artillery, and on the morrow the Turks were in full and undisputed possession of the place, which, well equipped and fortified, strongly armed and manned, and ably commanded, was to give the ruthless invader such an amount of trouble as nobody in Europe had foreseen or suspected. A day later Omar took up his residence in Calafat, but Widdin continued to be the base and centre of operations, the *vis-à-vis* being merely the fortified bridgehead of the larger town. Ceaselessly Omar and Ahmed added to and strengthened the defences of Calafat, having in their service several trained Austrian and Polish engineers.

"*If the mountain will not come to Muhamed, Muhamed must go to the mountain,*" thought the restless Omar. The enemy seemed inclined to allow him undisturbed possession of the dirty Wallachian village; so, he went forth to seek and beat him.

Leaving Ahmed in command of Calafat, he travelled post-haste to Turtukai, a fortified little town on the right bank of the Danube, half-way between Rustchuk and Silistria. He arrived on the 2nd November, and two days later he had fought and won the Battle of Oltenitza, the first encounter in the war. This accomplished, he returned with the same speed to Calafat.

Here, during November and December, more troops were concentrated, and with the new year Omar counted on this spot 25,000 regulars, 10,000 irregular cavalry, and 50 field-guns. The defences of Calafat, having been extended to a semicircle with a radius of over three miles, had been strengthened in such a manner that the town, supported as it was by Widdin with its heavy ordnance and huge stores, was practically impregnable. And such the Russians found it when, at the reiterated command of their exasperated *Czar*, they made that series of futile attempts on the place, extending over a period of nearly five months, which is known to history by the somewhat misleading name of the Siege of Calafat, and which was inaugurated by the Battle of Chetaté, on the 6th January, 1854, the subject proper of this memoir. The action of Oltenitza had already made a great stir in Europe, and placed Omar Pasha's name on everybody's lips; the fight of Chetaté aroused the whole newspaper-reading world to the highest pitch of excitement and enthusiasm. Owing, however, to the total lack of impartial onlookers in this quarter, the versions which have reached the Western public are garbled, exaggerated, and misleading; even to this day the historians give each other the lie direct. I cannot do better than record the details of the action as I collected them on the spot. I had speech in Widdin in 1877 with participators and eye-witnesses, and with many citizens who were old enough to remember the events of twenty-three years ago. The following is, in substance, the account which I gathered as the harvest of my investigations:—

To commence with, Chetaté was at that time a large, straggling, dirty, poverty-stricken village of Little Wallachia, situate on the left bank of the Danube, about nine miles upwards of Calafat, and eighteen miles below the Timok mouth. It consisted of a single street over a mile long, and counted some 1,200 inhabitants (a populous place for that part of the world), mostly Wallachian fishermen and petty farmers of the poorest class, with a small sprinkling of Turks. The surroundings are flat, green, and fertile, but so sparsely inhabited as to be almost a wilderness, even at the present day, 1901. There was at that time no direct communication, not even track or path, between Calafat and Chetaté; the road led *via* Golentzé, a detour of ten miles or more.

It was late at night on the 5th January when the outposts of irregular cavalry brought into Calafat, *ventre-à-terre*, the astounding and wholly unexpected news of the occupation of Chetaté by the Russians, who were supposed to be still in Crayova, fifty miles to the north-east. Omar Pasha, who happened to be in Calafat, called at once a meeting of his principal officers, and an expedition for the early morrow was decided upon.

This was to be twofold. A force of 1,000, mostly regular infantry, with a few guns of light calibre, set out from Widdin before the 6th January had dawned, in craft which the far-seeing *Mushir* had caused to be got ready some time before, equipped with oars and Danube experts in the persons of local fishermen. There were some fifty of these boats and barges, and they rowed slowly upstream in the cold grey dawn of a bitter winter day. An hour later—in time to keep tryst with the river force—three battalions of infantry, 2,000 irregular cavalry, and three field-batteries of six guns each, started from Calafat along the river meadows.

The force in the boats was led by Ismael Pasha, the land force by Ahmed Pasha, who, being also commander-in-chief of the undertaking, deserves to survive to posterity as Victor of Chetaté. Omar himself followed at a march-hour's distance with a strong reserve of regular cavalry, and a battery of light guns. With Ahmed's detachment was a body of Polish and Hungarian volunteers, led by two noblemen of the former nationality, named Constantin von Yacoubowski (Yakub Bey) and the Count Alexander Illinski (Iskender Bey) while the large horde of irregular cavalry was officered by Ishmahil, a notorious Circassian chief. The artillery was under the command of an English adventurer by name Samuel Morris (Moussa Bey), who was popularly supposed to be a deserter from the British army, and who proved himself to be a clever, capable, and courageous leader.

The following men—all, like those already mentioned, conspicuous characters in the peninsula at that time—also took part in the fighting on the Turkish side:—Halim Pasha, to be mentioned hereafter; Sami Pasha, the civil governor of Widdin, the well-known advocate of an alliance between Turkey, England, and France, who later brought his powerful influence to bear upon the *Sultan* in this direction; two Austrian military engineers, Holzwege and Teutsch; and lastly, a renowned Kurdish chief and warrior named Iskendjer, who, having been captured by Omar Pasha some years before, and, at the instigation of England, banished to the Danube swamps to atone for countless atrocities committed upon the Armenians, asked, and was allowed, to take part in the fighting.

The Russian force then in possession of Crayova was composed of two divisions (23,000 men) with 48 guns, and was commanded by General Anrep. The troops detached from this to occupy Chelate consisted of six battalions of infantry, three squadrons of cavalry, and 16 guns—about 6,000 men; the Turkish force which came into action had about the same strength. The Russian leader at Chetaté was General Fischbach. The appointment was admirably kept by the two separate" Turkish forces, and the plan to surprise the enemy succeeded completely. Hardly had the river force landed unperceived and commenced to attack the village on that side, when the land force arrived and assailed at once impetuously on the other.

Most of the Russians were still resting in the houses from the exertion and the fatigue of the previous day's exhausting march from Crayova, when the first shots exchanged, between the *têtes* of the

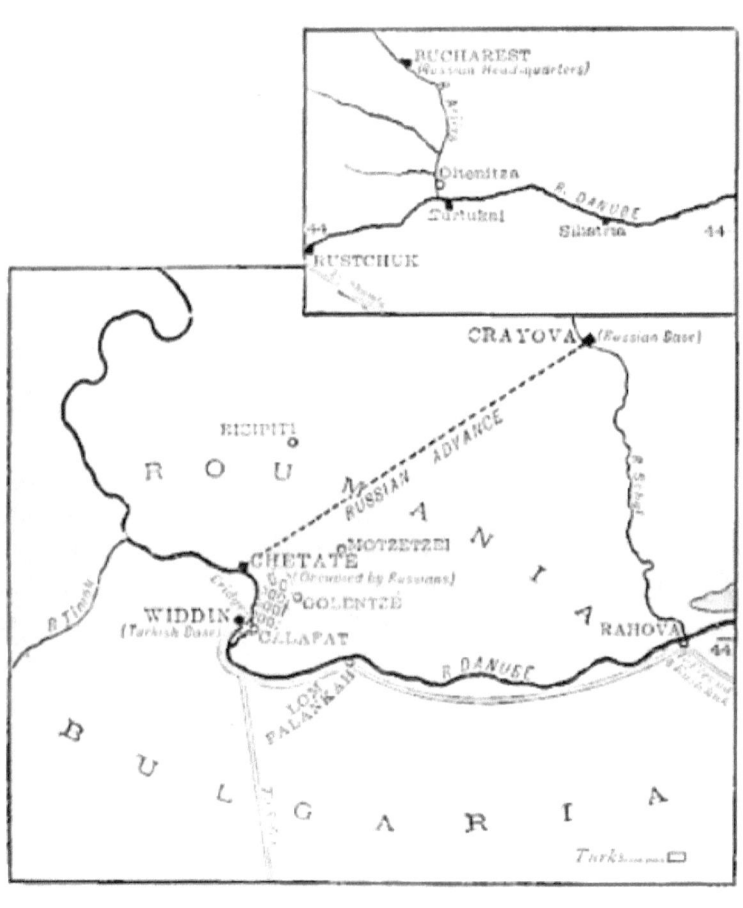

Turkish columns and the sleepy sentries, posted at both ends of the village, alarmed them. Many of the soldiers took part half-dressed in the ferocious fighting that ensued. The open ends of the street had been hastily barricaded and entrenched the evening before; but what the Russians trusted most to for protection against surprise was the river on one side and a large pond with some swamps on the other. Both these natural defences turned out to be imaginary; for as to the former, we have seen that the Turks utilised it for transport, and as to the latter, the obstacles were successfully circumvented.

The struggle was of the most desperate description. Hardly ever has action exhibited greater personal bravery of either combatant. As if conscious that the eyes of Europe were upon them—which, indeed they were—both sides fought ferociously, and the result was simply murderous. Each house, hovel, and shed was converted into a fortress and staunchly defended; each foot of ground was contested. In the end the Turks were left masters of the village, having carried it almost entirely at the point of the bayonet. The action, which had commenced at about an hour after daybreak—that is, at 9 a.m.—was over shortly after noon, and the surviving Russians fled hastily across country northeastward, leaving two guns in the hands of the enemy and nearly one-half of their force, dead or dying, on the ground and in the burning houses. So desperate had the fighting been that the Russians lost all the horses and almost all the men of their two batteries; the guns had to be served by infantry and removed by Cossacks. That fourteen pieces out of sixteen were saved in the turmoil and confusion of such a defeat is to their credit.

The Turks had lost 1,000, the Russians 3,000 men in killed and wounded; thus, the casualties amounted to 25 *per cent,* of the forces actually engaged. The former had taken many hundreds of wounded prisoners: what they did with them is not recorded. The village was almost destroyed by fire, and it is to be feared that many disabled men of both nationalities perished in the flames.

The weather on this day, as well on the three fighting days that were to follow, was bitterly cold, with the peculiar icy north wind of the Bulgarian winter; the ground was soaked by many weeks of incessant rain, and although snow and slush came down at intervals, the frost was not sufficiently severe to create a hard crust on the ground, which latter is always preferable for fighting purposes.

As in almost all the countless victories which the arms of the Crescent have won in the course of five centuries, pursuit of the beaten enemy by the Turks was sad to seek. That means, the victory was not utilised, and might as well have been non-existent for all the difference it made in the progress of the campaign. This is the more astonishing in the case of Chetaté, as Omar disposed of a splendid body of horsemen, greatly exceeding that of the Russians at Crayova in numbers.

That there was not even the faintest attempt or semblance of a pursuit is made manifest by the fact that on each of the three following days (7th, 8th, 9th January) the Russians sent large detachments from Crayova for the purpose of recovering Chetaté—first a fresh brigade, then an entire division, and finally almost the whole of Anrep's corps. But the Turks clung to their newly acquired possession with all the obstinacy which is their distinguishing characteristic in warfare, and the Russians were beaten off each time. The Turks lost another thousand men, the Russians nearly double that number. Thus, the four days' fighting at Chetaté (which was said to have exasperated the *Czar* in no small degree) involved a total loss in life and limb of 6,000 human beings, the aggregate of fighters actually engaged having been below 25,000.

In Turkey, the four days' Battle of Chetaté made an enormous sensation, and Widdin celebrated the victor of the first field-day, Ahmed Pasha, by building a huge mosque and dedicating it to him in naming it Ahmed Djami.

To such an extent grew Omar Pasha's popularity in Europe, that countless volunteers of all nationalities flocked to Widdin to join his banners. Wherever there was an adventurer, a runaway, a social outcast, a *blasé*, any man with a love of fighting and no other opportunity for exercising it—Austrians, Germans, Italians, French, or English (for these events happened three months before the consummation of the French-English-Turkish alliance)—he found it incumbent upon him to link his fate to that of the now famous renegade. For at that time Russia was heartily disliked by all countries and peoples, and her Czar, Nicholas I., was held in particular execration, although whether rightly or wrongly cannot here be determined.

We have now arrived at the second portion of our subject—the struggle for Calafat, January to May, 1854.

It has already been intimated that the Calafat of 1854 was a very different place from the clean and sober European town which I was to behold in the year of war 1877, when it was quite a modern creation, built on the site of the historic objective of many a sanguinary struggle. That which Omar's force defended so bravely was a long, extended, squalid, poverty-stricken Wallachian village, of which no trace remains at the present day. The strategical importance of this place, considered by itself, was nil; but in conjunction with its neighbour across the road, the impregnable fortress of Widdin, it was of enormous value to both belligerents, since the latter city was the key to the Danube and the door which barred the two great roads into the heart of the country—that to Sofia in the south and the other to Rustchuk in the east.

Widdin was a thriving town of 12,000 inhabitants, three-fourths of whom were Christian Bulgarians. But the sympathy of the latter, from causes which can find no space in the present narrative, was wholly with their Turkish masters throughout that war. Widdin had two concentric lines of fortification on the land side and many gun-spiked quays on the riverbanks, was armed with some 400 guns of heaviest calibre, held huge warlike stores of every description, was in easy and uninterrupted communication with the heart of the country, and was altogether a most formidable foe to tackle.

In the campaigns of 1737 and 1790 against the Austrians, and in that of 1828 and in 1829 against the Russians, it had stood unconquered, although in 1700 and 1828 the enemy had possessed himself of the bridge-head, Calafat. In conjunction with the latter it was impregnable, which fact Omar Pasha recognised with his wonderful gift of mental far-sight (hence his determination to retain Calafat at any cost), and which the Turkish wirepullers would have done well to remember in the later war—that of 1877.

General Anrep received reinforcements from Bucharest shortly after the disaster of Chetaté, and, having in the first instance concentrated his forces (three divisions, with a large body of Cossacks and other cavalry, and 100 pieces of artillery) in Crayova, he moved slowly up to Calafat. The Turks, too, were reinforced from Sofia, and counted presently 35,000 men—about 5,000 less than their opponents.

A number of minor actions were fought in this district during January and February, 1854 (at Golentzé, Motzetzei, Risipiti, Chiupercheni, and other places), all of which were more or less successful for the Turkish arms; nevertheless, the Russian belt of investment approached and pressed hard upon Calafat. The Turks had to abandon the outlying positions (among them Chetaté) and concentrate their strength. Soon (middle of February) the place was surrounded by a semicircle of entrenched Russian bivouacs, concentric with that of its fortifications.

Omar Pasha, by virtue of his office as commander-in-chief, found it impossible to devote himself to the details of the defence of the now practically invested Calafat (or, rather, semi-invested, for the communication with Widdin remained open), and he ceded the conduct of operations to his bosom friend, Ahmed Pasha, continuing to reside, however, for the greater part of the winter in Widdin, which he considered, erroneously, to be the objective of the enemy's movements in the principalities.

All through the winter and the spring the senseless struggle for Calafat dragged its weary length. The stubborn Turks yielded not an inch of ground, and both sides suffered severely from cold, exposure, privations, and disease. Ahmed, although at that time probably the most highly educated officer of the Ottoman Army, was not so resolute in his sallies and sorties as the rabble wished: ugly and persistent, though quite unfounded, whispers of corruption made themselves heard. Omar, responding to popular clamour, replaced him by the less-educated but more dashing Halim Pasha, Ahmed retaining, however, the command of the artillery and the engineering operations. This compromise worked well.

Instigated by the constant pressure emanating from the vain, ambitious, and energetic Omar—whose European reputation was at stake, and who knew his person to be the focus of the eyes of the newspaper-reading world—driven also by the lash of an acclaiming and presumptuous populace, the two leaders, in command of brave and spirited troops, harassed the enemy to such an extent by frequent petty sallies—although after Chetaté only one action worthy of the name was fought, outside Calafat on April 19th—that the Russians had sacrificed over 20,000 men (nearly half of their number) by death or disablement from shot or disease, before they finally (in May, 1854) gave up all attempts to capture Calafat. But the Turks, too, had lost severely: their defence cost them, from first to last, 12,000 men—a third of their strength.

The Englishman, Morris, was badly wounded in the action of April 19th, and was brought to Widdin, where he died a few weeks later. The Turks, with whom he had been *persona grata,* caused him to buried in one of the *intra-muros* cemeteries (recently demolished; 1901), where his grave was shown to me in 1877. A crude stone slab, erected—so I was told—by Sami Pasha, a sworn Anglophile, exhibited the following extraordinary epitaph—

SAM MORRIS

Kapitain of Artilrie
30 year old
Fell in Bataille
AT
Kalafatu
April MDCCCLIV,

with the addition of a Turkish sentence, which, translated, ran thus—

"He loved, but death came."

Vividly I recall the impression of sadness and utter desolation which the fertile desuetude of that lonely graveyard, the curt testimony of that neglected tomb, wrought upon my youthful fancy. Who was he that died in a foreign land, fighting for an alien race, and what tragedy is so imperfectly) indicated by that forgotten grave?

The gun-spiked quays on their own shore, all cleverly utilised; the well-fortified islands; the threatening ordnance of Widdin; the conviction—constantly demonstrated—that the harder nut to crack awaited them on the other side of the river, induced the Russians to abstain from a general assault on the Calafat position. And if such a one had been undertaken and had succeeded—*cui bono?* The ease to swing a pound weight does not presuppose the ability of lifting a hundred-weight. It would have required a stronger force, and a better, than that which Generals Anrep and Fischbach commanded to carry Widdin.

If the reader will reflect upon the *locale* of this struggle—the defenders but a bridge-length removed from their base, which was in uninterrupted communication with the interior of the empire, the assailants operating hundreds of miles away from their stores in an ill-cultivated, sparsely populated, alien country—he will perceive the uselessness of this "siege," will understand its failure, and grasp the difficulties the beleaguers had to contend against. As a matter of fact, Calafat could never have been besieged—in the proper sense of the word—as long as Widdin stood unconquered.

For the Turks, the episode was highly creditable, and Omar Pasha became one of the most popular men of the day, in the Orient as well as in the Occident. But a great deal of bombast and arrant nonsense was written anent both man and event—for and against—in the contemporary press, as also by later chroniclers; and to the historian it is extremely puzzling to find the truth that lies midway. I have endeavoured to hold the balance of contradictory records, and have soberly stated events as the result of my researches, my discrimination applied thereto, and information locally collected have painted them to me.

In May, General Anrep withdrew his forces from the neighbourhood of Calafat and retreated on Bucharest, leaving Fischbach and his division in observation at Crayova. On the 15th of June, the bulk of Omar Pasha's Widdin army commenced its eastern march to help to defend Silistria against its besiegers.

Ismael Pasha was left in Widdin and Calafat, having 6,000 men (half of them irregulars) to hold the towns against a renewal of the enemy's attack. But none was undertaken, and in this quarter operations were at an end. Soon afterwards the Russians evacuated the principalities, retreating before the Austrian occupation. Calafat received a small Austrian garrison, which was not withdrawn until after the peace (1856).

Omar Pasha had already in April gone to Shumla to hold a consultation with the French and English commanders, and Widdin knew him no more. By clever concentration of troops, he effected the raising of the siege of Silistria, and by allowing the Russians unchallenged possession of the fever haunted Dobrudcha swamps he inflicted upon them losses more severe than pitched battles would have had in their train, without the cost of a single life to his own army. When the Russians retreated, he followed them to Bucharest.

The theatre of war was shifted to the Crimea, and Omar commanded the Turkish troops which accompanied the allied armies. He led his forces to victory in the Battle of Eupatoria (March 21st, 1855), and assisted in the siege of Sebastopol. When this town had fallen (September 8th, 1855) he repaired to Batum in Asia, and commanded the corps sent for the relief of beleaguered Kars, but was not in time, through which fact he incurred, momentarily, the imperial displeasure. That fortress succumbed to the Russians (November 27th, 1855), who, their military honour being now vindicated, were ready to listen to pacific proposals, and lay aside their battered arms.

The treaty of Paris (March 30th, 1856) put an end to the useless war. But it terminated not the military career of the Renegade of Widdin, who was destined to employ his courage, prowess, and cruelty in the interests of the Crescent for eleven years longer, chiefly in the congenial task of quelling the rebellions of his former co-religionists. But in 1867, having been unsuccessful in suppressing the revolt of the Cretan Christians, in spite of merciless rigour, he was compelled to retire from active service. The imperial ill-will did not last long. He died in Stamboul in 1871, at the age of sixty-five, in possession of wealth, honours, world-wide fame, and his sovereign's fullest favour.

That the Renegade of Widdin was a great general cannot, in the face of history, be doubted. But personally, he was not an amiable or even estimable man, being, indeed, unscrupulous, brutal, and ruthless to a degree, fond of inflicting pain, innocent of even the faintest vestige of love, pity, or humanity. Next to cruelty greed was his ruling passion. He was also hypocritical, licentious, and not free from the old Ottoman taint—sowing corruption. Many traits in his sordid character, many deeds of his heavy hand, many events in his stormy career, are best forgotten.

OMAR PASHA

The Second Italian War of Independence
1859

MacMahon at Magenta
4 June, 1859
By Stoddard Dewey

It was noon of the 4th of June, 1859, before the French general, Trochu, at the head of his division, could move out in turn from Novara along the high road leading to Milan across the River Ticino. The Emperor, Napoleon III., was commanding in person the united French and Italian armies. He had gone on ahead, and was himself preceded by several divisions of the French troops. It was known, in a general way, that the Austrian enemy was not far distant to the south and eastward beyond the river. An attack was expected, but it was uncertain where it would be made.

Suddenly the noise of cannon was heard from the front, several miles away. It went on steadily increasing.

"What is the meaning of that?" inquired Trochu of an officer he

met watering his horse by the roadside.

"At first we thought it was a fight," was the answer; "but it is only General Leboeuf trying his cannon."

"Cannon would net thunder like that under trial," replied Trochu. "Those guns are loaded with something heavier than powder."

He hastened the march of his troops with not a little anxiety. Soon another officer, in the sky-blue uniform which marked the personal staff of the Emperor, dashed up.

"Ah, General, what a fearful surprise! The Emperor has been attacked by the Austrians when he least expected them. We are all but beaten."

"Where is MacMahon?" asked the general.

"MacMahon had orders to march forward, no matter what happened, to the church-tower of Magenta."

"Then nothing is yet lost. MacMahon is not a Caesar, but he is stubborn. If he has been told to march on the tower of Magenta, he will reach it in spite of all. And then it is we who shall have outflanked the Austrian army."

Several hours passed before the guns of MacMahon made themselves heard. It was late at night before the Emperor learned what MacMahon and his men had been doing. Generals and soldiers, wearied out with the afternoon's bloody fighting by the river, could not believe that a great victory had been won in the evening without them over by Magenta. In the morning, when they looked for the battle to be renewed, they found that the enemy was indeed drawing off, sullen and beaten.

Even afterwards, when each movement of the hostile troops was known and could be followed on the map, great authorities in practical warfare, like the Prussian general, von Moltke. criticised the winning of the battle. MacMahon at Magenta is an instance of a battle won contrary to rule.

1.—The Preparations of Battle.

The enmity between Austrians and Italians was of old date. It belonged to the great popular movement in favour of a common government for all of the Italian race and language. Until now the whole of Italy had been divided up piecemeal among many rulers. To the north-west Victor Emanuel had his kingdom of Sardinia, or Piedmont. He represented the Italian hopes in this war with Austria which held possession of the rich provinces of Lombardy and Venice

General Lebœuf dashed up

to the east of his dominions. Toward the south were the petty duchies of Parma and Modena, the grand-duchy of Tuscany, the States of the Church, and the kingdom of Naples, or the Two Sicilies. All these were at one with Austria in striving to keep things as they had been so long; but their people were ripe for the revolution which was bound to come. Magenta was the first decisive victory won, after an invasion of the Austrian territory, in the name of United Italy.

The war had been long preparing. In 1849 the Austrians crushed for a time the Italian uprising by a victory over the Sardinians here at Novara. For many years, nothing could be done but by way of diplomacy. This was the work of Cavour, the Minister of King Victor Emanuel. From 1852 he had been persuading the governments of Europe that there was an Italian question which would soon have to be settled.

Louis Napoleon, who was now Emperor in France, had himself been a revolutionist in Italy when he was only a needy adventurer. That was in 1831, when he took part in an insurrection in the Papal States. He then became a *carbonaro*, or member of one of those secret societies in which the chief obligation was to forward the cause of Italian unity. For a long time after he became emperor he shrank from precipitating the war to which his oath obliged him. The explosion of a bomb under his carriage in Paris by Orsini, the son of the man who had stood sponsor for him in the revolutionary society, reminded him that the *carbonari* were relentless in their vengeance on traitors to their cause. In July, 1858, it was made known that the Emperor of the French had entered into close alliance with the King of Sardinia.

Austria, seeing that war was inevitable, preferred that it should come sooner rather than later. On the 19th of April, 1859, she summoned Sardinia to put her army on a peace footing within three days. Cavour refused, and on the 29th the Austrian commander Gyulai invaded the Sardinian territory.

Napoleon III. now announced that the acts of Austria constituted a declaration of war on France, the ally of Sardinia. At once he set about organising his army for the Italian campaign. On the 4th of May, his troops were entering the valley of the Po, along which lay the open way to Lombardy. On the 10th the emperor himself left Paris for the seat of war, to command the allied armies in person.

The news of Napoleon's coming was enough to send Gyulai back from the threatening movement which he had already made on Turin, the capital of Sardinia. Napoleon had not yet his artillery, but the

Austrian commander did not know the essential weakness and confusion of the forces that were coming to meet him. Until the battle of Magenta, when consistent and energetic measures were already too late, the Austrian movements were a strange alternation of forward marches leading to no decisive action, and of hasty and fatiguing retreats when no enemy pursued.

General Gyulai's mind in the matter is now known. He was continually urged from Vienna, and afterwards from Verona, in Italy, where the Austrian Emperor had placed himself to direct the campaign, to push forward with his numerous, well-drilled, and well-equipped troops, and take the offensive. He himself was beset with fears that the enemy might pass him by and take Lombardy unprotected. He was not reassured when a division of his army in the north had succeeded in driving the free bands of Garibaldi to the very edge of the neutral Swiss territory. He gradually drew back to the region where the River Ticino, in its lower course, separated Lombardy from Sardinia. There he gave all his attention to concentrating his forces around the strong defensive positions which he had already prepared. But all this gave time to the French Army to perfect its order and equipment, and to concentrate its own strength in line with the Sardinian troops.

Such was the general situation of things on the 1st of June, when Napoleon was directing the main body of the allied troops along the great highway leading to Milan, the capital of Lombardy, only twenty miles beyond the Ticino. On that day Gyulai again retreated with all his forces, leaving the astonished French Emperor free to enter Novara. Napoleon could not believe that the Austrians would long delay their attack. On both sides the service of scouts was so ill-organised that neither commander had any clear idea of the other's strength and position.

On the 2nd of June Napoleon sent forward two divisions of MacMahon's corps to see what was awaiting them along the Ticino. General Camou reached the river, with his light infantry, at Porto di Turbigo, six miles to the northeast of Novara. He found no one facing him from the Austrian side but the single Customs officer, who was still faithful to the post which he had occupied in time of peace. From the yellow and black flagstaff beside him floated one double-headed eagle of Austria. Camou ordered first one, and then a second cannonshot to be fired. The functionary disappeared open-mouthed. General Leboeuf, who was in command of the artillery, dashed up, pale with indignation.

"General," he cried to Camou, "what are you firing at? It is lucky there is no one in front of you. Do you wish to bring the enemy down on us?"

In this campaign of blunders fortune steadily favoured the French and Italian armies. Unmolested by any sharpshooters that might have been hidden in the marshy thickets across the river, the bridge of pontoons was completed, boat by boat, and at half-past six in the evening a division of the light infantry was safely established on the enemy's ground.

General Espinasse, with his division, had gone forward along the high road to Milan as far as the stone bridge of San Martino. This was expected to be a strong defensive position of the Austrians. To his surprise, he found that it too had been abandoned, after an ineffectual attempt to blow it up. The only two arches that had been seriously injured were repaired that same afternoon, and another way lay open into the enemy's country.

It now seemed evident that the Austrians would make their stand along the Naviglio Grande—the broad and deep canal which here follows the general course of the Ticino, at from one to three miles' distance toward Milan. The indecision of the French Emperor was still great. He could not determine on any general advance of the allied armies further to the east, fearing always that the invisible enemy might be turning back to attack him from the south.

At three o'clock in the morning of the 3rd of June, the light infantry reached a bridge over the canal. It was untouched, and the Austrians were not there to defend it. Two companies of the French troops at once installed themselves in houses on the bank, and, by mattresses at the windows and otherwise, prepared a defence against any sudden attack. The remainder of the battalion crossed the bridge and disposed itself behind the stone walls of the gardens and the haystacks which were near at hand.

In this way, an enemy would be covered by the fire from each bank. MacMahon's entire corps, comprising the divisions of Generals Espinasse and Lamotterouge, besides the light infantry of Camou, had been ordered to cross the river and rana; by the bridges which had thus been secured. While the greater part were still at the pontoons, MacMahon and Camou, with a large body of troops, pushed on beyond the canal to Turbigo, a village farther north. The corps thus took the position, which it kept through all the subsequent fighting, of left wing (farthest to the north and east) of the long, scattered line of the allied armies.

General Mellinet, with the Grenadiers of the Imperial Guard, was substituted for Espinasse at the bridge of San Martino to the south. The Austrian division of Clam-Gallas, which was occupying Magenta, faced all these troops approaching it from the north and west.

The Turcos, whom MacMahon had brought with his other soldiers from their posts in Algiers, soon dislodged the few Austrian companies that were on guard at Turbigo. Seeing the way clear, MacMahon, with Camou and a small escort, rode forward to the hamlet of Robecchetto, where the two generals climbed the church-tower with the hope of ascertaining the position of the enemy. Instead, they saw a large number of the Austrian troops charging down on them. They had barely time to get to their horses and ride away, with the Austrians behind them in hot pursuit. The Algerian sharpshooters came to the rescue, and soon a serious battle was raging around Turbigo.

At the same time a column of 4,000 men, preceded by a battalion of Tyrolese sharpshooters, was directed against the bridge over the canal, which the French troops had occupied in the early morning. The Austrian commander now foresaw the results of the negligence which allowed the allied troops to cross both river and canal above the positions on which he relied for defence. It was too late. Before the Austrian attack could dislodge the French infantry, who answered their fire from each end of the bridge, MacMahon had gained the day at Turbigo, and his cannon sounded nearer and nearer. The enemy, fearing to be cut off from their main body, hastily retreated. It was seven o'clock in the evening. The combat of Turbigo, which was the prelude of the morrow's work, had been fought and won. Napoleon, who came up during the fray, gave the name to one of the broad, new streets he was opening in Paris.

The emperor returned to Novara for the night, and made out the necessary orders for a general movement forward of the allied armies on the following day. These orders were changed next morning in several of their details. As they were based on no precise knowledge of the enemy's position and movements, they were again upset by the fighting and surprises of the mid-day.

2.—The Ride of the Commandant.

At six o'clock in the morning of the 4th of June, Napoleon despatched Commandant Schmitz of his staff with his final orders.

Go first to the king. Inform him of my march forward, and tell him to begin moving his men, following Camou over the left side of the river.

This was for Victor Emanuel, who was in command of 22,000 men, one-half of the Italian regiments of the allied armies. He was but a short distance to the west of the pontoon bridges which had been thrown across the Ticino at Porto di Turbigo.

Go on next to the Ticino. I have ordered two of the bridges to be brought down to San Martino, to hasten what will be the long crossing of our own troops.

The emperor referred to the main portion of his army, made up of the 41,000 men of Canrobert and Niel, who were still back of Novara, and of 40,000 more belonging to the corps of Baraguey d'Hilliers and the second Italian division. The latter were so many miles in the rear that they could be of no use in any battle to be fought that day.

Then find MacMahon, who must be already beyond Turbigo. Ask him what he counts on doing if he has the enemy in his front. Inform him of the march and position of the Guard, which he has at his right.

This was General Mellinet's division, which had been detached from Camou and was already across the river at San Martino. With the remainder of the Guard under Camou, and the entire divisions of Espinasse and Lamotterouge, this brought to 32,000 the number of men sharing in MacMahon's offensive movement on Magenta.

"I shall be at Trecate" (halfway from Novara to the bridge of San Martino), continued the emperor "at noon precisely. Make the entire round, and be exact in reporting to me at that hour."

The line of march thus formed left MacMahon in command of the left wing of the army. This was already in great part across both river and canal, and was to be followed closely by King Victor Emanuel with his Italian regiments as a reserve. The emperor was commanding in person the centre and right—that is, the long line of troops which was to advance, division after division, along the high road of Milan. He had to expect a sharp fight in forcing the strong defensive positions held by the enemy where the road crosses the canal, before reaching Magenta. The movement of MacMahon's corps on Magenta from the other side was designed by him to divide the Austrian forces during this attack.

In the absence of all precise information, Napoleon still believed

ON THE TRACK LAY A BODY COVERED WITH A BLUE CLOAK

that the bulk of the Austrian army was disposed in a long line parallel to his own, and several miles to the south. To avoid a possible general attack all along the line, he had arranged the march of his troops so that division trod on the heels of division from far beyond Novara. He hoped, by forcing back the right wing of the Austrian army, which alone he supposed to be defending the approaches to Magenta, to be able to pass by the main body of the enemy and march on Milan. At least, this is the only way of explaining the emperor's orders for this 4th day of June. As a line of battle his forward movement was preposterous, straddling a river and canal, which were not easy of passage, and without any defensive positions to support him in case a concentrated attack should be made in the meantime.

General Gyulai did not know the advantages of his position. The line of battle which he opposed to the French advance admitted of a quick concentration of his troops which might, by the mere force of numbers, have crushed the corps of MacMahon and the Guard before the divisions of Novara could have marched up to their aid. Around Magenta the troops of Clam-Gallas faced MacMahon to the north, and the high road from San Martino to the west. There was a strong body of cavalry at Corbetta close at hand. The divisions of Liechtenstein were at Ponte Vecchio (the Old Bridge) and Robecco, along the canal below where the road crosses it.

These, which formed the right and centre of the line of the Austrian Army as it was actually engaged in battle, numbered 36,000 men. The left was in the immediate neighbourhood, with Zobel not two miles to the south and the rest just beyond at Abbiategrosso, 28,000 in all. At Vigevano across the Ticino there were 24,000 more, quite as near as the central divisions of the French. The remaining 25,000 men of the Austrian Army, like the extreme rear of the allies, were too far away to be counted on for this day's work.

As it was, between ignorance and indecision, the battle was to be fought with about equal forces on either side. It was to be an instance of an adage often in the mouths of military men—

"Victory belongs to him who makes the fewest blunders."

Commandant Schmitz galloped off on his long morning ride. He warned the king to hasten the movement of his troops, which would be needed as a reserve in case MacMahon should be attacked. Only one of the pontoon bridges would be left him for the tedious crossing over the Ticino. Beyond the river he found the division of Camou

IN THEIR FRENZY HIS ZOUAVES BROKE THROUGH THE DEFENCES

already on the way to follow the main column led by MacMahon. It was half-past ten o'clock before he came up with MacMahon himself, riding at the head of the division of Lamotterouge.

"The emperor asks what you reckon on doing if you meet the enemy."

"I have no news yet, and there is no attack along the front. On account of the narrow road I have only the division of Lamotterouge with me. I have sent Espinasse by a roundabout way at a half-hour's march from my left. He is keeping up with me. Camou is behind. Tell the emperor that I count on being at Magenta at two o'clock."

The *commandant* rode back, after warning MacMahon that the king had not yet begun crossing the river with the troops which ought to be his final reserve for the day. He reached Trecate at noon, just as the emperor was alighting from his carriage. All along the way he had heard the noise of cannon from beyond San Martino. Napoleon received his report, mounted his horse, and rode off hastily with his escort in the direction of the firing.

It was the portion of the Guard which was under General Mellinet that had been violently engaged beyond the bridge at the village of Buffalora by the canal. Napoleon sent back at once to hurry on the corps of Niel, which was marching forward along the road from Novara. The disposition which had been made of the troops rendered this no easy task, and Mellinet was obliged to hold his own as best he might for three hours longer.

At half-past four the emperor, more and more disquieted at hearing nothing from MacMahon, sent Commandant Schmitz once more by the weary round of the morning to get news of him. There was no nearer way by which he might escape the enemy's fire in crossing the canal. At six o'clock the *commandant* reached the pontoons, which the Italian regiments had not yet finished crossing. Victor Emanuel asked if it was Canrobert who was attacked.

"No, sire: it is the whole army. Have you nothing from MacMahon?"

"Yes; a word in pencil, signed by his *aide-de-camp*; but it is not pressing."

Commandant Schmitz could only conjure the king not to lose a moment of time, and asked for an officer to keep him company in his own search. As they rode off, the Piedmontese infantry was straggling over the pontoons. Some of the men were stopping to heat their soup in the islands of the river, and all, when a new burst of artillery

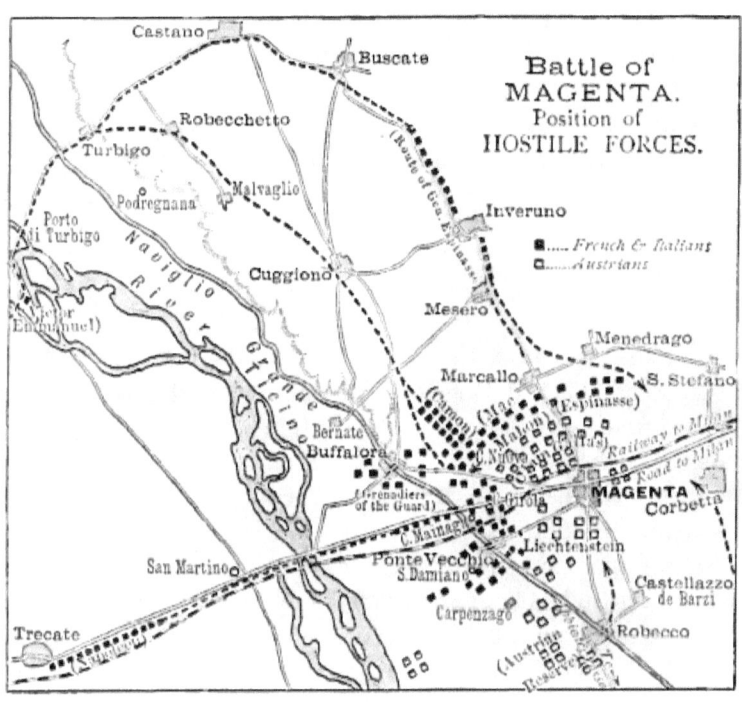

was heard from the distance, gave vent to their patriotic cry—"*Viva l'Italia!*"

It was eight o'clock and night was falling when Commandant Schmitz reached the line of railway from Milan, just beyond Magenta. On the track before him lay a body covered with a blue cloak and guarded by a staff-officer in tears. It was General Espinasse, who had been shot dead as he entered Magenta. At the other end of the town a sharp fusillade was still going on. In the confusion, it was some time before MacMahon could be found; and it was half-past eleven at night before the *commandant* arrived with his news at Napoleon's quarters by the river. The emperor was lying, dressed, on the bed in an attic room of the little inn. He arose, and by the light of a candle dictated the telegraphic despatch to the Empress Eugenie which set all Paris rejoicing next day. "A great battle—a great victory! "

3.—The Fight at Magenta.

From the beginning, the task assigned to the troops of MacMahon was long, difficult, and dangerous. After crossing both river and canal, they had to march down toward Magenta in a line trending always to the right. They would thus be ready to aid in the attack which the divisions under the command of the emperor were bound to make on the enemy's positions along the canal.

Shortly after Commandant Schmitz left him in the morning, MacMahon came suddenly on the enemy in front of Buffalora. This small village, situated on both sides of the canal, was one of the strongest Austrian positions, and the first serious obstacle which Napoleon would encounter in his own movement forward from the other side. MacMahon at once ordered the attack. It was made, with their wonted violence, by the Turcos and the foot-soldiers of the 49th Regiment of the line.

They were in the thick of the fray when a strong column of the enemy was discovered moving up to attack the divisions of MacMahon from the right. So far as he could discern, he would have to face the main body of the Austrian Army. The smoke of battle already clouded the air, heavy from the damp rice-fields by the river, and it would be no light task to bring his various divisions into line from their march across country. The enemy's advance already threatened to separate him from the troops led by Espinasse, and from Camou, who was not yet in sight.

Before him, where the combat was actually engaged, disorder had already begun. The shells, on which the Austrians chiefly relied in this campaign, were whizzing through the air and leaving clouds of smoke and dust that added to the difficulty of his movements. One regiment, which had been ordered to fall back, found itself marching straight on the enemy; and another, wishing to rush forward to the attack which had been begun, turned back in the opposite direction.

MacMahon now gave orders that the Turcos and foot-soldiers should give over the attack on Buffalora and rally to his main column. This was a work of time. It was necessary to tear the men from a mortal combat which they were sharing with the Grenadiers of the Guard. These, at the head of Mellinet's division, had come up from the other side and were already taking their position in the village. MacMahon next ordered Espinasse to move his men steadily to the right until he should be able to act in concert with the division led by himself. He then suspended his own movements until he could enter into communication with Camou, who was approaching but slowly from behind.

In these first movements of the day. General MacMahon has been reproached for his sudden attack on Buffalora; but this seems to have been in harmony with the essential plan of the Emperor, who had little idea of the real strength of the Austrian troops concentrated round Magenta.

He is next blamed for withdrawing his men from the attack when the Guard was in most danger; but it was the business of the emperor to protect his own line of attack. MacMahon had been made responsible for the important attack on Magenta itself; and the advance of the enemy on his right threatened to render this impossible. Besides, the Grenadiers of Colonel d'Alton-Shee had already secured possession of Buffalora, which they had now only to defend.

Most of all, MacMahon is criticised for the long pause which now ensued in his operations, while the enemy was attacking in force close at hand. This was contrary to the tradition of the French army, praised by Moltke, that haste should be made where the cannon sounds. It can only be answered that MacMahon had been positively ordered to march forward to the church-tower of Magenta; that he was not responsible for the slowness of Camou which retarded his own movements; and that the victory which he won when he did move on the enemy shows who it was made the fewest blunders on that day.

In directing the movements of his thirteen battalions. General Camou, whose experience of war went back to the First Napoleon,

HE DICTATED THE TELEGRAPHIC DESPATCH

had been following all the rules. At the sound of the cannonading in front, he marched straight across the fields toward the church-tower of Magenta, on which he knew MacMahon was advancing before him. The fields were separated from each other by dense thorn-hedges, and divided into small patches of maize. These, in turn, were separated by rows of mulberry trees bound together by wires, along which grape-vines were trained. At each moment the Sappers were called on to use their axes, and the other soldiers their sword-bayonets. This needed no great time; but, at every open space, the command of the tactician Camou was heard, stopping all movement in order to straighten properly the line of his advance.

At half-past four o'clock MacMahon himself, with his uniform in disorder and accompanied only by a few officers of his staff, dashed up to hurry forward this reserve which was necessary to his own attack. On the way, he had run into a body of Austrian sharpshooters who saluted him as one of their own commanders, not dreaming of the presence of the French general. Hastening back to give directions to Espinasse, he again barely escaped being captured by the *Uhlans*. Camou had taken six hours for less than five miles of march.

The drums now beat the charge, and a determined attack was made on the enemy's main column. It was taken between two fires, from the division of Espinasse on one side, and from that of Lamotterouge, led by MacMahon in person, on the other. Step by step, resisting desperately to the end, the Austrian troops fell back on Magenta, where their general and his staff were watching the fortunes of the battle from the church-tower.

Espinasse, by order of MacMahon, hastened his movement on the town from the side of the railway, to stop the fire of artillery which fell obliquely on the troops of Lamotterouge. A company of Tyrolese sharpshooters had entrenched themselves in one of the first houses. General Espinasse and his orderly fell dead under their unerring shots. In their frenzy, his *Zouaves* broke through the defences of the house and put to the bayonet each man of the three hundred Tyrolese. The bloody fight was continued around the railway station and through the narrow streets of the town. It left everywhere dead bodies clothed with the hostile uniforms, the red breeches of the French mingling with the white jackets of the Austrians.

On his side, MacMahon charged again and again, but the resistance was still obstinate around the church. At last, from the tower, the Austrian commander caught sight of the four regiments of

Camou advancing in that regular order which became old soldiers of the Guard. They were impatient to share in the fray, but the Austrian general abandoned the place before them. Not one of their number had burned a cartridge or received a scratch. Their coming two hours earlier would have saved no end of good French blood. The Italian reserve, under King Victor Emanuel in whose cause the war was waging, did not appear all this day.

With nightfall, the soldiers of MacMahon—those who had fought and those who had only marched bravely—bivouacked as best they could outside the town. The doctors began their all night's work among the wounded in the church.

General Trochu had brought his battalions forward at quick step along the road from Novara. At the bridge over the Ticino he found the emperor quite alone, listening intently to the sounds of the battle. The officers of his escort had been despatched in every direction for information to relieve his uncertainty. Trochu asked for directions. Napoleon, white and trembling, could not answer. At last, in a scarcely intelligible whisper, he said, pointing to the bridge—

"Pass!"

From General Regnauld de Saint-Jean d'Angély, who was in command on the other side, Trochu learned that the enemy still held out at the Old Bridge (Ponte Vecchio) over the canal, in spite of Canrobert's impetuous onsets. He ordered his men to move forward, rifle on shoulder and all the drums beating and trumpets sounding. The Austrians, believing in the arrival of a large body of fresh troops, abandoned their last positions. At four o'clock in the morning Trochu followed them to the south with his artillery, and their defeat became a rout. When Napoleon, on this day (the 5th of June), sent 50,000 men against what he still supposed to be the main body of the enemy, not an Austrian was to be found.

After a day for rest, on the 6th, MacMahon, with his corps, was off to check the advance from the north of General Urban, who was hurrying back from his chase of Garibaldi. Napoleon stood at the bridge of San Martino to see the troops pass by. Calling MacMahon to alight from his horse, he said:

"I thank you for what you have done. I name you Marshal of France and Duke of Magenta."

At the request of the generals who could not yet understand how the battle had been won without them, the dignity of Marshal was, also bestowed on the modest and valiant commander-in-chief of the

Imperial Guard, General Regnauld de Saint-Jean d'Angély. It was the heroic resistance of General Mellinet and his Grenadiers of the Guard, left unaided for hours at Buffalora. that allowed to Camou all the time he required for bringing up his men according to military rules. It also gave MacMahon the shorter time needed to march forward and to reach the church-tower of Magenta.

THE DOCTORS BEGAN THEIR ALL NIGHT'S WORK

The Second Italian War of Independence
1859

The Battle of Solferino
24th June, 1859
By Major G. Le M Gretton

Used as he was to splendid pageants, Napoleon III. can seldom have seen anything more impressive than his reception by the people of Genoa 12th May, 1859. He was welcomed as the friend of Italy, who had come to deliver two of her fairest provinces from the Austrian yoke. His troops had preceded him. Some had crossed the Alps over the pass of Mount Cenis, by a road first built by the Great Napoleon; others had been disembarked at Genoa from Algeria and Toulon. And now the Emperor of the French himself was landing, to take the command of the armies of France and of Piedmont, the kingdom of his ally. King Victor Emmanuel.

The harbour, one of the most beautiful in the world, was crowded with merchant shipping, anchored in long straight lines—perfect streets of ships; and at the breakwaters lay squadrons of French and Piedmontese men-of-war. As Napoleon left his yacht to take his seat in a gilt state barge, the warships manned their yards and thundered out the royal salute of 101 guns; the batteries along the water's edge replied; and then the forts which crown the amphitheatre of hills around the bay caught up the fire. The ships were all dressed with flags; the vessels between which he passed were gay with music; flowers were strewn upon his watery path; men swam before his barge; hundreds of rowing-boats put out to welcome him.

On shore a transformation had been effected in the narrow streets of imposing palaces through which the procession wound its stately way. Every window was a flower garden; costly tapestries fluttered in the breeze; garlands of roses were festooned from house to house; flags hung across the streets. Every window, every roof, every inch of standing-room ill the densely-packed streets was occupied by handsome, dark eyed Italians, vociferously welcoming the chivalrous Frenchman, who, they were assured, was pledged to rid Italy for ever of the hated presence of her Austrian tyrants.

There were few Piedmontese troops left in Genoa to receive the emperor, for Victor Emmanuel's little army was facing the Austrians in Piedmont; but enough remained to make the French soldiers familiar with the uniform of their allies. The heavy cavalry wore huge brass helmets, with brightly-coloured horses' tails hanging from their crests, dark grey-blue tunics, and grey overalls. The infantry of the line had long, flapping grey coats, buttoned back at the hip to clear the knee in marching, baggy grey trousers gathered in at the ankle, long gaiters, and a *kepi*.

The *Bersaglieri*—riflemen—were certainly the most picturesque corps in the Piedmontese service, as their successors are now in the army of United Italy. Short men, chosen for great strength, activity, and depth of chest, they were trained to perform forced marches against time, while carrying their heavy kit upon their backs; to swim with their rifles and cartridge-pouches held above their heads; to scale almost inaccessible mountains—in a word, to go anywhere and everywhere and to do anything. They were the idols of the Italians in 1859[1] and to this day their uniform of rifle green, with a huge round hat, worn over the right ear, and a plume of cock's feathers streaming down their backs, is the popular ideal of military beauty in Italy.

For a few days before the emperor arrived Genoa was full of French troops. They were encamped on every fairly level piece of ground within miles of the harbour. To walk through their camps «as to see contingents of nearly every branch of the French army as they lived on active service. The stately Grenadiers of the Imperial Guard, fresh from their luxurious quarters in Paris, roughed it on the dry bed of a river: their camp was always thronged with admiring Italians, for as a martial spectacle it is difficult to conceive anything more attractive than these, the picked infantry men of France. Napoleon III. had revived for them the uniform of the Old Guard of his uncle, the Great Napoleon—huge bearskins, dark blue *coatees*, white breeches and gaiters.

Splendid as was their appearance, it was equalled by the splendour of their manners—to ladies, at least, for to their brothers of the French line they were condescending, and to all civilians, except the English, superbly insolent. To a party of Englishmen who visited their camp they were affable, though a trifle patronising. They exhibited

Genoa

the Crimean medals which the British Government had distributed among the French troops who had taken part in the Crimean War. "*Medailles de sauvetage*" (life-saving medals) "we call them," said a grim old sergeant: "the Queen of England sent them to us because we prevented the Russians from killing all her soldiers at Inkerman!"

Near them were cavalry fresh from Algeria—Hussars in light-blue tunics and baggy red trousers strapped over the foot. Lean and tanned by their African campaigns, and mounted on beautiful Arab chargers, they looked the *beau-ideal* of light horsemen.

A mile or two away were the Algerian sharpshooters, or Turcos, as these swarthy Africans were called throughout the army. In their fantastic uniform of jacket and baggy knickerbockers of light blue, yellow leggings, red sashes and turbans, they looked picturesque, but savage to a degree. Indifferent to minor punishments, death was the only sentence they respected; and even a firing-party in the grey of the morning had little terror for them. One of them, sentenced to be shot at dawn the next day, sat cheerfully smoking and drinking coffee with his friends at the door of his tent, and chatted in guttural tones with the sentry, who with loaded rifle and fixed bayonet mounted guard over him.

The *Zouaves* also camped for several days near Genoa. They were the very opposite to the Grenadiers of the Guard, except as regards politeness to women, in which the whole of the emperor's army excelled. The Grenadiers were spick-and-span, well drilled, correct, decorous; the *Zouaves* were slouching, rollicking madcaps, who disembarked at Genoa from Algeria with a menagerie of pets attached to each battalion. As they marched along the quay from the steamers, monkeys and parrots chattered from the men's shoulders, and dogs trotted beside their masters in the ranks. Their uniform was the same as the Turcos, but of different colours; and the men were French—often, it was said, young gentlemen who had exhausted the patience of their relations before they became soldiers.

Artillery was there in abundance, but the public were kept as much away from it as possible, as the French were anxious that no information as to the rifling of their new guns should reach the Austrians before the fighting commenced.

Needless to say, that the infantry of the line were found at every turn—wiry, cheerful little men, who marched all day with huge weights on their backs without fatigue or grumbling, and who, like the French soldiers of every age, excelled in the art of making them-

BERSAGLIERI

selves comfortable. You would see a regiment led to a dried-up plain and ordered to encamp.

At once the men piled arms, and took off; their knapsacks; fatigue-parties filed off to fill the kettles carried on the march by the men themselves; and the little shelter-tents, which the men also carried in pieces between them, were run up like magic. Some parties made little cooking-places with stones, others collected wood and started fires; the water fatigues returned; meanwhile the food had been prepared, and in about half an hour the *piou pious* had a comfortable meal cooking in their camp-kettles.

As fast as possible the French troops, as they landed at Genoa, were pushed up towards Piedmont, which had already been invaded by the Austrians. At one time fears were entertained that the Austrians would be able to reach Turin before the French columns, which were pouring over the Alpine passes, had arrived there; but the quick marching of the French, and the procrastination of the Austrians, combined to save the capital of Victor Emmanuel from capture.

Eight days after Napoleon landed in Italy was fought the first of the series of battles which culminated at Solferino. At Montebello, and again at Palestro, the Austrians were worsted by the allied armies. On the 4th June, at Magenta, they made a gallant, though unsuccessful stand; and after this fresh defeat retreated slowly to a strong position east of the Mincio, their front covered by that river, their flanks guarded by the fortresses of Peschiera and Mantua.

The Franco-Piedmontese Army, much hampered by want of transport, slowly pursued them, and on the 23rd bivouacked on both banks of the Chiese River, about fifteen miles to the west of the Mincio. Short were the hours of sleep allowed that night to the French and their allies, for at two o'clock in the morning the leading divisions resumed their march. Napoleon's orders for the operations of the day were based upon the reports of his reconnoitring parties and his spies. These led him to believe that, although a strong detachment of the enemy might be encountered west of the Mincio, the main body of the Austrians was awaiting him on, the eastern side of the river.

But the French intelligence department was badly served. The Austrians had stolen a march upon Napoleon. Undetected by the French scouts, they had re-crossed the Mincio, and by nightfall of the 23rd their leading columns were occupying the ground on which the French were ordered to bivouac on the evening of the 24th. The intention of the Austrian emperor, now commanding his army in person. had been to push forward rapidly and fall upon the allies before they had completed the passage of the river Chiese. But this scheme, like that of Napoleon, was based on defective information. The allies broke up from their bivouacs many hours before the Austrians expected them to do so; and when the two armies came into contact early in the morning of the 24th June the Austrians were quite as much taken by surprise as the French.

The march of the allies was in the following order:—Baraguay d'Hilliers was leading the 1st Army Corps from Esenta to Solferino; one of his divisions followed a country road along the crest of the hills, the other two marched by the plain. McMahon, with the 2nd Army Corps, had bivouacked at Castiglione, and was moving upon Carriana. Niel was ordered to proceed with his corps—the 4th—through Medole to Guidizzolo. Canrobert's corps—the 3rd—which had been encamped on the western side of the Chiese, crossed the river on a bridge thrown over in the night by the Piedmontese engineers, with orders to march to Castel Goffredo, and thence to Medole. The Imperial Guard, the reserve of the army, was in rear, on the road west of Castiglione. The Piedmontese contingent, under the command of Victor Emmanuel, were on the left of the French, and commenced their share in the day's work by sending out strong reconnaissances from their camps near Lonato, Desenzano, and Rivolta, in the direction of Pozzolengo.

The Austrians finding that the French had already crossed the Chiese, had occupied a position which ran from north to south through the village of Pozzolengo, Solferino, Carriana, and Guidizzolo. Guidizzolo stands on the level plain of Medole; the other villages are perched on the highest points of the triangular upland which juts out like a wedge from the shores of the Lake Garda for ten miles south into the plain. To the care of the First Army, under Wimpffen, was committed the defence of Medole and its surroundings; the task assigned to the septuagenarian Schlick with the Second Army was to maintain the position on the hills.

The hill of Solferino, the key of the position, is a formidable stronghold. It stands at the head of a network of valleys, so steep that the roads along them are locally known as the "Steps of Solferino." On the dividing spurs are strong stone buildings: a church, a convent, a high-walled cemetery, an old feudal tower, all command the approaches to the hamlet. The village itself is well adapted for defence.

The houses, built on terraced gardens standing in walled enclosures, rise tier above tier on the slope of the precipitous hill. Early, in the day the Austrians occupied the place in force. Each wall was loop-holed, and at every loophole was posted a picked shot, with men behind him loading and capping the muzzle-loading rifles then in use. Solferino became a series of miniature fortresses which had either to be breached by cannon or taken by escalade. Yet, formidable as it undoubtedly was, it presented a grave tactical disadvantage. The back of the hill is so steep and scarped that it can only be descended by one winding path; and consequently, when the French had succeeded in establishing their artillery on the heights commanding the flanks of the village, and it became untenable, there was no way of escape for the garrison, whose only alternative was to die fighting, or to surrender as prisoners of war.

It has been already shown that the French, marching in several columns and on every available road, all unconscious of their enemy's sudden return across the Mincio, were moving straight for the very positions on which the Austrians were encamped. Very striking was the view which met the French columns as day broke upon their march. To the left rose the broken ground, with the old grey tower of Solferino looming high against the sky-line through the morning mist. In every other direction, the plain of Medole stretched away before them. Long lines of poplars marked the roads; the red-tiled roofs and white belfries of many a town and village showed in the distance. In the foreground, solidly-built farmhouses rose like islands out of a sea of vines, mulberry trees, and Indian corn.

Flat as a board, the plain was eminently fitted for the action of cavalry, and in this arm the Austrians excelled; yet during the day they executed no grand charges crushed. He wished at once to turn to his left they performed no feats such as live in history, to aid them. But if he did so, the gap, already Apparently, the cavalry arm was demoralised by dangerously wide, between his own army corps the defection of Lauingen, who, seized with panic early in the day, withdrew his whole division of splendid horsemen from the field of battle, before the day's work was even well begun!

Soon after sunrise the advanced guard of Niel's army corps, the 3rd, met a strong detachment of Austrian cavalry in front of Medole. After a sharp skirmish Niel drove them off the road and took the place, though stoutly held, by storm. As he was directing his attacking columns, two staff-officers arrived at a gallop to report that about a mile and half to the north McMahon, with the 2nd Corps, was held

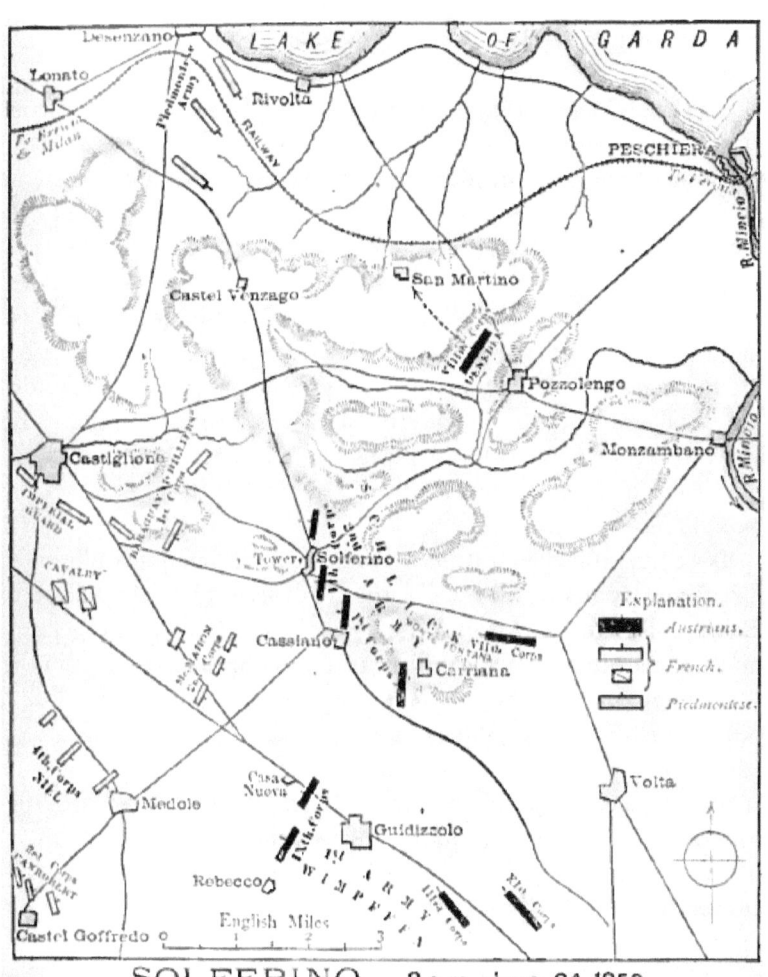

SOLFERINO,—8 a.m. June 24. 1859.

in check by large numbers of the enemy. Some were debouching into the plain at Cassiano; others already crowned the heights in every direction; and McMahon feared that the 1st Corps, under Baraguay d'Hilliers, would be crushed. He wished at once to turn to his left to aid them. But if he did so, the gap, already dangerously wide, between his own army corps and Niel's would necessarily be increased, Would Niel conform to McMahon's movement and himself move off to the left?

To this Niel, like a loyal comrade, instantly assented, on the condition that he should first secure himself by taking Medole, and that Canrobert, who commanded the 3rd Army Corps on the extreme right, and who was also moving on Medole, should guarantee Niel's outer flank from attack. But Canrobert was unable to help his colleague till late in the afternoon. Orders from the emperor had reached him to watch for 25,000 Austrians who were said to be threatening the French right from Mantua. The Austrians did not appear, but the necessity of guarding against a possible attack paralysed Canrobert. Until after three in the afternoon he took no part in the battle, and Niel was left unaided for many hours to bear the brunt of the heavy and determined onslaughts of the First Austrian Army, under Wimpffen.

Soon after Niel had stormed Medole he ascertained that Wimpffen had thrown out brigades on all the roads leading to the village of Guidizzollo, that he was, moving a whole division towards a farmhouse, Casa Nuova, about a mile out of Guidizzollo on the road to Castiglione, and that he was receiving large reinforcements. After a weary time of inaction, skirmishing, and distant cannonading, a welcome reinforcement of artillery reached the French general, and he at once concentrated his guns on the Casa Nuova farm. It was surrounded by trees, hedges, and ditches; its outbuildings gave a flanking fire; the Austrian engineers had improved these natural advantages and converted the homestead into a formidable work. By noon things looked very ugly for Niel: he had made no impression on the defence, and a fresh Austrian corps was seen advancing against him; but the Scotch blood which he inherited with his name was not to be daunted. He saw that he must either take the Casa Nuova or retire. The farm was fiercely shelled.

Suddenly the guns ceased, for a moment the hoarse roar of the battle was hushed; and then column after column of active little Frenchmen sprang forward to the assault. The Austrians stood well and firmly, they shot straight and plied their bayonets vigorously; but Niel was not to be denied. The green-coated 6th Chasseurs, with part of the 52nd and 85th of the line, threw down the barricades, smashed in the doors, climbed through the windows, and hunted the garrison from room to room. Casa Nuova was taken; and the tricolour now floated where the Imperial standard of Austria had flaunted its black and yellow colours in the breeze. A detachment of sappers were hurried into the farm to loophole its walls on the side facing the enemy, and the *Chasseurs* were ordered to hold the farm at all hazards and against all odds.

Several times during the remainder of this hard-fought day did Wimpffen make strenuous efforts to regain Casa Nuova and Rebecco—a hamlet to the south of the farmhouse, which Niel had occupied early in the day. In spite of great gallantry, however, the First Austrian Army failed to retake them.

Among the many episodes recorded of this part of the battle is the following:—A French battalion, surrounded by greatly superior Austrian forces, was retiring, with the eagle proudly carried in its midst by a young lieutenant. Hard hit, he fell, clasping the colours to his breast. A grey-haired sergeant stooped to pick up the standard, when a shell swept off his head; a captain, bronzed by the sun of Africa, snatched up the pole, which fell, broken by the same shot that struck him down. Every soldier who attempted to save the eagle was shot down. But the flag was not destined to fall into the hands of the enemy. When the battle ceased, it was found buried under a mound of dead.

Early in the afternoon Niel's position was becoming critical. His men were worn out by fatigue, by hunger, and by the extraordinary heat of the day. His formations were broken; his troops were in great confusion, and the pressure along his line was so continuous that he had no time to restore order. Even the forty-two guns which he had in action could not obtain for him the momentary respite necessary for reorganisation. The gap between his left and McMahon's right had, by the emperor's orders, been filled with the cavalry of the Guard and two cavalry divisions; and two regiments, the 2nd and 7th Hussars, were ordered to charge the enemy and distract his attention from the infantry. The Hussars rode straight and well; the Austrians staggered under the blow; and while the enemy were recovering their formations Niel rapidly restored order in his ranks.

So much did he recover himself that, on the news that Canrobert was at last about to reinforce him, he collected seven battalions of infantry, and hurled them at Guidizzolo—a gallant enterprise, but

EVERY SOLDIER WHO ATTEMPTED TO SAVE THE EAGLE WAS SHOT DOWN

unsuccessful. The head of the column reached the first houses of the village, but there meeting masses of troops, formed up for a counter attack, the leading ranks were crushed by a withering fire, and the French retired, overmastered by superior numbers.

It is now time to trace the progress of the fight on the other portions of this straggling battlefield, of which the total length was about eleven miles. The contending armies were of about equal strength: each side numbered some 50,000 combatants.

In McMahon's march across the plain towards Carriana his advanced guard early met the Austrian outposts, and the first actual contact between the scouting parties is thus described:

"A detachment of French cavalry in front observed what seemed through the mist of the morning a giant hussar watching by the wayside. The figure for an instant disappeared, jumped over a ditch into the road, crossed it, then turned, and assaulting the French officer at the head of the detachment on his left or unprotected side, dealt him a tremendous cut across the head, followed by another equally well directed. A volley from the troops behind rattled after him, and brought him down. The echo of the fire was repeated by the hills, and was the signal that two hostile armies had met."

We have already seen how McMahon applied to Niel to assist him in aiding Baraguay d'Hilliers, and that Niel was prevented from giving his help by Canrobert's enforced idleness on the extreme right of the French line, where he was condemned to watch for 25,000 Austrians who never appeared. Thus, McMahon for several hours, unable to advance, was forced, much against his will, to remain strictly on the defensive. In this part of the field the battle was for long confined to the artillery, and in this duel the French, thanks to the sound views which the emperor had instilled into the generals, were able to hold their own. Louis Napoleon was not a great captain. There were many of the secrets of his uncle's marvellous success which he had not mastered: for instance, the employment of cavalry reconnoitring parties forty, fifty, or even a hundred miles ahead of the main body was a lost art in the French army. But to do the nephew justice, he had thoroughly grasped the Napoleonic idea that artillery fire to be effectual should be overwhelming and concentrated under the direction of one commander.

The French grouped their artillery in masses; the Austrians fought their batteries independently. The result always proved the eternal truth that unity is strength. Thus, a solitary Austrian battery was in action against twenty-four of the new rifled guns of the French, which were punishing it severely. To distract the French gunners, and enable the battery to retire, two or three horse-artillery batteries, supported by three brigades of cavalry, made a demonstration; but the batteries came into action singly. At about 1,700 yards range the French opened fire upon the first that opposed them, and in a very few minutes had dismounted five out of its six guns. Another battery galloped up to its help, but in the space of one minute half its guns were silenced by the weight of shells hurled against them by the French rifled cannon. While the debris of these two batteries were making the host of their way to the rear the French guns were turned on the cavalry, and it is said that 500 out of the cavalry and artillery horses were hit in this affair, which lasted altogether about a few minutes.

Meanwhile, the 1st Corps, under Baraguay d'Hilliers, was hotly engaged round Solferino. Very early in the day this general received orders from the emperor to take the village. Slowly and painfully, after many a check, he had by noon succeeded in winning the lower slopes of the cone-like hill of Solferino. Further he could not go. The Austrians, with dogged courage held to the crests of the spurs which commanded the valleys. Foret, one of the generals of division, led a fierce assault upon the old tower; but his columns, crushed and withered by the fire of the enemy, who overhung them in every direction, failed to attain their object. With equal firmness, but with less success, did the soldiers of Austria-Hungary defend the convent and the cemetery. The infantry attacks failed, but the artillery, playing against the walls at 300 yards' range, made a practicable breach through which the French poured furiously, and then settled matters with the bayonet.

The emperor now determined to reinforce the first corps with part of the Imperial Guard, and the Chasseurs de la Garde were thrown into the fight. Formed up in the dense columns which had survived in the French Army since he days of the Great Napoleon, they awaited the signal.

> The bugles sounded the charge, and the hoarse voice of the colonel could be heard as he placed himself at their head, *'Bataillon en avant—pas de gymnastique!'* *'En avant, en ayant! Vive l'Empereur!'* burst from every throat, answered by the fierce hurrahs of the Austrians; and in a perfect transport of military frenzy the whole mass sprang up the hill. The thunder of the guns, mingled with the wild cries of the combatants and the

shrieks of the wounded, made an awful medley of sound. The men dropped cruelly fast: the dark forms of the *Chasseurs* were marked by the glancing of the sunbeams on their sword bayonets. The supporting columns pressed on. As they neared the village the puffs of Austrian smoke became less frequent. Now the French reached the first houses, and for a moment the column wavered; then with one mad rush the *Chasseurs* swept the white-coated linesmen and the Tyrolese *jagers* before them into Solferino; and the edge of the village was won.

But every house, every garden, every vineyard, was a fortress, and had to be taken separately by storm. A newspaper correspondent said:

> These small enclosures had to be carried at the point of the bayonet. I saw several of them which were literally covered with dead bodies. I have counted more than 200 in a small field, not 400 yards in length by 300 in breadth.

It was not until 2 o'clock, after several more assaults and much hard fighting, that the French really became masters of Solferino; but once they had accomplished this, they had pierced the Austrian centre.

While this sharp work was going on at Solferino, a body of Voltigeurs of the Guard and other troops were slowly forcing their way along the heights towards Carriana. It was a series of hand-to-hand fights, in which the personal qualities of the French soldier, his courage, his intelligence, his *élan*, all stood him in good stead. Monte Fontana, a hill in front of Carriana, was the scene of a fierce conflict between the Turcos and the Austrian infantry. The Africans, who hated firing and loved the bayonet, were launched in the attack. Bounding like panthers from rock to rock, crawling like beasts of prey from cover to cover, rushing with horrid yells upon their astonished antagonists, they seized the hill; the Austrians, reinforced, took heart of grace, and after a sharp struggle hurled the assailants down the slopes.

The Turcos reappeared, again drove all before them, and again the defenders by a supreme effort regained this much-disputed hill, which they held until the French, crowning the opposite height with artillery, made Monte Fontana untenable. To crown that height with artillery was no mean feat. So steep were the slopes that the gun-teams could not scramble up them. The Grenadiers of the Guard cast their usual dignity to the winds: they threw themselves on the guns and hauled them to the crest; then forming a chain, they passed from hand to hand the cartridges and shells from the waggons in the valley to the

RUSHING WITH HORRID YELLS THEY SEIZED THE HILL

gunners on the top of the hill.

Soon after the Austrians had been shelled out of Monte Fontana, the French emperor, who had exposed himself freely to danger throughout the day, came up to a line regiment fighting to get into Carriana. The emperor, followed by his escort of Cent Gardes, splendid men in bright steel *cuirasses* and tall helmets:

> Proceeded to the head of the battalion, and the fire became warmer as the uniforms and the breastplates of the body-guard served as points to aim at. The colonel threw himself in front of the emperor, and said: 'Sire, do not expose yourself: it is at you they are aiming.' 'Very well,' replied the emperor, with a smile; 'silence them, and they will fire no longer!' The expression gave us fresh vigour, and, I know not how it was, but at a bound we gained a hundred yards, and twenty minutes later we had taken Carriana.

A hapless Austrian cavalry regiment, in protecting the retreat towards Carriana, suffered great losses. They charged the French mounted skirmishers, and in doing so passed the 11th Chasseurs-à-pied, who were lying down among the standing corn. As the cavalry went by, the *Chasseurs* sprang up and poured a deadly volley among them. Two French batteries completed their confusion by firing upon them in flank.

While the Austrian left and centre were thus hotly engaged with the French, their right was no less actively occupied with the Piedmontese. Victor Emmanuel, whose little army had been encamped about Lonato and Dezenzano, commenced his share in the day's work by sending out strong reconnoitring parties of all arms towards Pozzolengo, the village where by Napoleon's orders the Piedmontese were to bivouac on the night of the 24th. Very early in the morning these detachments encountered the Austrians at various points of the plateau of San Martino. They attacked bravely, but haphazard, without combination and without supports, and they soon found themselves thrust backwards down the hill.

By midday the Piedmontese received reinforcements, and fiercely assailed the village of San Martino, which had been solidly occupied by the Austrians. At first, they carried all before them. They stormed outlying farms, the church, and some of the houses; and then in wild enthusiasm, cheering for Italy and for Victor Emmanuel, they surged forward against their enemy's main line. The Austrians stood firm. A storm of musketry swept away the heads of the Piedmontese columns, and guns, suddenly brought up within 250 yards of their left flank, mowed them down with grape shot. There was a panic; some of the troops thus roughly handled ran two miles before they could be stopped; but to their honour be it said, they rallied sufficiently to take a distinguished part in the final capture of San Martino. On the centre and right the Piedmontese retired, but with deliberation, and only as far as the railway line, behind which, while waiting for reinforcements, they hastily entrenched themselves. At length, late in the day, came the welcome aid.

Victor Emmanuel had promised Napoleon that a division of Piedmontese infantry should operate in the French attack on Solferino; but on realising the desperate need of his own troops, he diverted the march of this division, and hurried them to the assistance of their fellow-countrymen. Again, and again the heights of San Martino were assailed, and finally with success. The Piedmontese troops captured the village; they beat back an Austrian counter-attack by a charge of cavalry, and then, exhausted by the want of food, by fatigue, and by the terrible heat, they wearily dropped to sleep among the dead and dying, whose bodies lay thick upon this hard-fought field. Out of 25,000 Piedmontese engaged round San Martino 170 officers and 4,428 men were killed or wounded—a heavier loss than was sustained by any of the French army corps of equal strength either on the hills round Solferino or in the plain of Medole.

Early in the afternoon the Emperor of Austria determined to make a final bid for victory. His centre was broken. Solferino was lost, Carriana was threatened; but his right flank was still safe, and his left was holding its own against the 4th French Corps. A bold counterstroke against Niel's tired men might yet retrieve the fortunes of the day. He accordingly ordered Wimpffen to hurl three army corps at Niel, and to crash through his lines. The Austrian troops displayed their accustomed qualities of courage and devotion, but the Fates were against them. Round the farm of Casa Nuova, the key of the position, raged much hard fighting, and in the episode of its attack are found interesting illustrations of the value of cavalry against infantry.

Prince Windisch-Graetz led a brigade against the farm, while other battalions were destined to attack it in front. To press home the frontal attack his columns deployed. Wave after wave of Austrians beat against the walls of the Casa Nuova, still held by the 6th Chasseurs who had wrested it from them in the forenoon. In all the confusion of the assault the prince fell mortally wounded. He insisted on continuing to command, supported in the arms of his faithful soldiers. Suddenly, with a hoarse shout, a French lancer regiment burst from its cover behind a belt of trees, fell upon the disordered Austrians, and drove them from the farm like chaff before the wind. At the same moment, the column intended to turn the farm was once more proving that cavalry may delay, but cannot break solid and unshaken infantry. The Austrian column was repeatedly charged by two brigades of cavalry, but on each occasion the infantry had sufficient time to form square, and thus beat off the French with little loss in men. But the necessity for halting and forming square had consumed so much time, that before this column had arrived near Casa Nuova the assault in which it was to have played an important part had failed.

In laconic language Wimpffen announced to Francis Joseph the failure of the counterstroke:

> I have twice attempted to take the offensive, and have used my best reserves. I can no longer hold firm, and must retreat, covered by the 11th Corps.

Francis Joseph received this report at Carriana, where, exposed to a heavy artillery fire, he was making strenuous but unsuccessful efforts to stem the tide of French success. With great difficulty was the emperor persuaded to give orders for a general retreat across the Mincio; with even greater difficulty did his staff induce him to leave the rear-guard, where he was furiously urging his beaten troops once more to turn and face their foe. The fighting was still continuing along the long front of this straggling battlefield when, to use Niel's words:

> A violent storm, preceded by whirlwinds of dust, which plunged us in darkness, put an end to this terrible struggle, and enabled the Austrians to retreat in safety to the east of the Mincio.

The victory cost the allied armies dear, however: their killed, wounded, and missing were about 18,000; the Austrian loss amounted to about 22,000 in all.

The Spanish-Moroccan War
1859-60

Spanish Battles in Morocco Castillejos, Tetuan, Guad El Ras 1859-60
By Major Arthur Griffiths

The hero of the Spanish war with Morocco in 1859-60 was General Prim, the celebrated marshal who was afterwards known through Europe as a kingmaker and politician. But he was before all a soldier, and a gallant one, ever ready to seek the foremost place in danger and venture his life upon occasion. The most marked trait in his character was his cool, calm courage: for although he could take the lead and head an attack like any subaltern, with all the fire and intrepidity of youth, it was done on profound calculation, as the best means of inspiring an enterprising, determined spirit. In one of the many sharply contested combats in this African war he found himself with infantry alone, exposed to the attack of a considerable force of Moorish cavalry. The Spaniards in this war were weak in cavalry, the Moors, on the other hand, strong. In the present instance, their horsemen were quick to discover a weak spot in the enemy's line.

This was where Prim was posted, with only infantry to withstand the charge. He was nothing daunted. "Men!" he shouted, with that brief, stirring oratory for which he was famous in the field—

> Men! here are cavalry coming down on us, and we have none to send against them. We will meet them and charge them with the bayonets. Form squares and let the music play!

So in solid masses, with bands and colours in their midst, the Spanish infantry marched to attack the attackers, and with such a resolute mien that the Moorish cavalry turned tail and would not wait to receive them.

Prim's had been an adventurous career. He began life as a private soldier, a volunteer in a Catalonian regiment at the time of the first Carlist war. Gaining almost immediately an officer's commission, he won rank after rank so rapidly that he was a colonel at twenty-five. The very next year (1840) he threw himself into the troubled sea of Spanish politics, was concerned in a military rising, took the losing side, and was compelled to fly to France. Three years later he returned and headed a small revolution of his own, which succeeded in overthrowing Espartero and gave Prim a title as count and the rank of major-general. Once more he joined the wrong side and suffered for his mistake; he was charged with participation in an attempt to assassinate the Spanish Prime Minister, and sentenced to imprisonment in a fortress for six years.

When pardoned he travelled much in England and Italy; he went to the Crimean war as the representative of Spain, then settled in Paris, and was there leading a life of inglorious ease when the war broke out between Spain and Morocco. A born soldier, he could not bear to be left out of such stirring business; he at once sought active employment, and was appointed to the command of the Spanish reserve.

This war was the result of perpetual disagreements between the two countries. Spain was a little stimulated to it, perhaps, by her desire to extend her African possessions. She held, and still holds, a number of fortified posts on the Mediterranean shores of Morocco—Ceuta, Melilla, Alhucemas, and others. These settlements were so often harassed and attacked by the turbulent mountain-tribes that Spain indignantly demanded reparation. The Moors gave way at first; then Spain claimed more territory, which was also granted; but as one side yielded the other grew more exacting, and finally the two nations quarrelled over the lands that were to be ceded outside Ceuta. Spain at once declared war, and prepared to advance into Morocco.

It was the late autumn—a season not quite propitious to military operations. Although the summers are hot in North Africa, the winters are very inclement; heavy storms of wind and much rain might be expected. Then the country was rugged and inhospitable—a network of hills sloping down from the Atlas Mountains and intersected by rushing streams, "without roads, without population, without resources of any kind." All supplies would have to be landed on the coast and carried up with the columns, or follow as convoys under strong escort. The enemy to be encountered might be semi-barbaric, with no great knowledge of modern warfare, but they had their own peculiar and

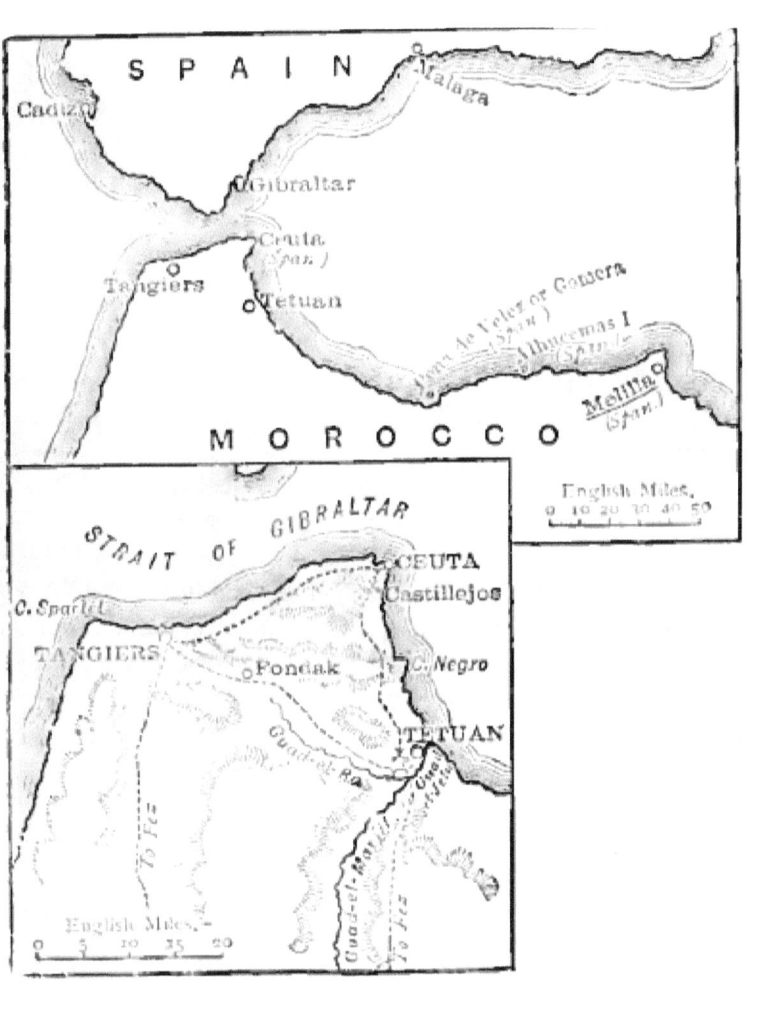

often effective tactics—clinging close to cover and using their long-barrelled flint muskets with deadly effect at long ranges, killing often at 400 yards, and when attacking using them as clubs.

These Moors were mostly fine stalwart men some six feet in height, very dirty, wretchedly clad in a white *naik*—a sort of loose, long tunic with a white hood. They were lightly equipped, active and swift of foot, knowing their mountainous country by heart, and being above all fanatics by religion—Mohammedans, the direct descendants of warlike ancestors, firmly believing, as they did, that the joys of Paradise awaited all who were slain in conflict with the *infidel*, they were likely to prove formidable foes. A writer who made this campaign says:

> Their stature, their wild and ferocious yells, might have been expected to have an intimidating effect upon troops the majority of whom are mere recruits.

How bravely the Spanish troops faced and encountered them will presently be told.

At that time the Spaniards were but little practised in war, had had but little experience of real campaigning. Although vexed continually with civil and fratricidal contests, Spain had not met a foreign foe since the old days of the Peninsular War. But she had a well-organised, compact army, made up of good materials. The Spanish soldier is willing, hardy, patient under trials and discomfort. He can march admirably—farther and faster, it is said, than the troops of any other European nation. In their light rope-soled sandals the Spanish infantry move always at a great pace, very much like the *Bersaglieri* or riflemen of Italy.

But in the early days of this Moorish war they failed rather in field manoeuvres; they did not encounter the Moors on the best plan; they were prone to rush out and engage in small skirmishes instead of awaiting attack, when their sturdy valour would have told most effectually. Again, they were bad marksmen; good shooting was not taught or encouraged in those days, and in the coming fights the Moors suffered more from artillery than infantry fire. It was, indeed, the artillery arm that did the greatest execution in the war; the Spanish cavalry was never very fortunate, and the infantry depended mainly on their bayonets, which, however, they used with excellent effect whenever they crossed weapons with the enemy, and that was often, as we shall see.

The sudden declaration of war found Spain unprepared to take the field; and as the Moors were at home on their own ground the first honours of the campaign fell to them. They quickly assembled in great numbers, and threatened Ceuta, the Spanish prison fortress, which was to be the base of operations. A line of redoubts was hastily thrown up across the isthmus—the neck of the narrow and rocky peninsula on which Ceuta stands. This brought out at once one of the many high qualities of the Spanish soldiers—their skill in manual labour. An immense amount of work fell upon them from first to last in clearing ground, road making, felling trees, throwing up earthworks; and their readiness, industry, and goodwill in these irksome but deeply important duties gained them high praise. In the earliest phases of the conflict it was hardly possible at first to move across the many obstacles presented by the ground immediately around Ceuta. Within a fortnight, the whole surface was transformed; the brushwood was cut down, good communication established between the redoubts, and it was no longer possible for the enemy to creep up to them unperceived.

Meanwhile, in the teeth of great difficulties, of hasty and, therefore, incomplete organisation, of the inevitable use of sea transport to ferry everything—men, horses, guns, food, material of every description—across from Spain, within a month a couple of army corps, each some 10,000 strong, and the reserve, another 5,000, had been disembarked at Ceuta, and had fallen into the defensive line. A third army corps was waiting conveyance at Malaga, but its movement was greatly impeded by tempestuous weather. These three corps were commanded as follows:—the first by General Echague, the second by General Zabala, the third (still at Malaga) by General Ros de Olano, and the reserve by General Prim.

The whole expeditionary army was under Marshal O'Donnell, another of the great soldier-politicians who in turn took such a prominent part in the government of Spain. O'Donnell, at this particular juncture, occupied the curious but authoritative position of Prime Minister, War Minister, and Commander-in-Chief of the army in the field. The possession of this supreme power no doubt helped him in the conduct of the campaign. It urged him, too, to the highest efforts; he knew he must achieve victory, for the first reverse would undoubtedly have been followed by his political disgrace and downfall.

November passed in desultory warfare along the line of entrenchments, during which the Spaniards held their own—no more. December, in its early days, saw no change; indeed, the situation grew somewhat worse, for the weather was always atrocious, and the rain

CEUTA AND ITS SEA-GATE.

fell incessantly, converting the ground into a quagmire, and putting the troops to the utmost discomfort.

They had no protection but the small *tentes d'abri*, of the French pattern—each for three men, and each only a few feet high—and through them the wind whistled and the water poured most uncomfortably. Such shelter was no better than lying in the open; the men sickened by hundreds, while cholera, that fell scourge, descended upon the camp and committed terrible havoc. All this time, too, there were constant skirmishes and combats of a more or less sanguinary character outside the fortifications. The Moors came on continually with great demonstrations, drawing the Spaniards beyond their entrenchments to fight at a disadvantage, and with no other result than a useless waste of life.

At last, as the year ended. Marshal O'Donnell felt himself strong enough to assume the offensive. The whole expeditionary force had now landed at Ceuta; there were troops enough to hold the redoubts covering the fortress-base, and yet to leave the main body free to march inland. Tetuan, the nearest Moorish city—if it deserved so grand a title—was the first point at which O'Donnell aimed; it was thought to be fortified and strongly held, and, although not by any means the capital of Morocco—it must be remembered that the principal object of an invader was to seize the enemy's capital—still, the fall of Tetuan would be a very substantial gain and an undoubted proof of Spanish prowess. The road to Tetuan was fairly open, moreover, due account being taken of the enemy that interposed; it followed the line of the eastern coast, and the Spanish ships of war and transports could accompany the march, giving aid if needs were to the land forces by disembarking seamen and supplies.

The order to march was issued on the eve of New Year's Day, and was hailed with delight by the Spanish troops. They were sick of Ceuta and its monotonous trench duty; they hoped to leave its narrow limits and breathe a fresher, higher air.

The advance was entrusted to General Prim, with the reserve division; an unusual proceeding, as the reserve generally follows in the rear. But Prim's fearless spirit, his indomitable energy and pluck, were so well known that he was naturally selected to lead the van. Zabala, with the second corps, supported Prim. The immediate head of the advance consisted of engineers, covered by cavalry and artillery, whose duty was to bridge the streams that came in the way.

Prim's command was on the move at daylight, their tents having

GENERAL PRIM.

been struck in the dark. By eight a.m. they were in collision with the enemy. The Moors, having seen the direction of the Spanish march, pointing as it was towards Tetuan, lost no time in assembling in strength to oppose it. They were soon seen in great numbers on a ridge in front, menacing an attack on Prim; but they gave way before his firm and resolute advance, and fell back, yielding position after position, until the hills seemed cleared of them. Prim now found himself in an open valley, hemmed in with heights, and studded with the ruins of two small white houses or "castles"—*castillejos*, as the Spaniards call them, which gave the name to the action now close at hand.

Here the enemy turned to make a fresh stand. A mountain-battery had galloped up to the front boldly, and might be supposed to have pushed on too far. The Moors were disposed to attack it, and came on brandishing their long guns, and shouting, "Dogs! Christian dogs!" till a burst of grape shot dispersed them. Then two Spanish squadrons charged. This charge, like that much more famous and more disastrous charge at Balaclava, seems to have originated also in a mistake. A French officer, who was acting as *aide-de-camp* to General Prim, brought them instructions to move out freely whenever they got the chance, adding, as he afterwards declared, that the Moors were "cowards" and would not face them.

The epithet was unhappily misconstrued and taken to apply to the Spanish horsemen. The cavalry commander, stung to the quick, immediately strove to disprove the calumny, and gave the word to charge. Away galloped the hussars into the very thick of the enemy, and tumbled in upon them in considerable strength on a plateau where their camp was pitched. But here, in this narrow and enclosed space, so unfavourable to the movement of horsemen, the Moors opened a fierce fire, and took them at a disadvantage. The hussars fought bravely against misfortune, but were presently compelled to retreat, after performing many acts of individual heroism. One of the most notable was that of the corporal, Pedro Mur, who, in the last stage of the struggle, when his comrades were already retreating, resolved to capture a standard he saw waving in the centre of a small group of Moors. With this rash idea, he turned, left the ranks, rode back alone and at full speed, charging sword in hand at the standard-bearer. He bore down everyone opposed to him, smote the Moor with the colour, killed him, seized the colour, and galloped away, unhurt, but splashed from head to foot with his enemies' blood.

Prim, it was said, should have been contented with the ground gained. But this unsuccessful charge led him to wish to renew the attack, and make a further advance. He was prudent enough to first seek further support, which O'Donnell refused, saying he would come himself to judge of the necessity, adding that Prim had gone too far already. It would be wiser, he added, to stand fast and entrench on the ground held. All doubts as to the proper course to pursue were solved by the enemy. The Moors had been receiving reinforcements, both horse and foot, and, about one p.m., were in such strength that they were emboldened to try a fresh onslaught. Prim's force, a mere handful of four weak battalions, further reduced by the day's casualties, had been on the move since daylight, without tasting food.

The men had lain down to rest and were in some danger. The Moors attacked both in front and on the flank, the direction of the latter being to cut off the Spanish retreat. The fight which followed was as fierce as it was momentous. The fire raged furiously; the smoke was so thick that the general's *aides* galloping to and fro were in touch of the enemy's line, yet unseen; the noise so deafening that it drowned the bugle calls. Prim was as usual cool, self-reliant, and quite undismayed; he gave his orders quietly, although always in the thickest part of the fight, often on foot, wearing two brilliant stars on his breast, and waving his gold-headed general's cane. His example was splendid; his excellent dispositions were well calculated to make the best use of his scanty forces, for the ground he occupied was too extensive for his numbers.

At the most critical moment help came in the shape of two fresh battalions, sent by O'Donnell, from the second corps, and that general himself, followed by all his staff, came galloping up like a small troop of cavalry, as though to take part in the fight. Prim had already utilised his new troops. He directed the men to lay aside their knapsacks, then, placing himself at the head of a battalion, and holding the other in support, he resolved to make a counter-attack. But first he seized one of the regimental colours, and, waving it on high, cried:—

> Soldiers! The time has come to die for the honour of our country. There is no honour in the man who will not give up his life when it is required of him.

With these words, he rushed on impetuously, caring little, it seemed, whether he was followed or not. Now his horse was badly wounded and staggered, but it recovered, and, as if imitating the noble impulse of its rider, galloped on. The Spaniards, fired by Prim's ex-

MOORISH HORSEMEN

ample, followed unhesitatingly, and with such energy that the enemy was at length forced to give way.

Prim afterwards gave his account of the episode in a letter to a friend:—

> At this supreme moment, I snatched up a colour; I spoke a few words with heartfelt emphasis. I called upon the remnant of my braves, and we rushed at the enemy. They were so close to us that the bayonet was the only weapon we could use. It is impossible to describe what followed. Moors and Spaniards mixed inextricably—bayonets crossing scimitars! But my men pressed on with loud cries of '*Viva la Reina! viva España!*' And for the last time that day we conquered again. The Moors fled, and our flag waved over a position we had carried three separate times.

O'Donnell officially reported that:

> The enemy, having been reinforced, incessantly attacked General Prim's position about three p.m. with great desperation. But Prim, with his usual serene courage, went out to meet them. A hand-to-hand, body-to-body combat ensued, from which our battalions emerged eventually triumphant.

The immediate result of the battle of Castillejos was the opening up of the valley and of the road to Tetuan, still some five-and-twenty miles distant. The enemy had withdrawn almost entirely, and a reconnaissance was pushed on to within a few miles of the city without being disturbed by them. But O'Donnell wisely sought to make good his position, and he halted while the necessary work of levelling ground was carried on to facilitate the bringing up supplies, much hampered hitherto and impeded by the return of tempestuous weather.

A more enterprising enemy might have done much damage during this delay, and afterwards when the advance was resumed, for the Spanish troops had to cross much rough country and thread many dangerous defiles. But the movement forward was steadily continued, with occasional combats—that across the heights of Cape Negro alone being of a serious character—until, upon the 17th January, the army reached and encamped upon the banks of the River Guad el Jelu, in full view of Tetuan, which glistened "snow-white on the rising ground at the extremity of the valley."

O'Donnell was now well placed for the attack of that city. His forces were well concentrated; the rear had come up with his main body, the guns also, notwithstanding the difficulties of the road and his baggage. The ships lay off the mouth of the river above-mentioned, and carried reinforcements, a fresh division ready to be disembarked when required. Still, he was circumspect; and feeling that he might be obliged to undertake a long siege, he set to work to strengthen himself by building redoubts, and collect his battering-train. The transport of the guns was hard work. As an artillery officer described it:

> When we leave the sand, we ascend the mountain; when we quit the mountain, we sink into the marsh.

A fortnight or more had elapsed before these preparations were completed, and in the interval the Moors had gathered fresh strength for the defence of Tetuan. Their numbers rose to 35,000 or 40,000 men. A brother of the emperor was in command, and around him was a portion of the famous black Moorish mounted guard. The whole of these troops occupied an entrenched camp covering the town—a camp carefully fortified with high substantial earthworks, along the front of which lay a swampy marsh.

There was water or muddy ground protecting one flank (the right), and on the other (the left) the defences rested on rising ground, with brushwood, which gave good cover to the Moorish marksmen. This position was strongly held by a garrison of nearly 30,000 men. It was armed with many batteries of guns, but the Moorish artillerymen were unskilled, and made but poor practice. Experts who saw this camp after the fight declared that, if manned by European troops, it would have proved almost impregnable.

The Spanish general soon realised that he must first crack this nut before he could get at the kernel—Tetuan. The 4th February was the day fixed for the attack.

There were two main lines of advance, right and left, and beyond the right an extension or flanking movement. The left attack was entrusted to General Prim, who was now in command of the 2nd Corps. He formed his troops in two lines, the first consisting of two brigades in echelon of battalions—one battalion behind the other, but stretching out beyond, so that the whole made a long line—with two brigades in column supporting. Between the two lines were the artillery.

The left attack consisted of the 3rd Corps, under General Ros de Olano, and it was formed in the same order as the right.

On the extreme right General Rios, with the division that had lately landed, was to circle round the left of the encampment continu-

A Moorish Soldier

ally threatening that flank.

The morning of the 4th dawned thick with fog; the night had been cold with severe frost. When, about 8 a.m., the mists lifted, the surrounding mountains were seen covered to their base with snow. The advance of the two attacks was made simultaneously, and both corps fell quickly into the dispositions already described. They moved steadily forward, notwithstanding the difficulties of the marshy ground undeterred by the enemy's guns, which opened fire as soon as the Spaniards came in sight. The Spanish batteries did not attempt to reply until well within range, and then did great execution. One shell set fire to the principal Moorish magazine, which exploded, scattering death and confusion within the lines.

The worst ground the assailants found was close up under the entrenchments. Here, too, the Moorish artillery, firing grape at very short range, did great execution. Prim's men were now a good deal harassed, too, by the sharpshooters in the wood. But as they neared the works the signal was given to charge, and all went forward gallantly with loud shouts and "*Vivas!*"

Of course, Prim led. On the eve of the fight he had said to some friends, "Happy the man who first enters the breach tomorrow."

Now he showed that he meant what he said; for he rode straight into a battery through an embrasure (gun opening), followed by four of his staff, and cut down with his sword the two first Moors who attempted to bar his passage. When Prim's men saw their general disappear inside the works, they dashed after him, cheering; and the enemy, astounded at the daring of the five mounted assailants, gave way entirely at the charge of the rest of the column.

Prim had made good his entrance about the centre of the line of works; next him, on the right, a brother of General O'Donnell's got in with his division. On the left the 3rd Corps made good progress, but were much impeded by a morass, and, while caught there, suffered much from the enemy's fire. The left division of this left attack, however, penetrated, and the men having thrown off their knapsacks, which greatly encumbered their movements, raced forward, bayoneting the Moors wherever they found them. On the far right, meanwhile, one of Prim's divisions, lending a hand to General Rios, had driven the Moors up into the hills.

The struggle was ended. It had been costly and gallantly fought on both sides. The Spaniards had borne a heavy fire with cool endurance, and had shown great dash when the time came to charge. The Moors, for their part, had made a tenacious resistance. The artillerymen especially had stuck to their guns to the very last, although altogether overmastered. The cavalry on neither side did much.

Three days afterwards Tetuan—at the urgent request of many of the inhabitants—was occupied by the Spanish troops. The Moors had gone; there was not a sign of their soldiers in or near the place. On the 9th February, General Prim made a reconnaissance forward in the direction of Tangier, but met no enemy. Hostilities were suspended. The only gossip was of overtures for peace. Spain had been entirely and rapidly successful; the Moors, dispersed and disheartened, were hardly expected to show fight again in the field. This impression was fully supported by the appearance of envoys in the Spanish camp, asking conditions, and negotiations began. These, as it afterwards appeared, were intended only to gain time. The Moors had not as yet abandoned hope. The resources of the empire could hardly be exhausted, even though they had lost one important town, and had been twice defeated in the field. They had still a vast territory behind and crowds of wild warriors to rally round their flag. Moreover, the terms demanded by the Spaniards were so intolerable that a proud people might well try another battle or two before yielding.

These peace negotiations dragged on for more than a month. Through the rest of the month of February, and all through the early days of March, the envoys came and went, and there were many references to Madrid and Fez. This delay was all to the advantage of the Moors, who employed it to bring up fresh and unbeaten troops, and in the collection of forage and supplies, which operations were greatly aided by the now fine dry weather. Presently it was borne in on Marshal O'Donnell, who had just been created Duke of Tetuan in reward for his victories, that he might have to do his work over again, and undertake another campaign, for the news came that the enemy had collected in great strength upon the road to Tangier.

This seaport town was to have been the next goal of the invaders, should the war continue, and now the road which was hilly and easily held would be probably barred. Accordingly, on the 23rd March O'Donnell abruptly broke off negotiations, and decided to appeal once more to the sword. On that day, leaving a small garrison in Tetuan, he marched out with the rest of the army, meaning to attack the enemy wherever he might find them. The troops carried six days' rations, and were in number about 25,000 men.

The order of march was as follows:—At the head were two bri-

MOORS AND SPANIARDS MIXED INEXTRICABLY

gades of the 1st Corps, that which had first landed at Ceuta, and had borne the brunt of the earliest fighting. The headquarter staff immediately followed; then came the 2nd Corps, under Prim; the 3rd Corps was in support. All these moved in the comparatively low ground, the valley formed by a river which constantly changed its name, and which at Tetuan is known as the Guad el Jelu or Martin, and yet four miles higher up is called the Guad el Ras. It is a long, rather narrow valley stretching east and west, and bordered on either side by commanding heights, especially on the northern. O'Donnell saw the necessity of occupying the latter, and for this purpose directed General Rios, with a division of the reserve, to crown them with a movement continually outflanking and protecting the right of the main advance along the valley.

The fighting began within two or three miles of Tetuan. A series of low hills crossed the valley, partly covered with brushwood, dotted with villages, and offering good defensive positions. These the Moors occupied one after the other, held stubbornly for a time, then yielded up lo the determined attack of the Spaniards. The Moors were counting much on the movement of their left wing—12,000 strong—which had been sent along the heights on their left, those by which Rios was marching, and this left wing was intended to first outflank, then cut off the advancing Spaniards from Tetuan. It was, however, met and checked by Rios, although the latter, finding the country very difficult, had had to make a wider detour, circling round to his right; and it was feared for a moment that the Moors might get in between him and the main body.

By 3 p.m., however. General Rios was reaching down and in touch with the nearest Spanish troops—those of the 1st Corps. By this time, too, the Moors had drawn off, retreating across the river Guad el Ras, and had re-formed there in a very strong position opposite the Spanish left. Prim was in command here. Dashing and indomitable as ever, he at once resolved to attack. The Moors held a village on the lower slopes beyond the river, and resisted obstinately. They contested the ground, inch by inch, losing it, regaining it, losing it again. Prim had, however, occupied a wood on one flank, and under cover of the trees made fresh dispositions, before which the Moors yielded, and the village was taken. The Moors fell back, however, upon a second village higher up, and much more, difficult of access. Here they again turned, again issued forth, charging Prim's people on both flanks, but without success. They were compelled to retire sullenly, reluctantly.

TETUAN

On no previous occasion had the Moors fought with such unhesitating courage. They were mostly new men, drawn from the wildest, most remote part of Morocco, and they had not as yet experienced the Spanish artillery fire or faced the Spanish bayonet. In the course of this fierce contest there were several instances in which bodies of Moorish infantry had boldly charged whole Spanish battalions. In one case "a mere handful of men rushed fearlessly upon the Spanish line, dying upon the bayonets, but not until some of them had actually penetrated the battalion." Wherever there was a position favourable to their irregular method of fighting the Moors stubbornly defended it, and were only driven out at the point of the bayonet. We are reminded of the reckless, indomitable courage of the Ghazis of our own Afghan wars.

Prim, having captured the two villages, moved steadily and irresistibly forward, and the movement was taken up by the whole line, until at last they were in sight of the Moorish encampment. In a twinkling the tents were struck, and the enemy, without baggage or impedimenta, had cleared off the ground. It was now about half-past four. The last shots had been fired, and the Spaniards were in occupation of the last stronghold of the Moors. This was at a point some six miles from Fondak, a great semi-barbaric *caravanserai*—the halfway house—between Tetuan and Tangier, and situated at the far end of a long defile which the Spanish would have to force the following day.

But there was to be no more fighting. Next day the Moors again tried negotiation. Envois from Muley Abbas, the emperor's brother, came in to the Spanish headquarters, and asked for an interview with Marshal O'Donnell. The Spanish commander-in-chief was not disposed to see them. He would have no more beating about the bush, he said. Either the enemy must make full submission at once, or he would press on to Tangier.

"I halt here today"—this was his ultimatum—"to send my wounded into Tetuan, and bring up more ammunition. The day after, I march forward. At 4.30 a.m., my men will breakfast, and all will be ready. But I will wait here till 6 a.m., if your prince chooses to come in by that time."

It so fell out, and the following morning Muley Abbas appeared. The conditions, which included an indemnity of four millions sterling and the surrender of a large slice of territory was settled, and the war was over.

MOORISH TYPES.

WARS OF ITALIAN UNIFICATION

Palermo: The Coming of Garibaldi
May 26, 1860
By Stoddard Dewey

The night of the 26th of May, 1860, came down on the city of Palermo, on the plains around it and on the hills which close it in beyond, amid anxious uncertainty everywhere. Everyone was asking, "Where is Garibaldi?"

The city itself was held in a state of siege by its king, Francis II. of Naples. The sympathies of the great mass of the inhabitants were known to be with the Thousand men of Garibaldi and the Sicilian insurgents who had joined him in his march from the western coast to the hills above Palermo.

No one was allowed to leave the city, or to walk through the streets

GARIBALDI

by day in company with others, or by night without a lighted torch or lantern.

Soldiers were picketed at the corners of the unlighted streets; companies of soldiers guarded each of the city gates which had not been walled up; and two lines of military outposts surrounded the whole city without.

On the plain to the west and north of the city 20,000 soldiers of the king were in camp; 4,000 more had for some days been pushing back the insurgents in the hills. Their general imagined it was Garibaldi who was retreating before them. No military man could understand how a thousand foot-soldiers, aided only by a few thousand ill-armed and untrained recruits, could give the slip to the pursuing columns of regular troops, and surprise the entrance to a city guarded at every point by battalions of trained men and commanded by the artillery of the forts and the warships in the bay.

Even now the descent of the Thousand into Palermo does not become plain until we go over carefully the condition of the city on that fateful night, the situation of the various bodies of troops that were guarding it, and the movements down the mountain side of Garibaldi and his men.

1.—IN PALERMO.

The Bourbons had now ruled over Naples, with the whole southern part of Italy and the island of Sicily, for 125 years.

Ferdinand II., who was dead but a single year, had been peculiarly unfortunate through the whole of his long reign. During its first years, after 1830, the secret societies of *carbonari* conspiring against him multiplied everywhere in Sicily. The cholera year of 1837 reduced the pride of Palermo; but in 1848, when France again gave the signal of revolution, the city rebelled and held out for a year and four months. For four weeks King Ferdinand had the city bombarded from his fort in the harbour. This did not help to make the citizens love him the more when he finally conquered, and his name was handed down as "King Bomba."

In 1850, his young and inexperienced son, Francis, found things in the worst possible condition.

In the north, Italians had united under the King of Sardinia against the Austrians and the petty princes who had so long divided up their country. With the help of France, the war was soon over. The Austrians were driven out of Lombardy; the Duchies of Parma, Modena, and

Tuscany expelled their reigning houses; and a good part of the States of the Church was taken from the Pope.

All these, with Sardinia, now made up the one kingdom of Italy, with Victor Emanuel as constitutional monarch.

It was a long step forward toward the realisation of what had hitherto been but a dream—a united Italy. And Garibaldi had been the one hero of its making.

In Sicily, a secret committee had been formed, under the name of the *Buono publico* (commonweal), to collect subscriptions among the nobles and property-holders for the purchase of arms and other munitions of war. It was in constant correspondence with the revolutionary committee existing at Genoa, of which Garibaldi was the soul. King Victor Emanuel was bound not to give open aid to any revolt against his cousin, the King of Naples, with whom he was supposed to be at peace. But it was known that his government would put no hindrance in the way. Everyone knew also that no revolution would break out in Southern Italy except in the name of Victor Emanuel and Garibaldi.

The counsellors of Francis II. had but one remedy for this evil state of things—the remedy of King Bomba and all the Bourbons before him. The city of Palermo was strongly garrisoned by troops from the mainland—Neapolitans or Swiss and Austrian mercenaries. Then fuller powers than ever were given to Maniscalco, the director of police, and his spies were placed everywhere. At Santa Flavia, eleven miles from Palermo by the sea, an armed insurrection suddenly broke out. It was crushed at once; but it was made the pretext for throwing several notable citizens into prison.

Next Maniscalco was grievously wounded at the door of the cathedral, and, in spite of all the efforts of the police, the would-be assassin escaped with the help of the people. A reign of terror was now begun, especially against the nobles and the rich. In every house searches were made by Maniscalco's *sbirri*, or detectives, for guns and swords and bayonets. It was felt that, among the 200,000 *inhabitants* of Palermo, only the soldiers, the host of government *employés*, and the countless members of the secret police were loyal to the king.

At last the Committee of Sicilian Liberties, as it was henceforth called, decided that the time had come to summon the citizens to revolt. Rizzo, a master mechanic of means, organised the movement. The rendezvous was given for the night between the 3rd and 4th of April, at the Franciscan convent of La Gancia, in the heart of the city. Rizzo's house was next door, and the arms which had been gathered

THE PICCIOTTI PICKED OFF THEIR MEN

were secreted in an unused well of his courtyard. A communication had been broken through the wall of the convent church. The friars were in the secret and in full sympathy with the conspirators. There was but one exception. He carried the news of what was going on to Maniscalco.

It was eight o'clock in the evening when the betrayal was made. General Salzano, who was in command at Palermo, was notified at once, and the convent was soon surrounded by troops. Rizzo and twenty-seven of his companions were already inside waiting for the coming of the others. Day broke, and no one had arrived. Looking out through the shutters, the little band saw the soldiers under arms, and understood that they had been betrayed. They resolved to sell their lives dearly, and Rizzo opened fire from the windows.

The troops brought their cannon to bear on the great door of the convent. Two shots were enough to batter it down, and the soldiers charged with their bayonets. They were met by the father superior, and ran him through on the spot. The insurgents held them back for a time, firing from the shelter of the friars' cells along the narrow corridors. Another friar was killed, and four more were wounded. Then Rizzo with his band made a last effort to escape in a determined sally through the courtyard, by the great door which the cannon had burst open. The troops were beaten back, but Rizzo fell with his leg broken by a bullet above the knee. The soldiers discharged their guns at him where he lay, inflicting lingering but mortal wounds. A dozen of his companions were taken prisoners with him; the others made good their escape.

The citizens, without arms and without a leader, kept to the shelter of their houses. The soldiers shot at anyone showing himself at a window. All who were connected with the conspiracy fled from the town into the fastnesses of the hills. The insurrection was again over in Palermo.

The *picciotti*—young men from fifteen to twenty-five years of age—had long been ready to join in the uprising. In the large town of Carini, ten miles to the west of Palermo, the impatience was so great that they anticipated the signal to be given at La Gancia. On the 3rd of April, the tri-coloured flag of United Italy was unfurled, and barricades were thrown up across the mountain roads. Misilmeri, a few miles to the east of the city, next took up the cry. With the two priests at their head, the insurgents drove out the Neapolitan garrison of four soldiers, eight mounted *gendarmes*, and eight of Maniscalco's

Palermo Harbour

sbirri. On the 11th of the month the *picciotti* swept down on a body of troops and forced them back to the bridge over the Oreto, almost within gunshot of the city. Soon all the villages along the coast and in the surrounding country were in full insurrection. The city began suffering from this blockade on the side of the land. All its provisions had to be brought in the king's vessels from Naples.

At Naples, the news of the revolt led to the taking of extreme measures. The vessels of the royal marine, along with merchant ships appropriated by the government for the occasion, were despatched to Palermo. All were filled with soldiers and munitions of war. In a few days, there were 13,000 of the king's troops in and around the city, to face the insurrection.

In spite of the vigilance of the police, a newspaper from northern Italy had been smuggled into Palermo, making known to the inhabitants that the committee at Genoa was organising an expedition to come to the aid of the Sicilian patriots. On the 10th of April, a secret messenger, Rosolino Pilo, who had been under proscription in his native bind for ten years, succeeded in landing safely at Messina. He made his way from village to village by night. In the morning, the sign of his presence was found written on the walls—"*Viene Garibaldi! Viva Vittorio Emanuele!*"

Soon, in Palermo itself, the very children cried after the *sbirri* as they passed— "Garibaldi is coming!"

Word was passed around that, on a certain day, all whose sympathies were with the revolution should walk in the fashionable promenade of the Via Maqueda—the broad, straight street that divides the city in two halfway up from the sea. Even the greatest ladies came on foot; there was no room for the splendid equipages for which Palermo has always been noted. No one was armed. All kept an ominous silence.

Maniscalco was at his wits' end. He sent a band of soldiers and *sbirri* along the promenade to cry from time to time, "*Viva Francesco Secondo!*" There was no response from the crowd. Then the *sbirri* surrounded a group of the citizens and ordered them to repeat the cry, "*Viva Francesco Secondo!*"

After a moment of deep silence one of the group, tossing his hat in the air, shouted, "*Viva Vittorio Emanuele!*" The soldiers bayoneted him on the spot, and then discharged their guns into the crowd. Two men were killed, and there were thirty women and children among the wounded. The mounted *gendarmes* charged on their horses, and swept the streets clear. But the next morning Maniscalco could read in huge red letters on every dead wall of the city, "*Garibaldi viene!*"— "Garibaldi is coming!"

2. WITH THE KING'S ARMY.

The regular troops were now kept constantly on the alert, and daily and nightly drawn by new alarms from the city toward the mountains, it was useless for them to give chase to the *picciotti* in their retreat along the winding goat-paths of the hills. In return, they brought their artillery against houses sheltering the helpless women and children of the insurgent villages.

It was on the 9th of May that the demonstration of the Via Maqueda took place, followed by the bloody police outrage on the people and the threatening prophecy written by night upon the walls. On the 13th word passed through the city that the prophecy was fulfilled.

Garibaldi has landed at Marsala!

It was on the 11th of May that Garibaldi and his expedition of a thousand men succeeded in entering the island. Two English ships stood between him and the royal cruisers, which gave chase, until men and arms were all safely on shore. The two Genoese merchant vessels that had brought the expedition were abandoned to capture, and the march began across the island. Nothing was left to the adventurous Thousand—old revolutionists and young university students from northern Italy, Hungarian officers of 1848, and French and Polish sympathisers with all that invoked the name of liberty—but to take Palermo or die.

The next day they were at Salemi, where, on the 14th, Garibaldi proclaimed himself Dictator of the island in the name of King Victor Emanuel. The guerilla bands and the *picciotti* began coming in from every quarter.

On the 15th the Thousand came face to face with the royal troops, which had taken strong positions along the hills overlooking the road at Calatafimi, fifty miles from Palermo. The only pitched battle of the campaign took place here. The: *picciotti*, with all their goodwill, showed that they would be of little use in open warfare. They could not endure the fire of regular soldiers, and still less execute the charges necessary for capturing the positions of the enemy. But the Thousand of Garibaldi were a host in themselves. The Genoese Carabineers were accustomed to his methods of fighting. Even the university students had been trained and hardened to practise his maxim, "Lose no time with artillery, but use your bayonets!

General Landi and his thousands of regular soldiers were driven back, and the next day they beat a disorderly retreat as far as Palermo. The *picciotti*, from the shelter of every rock and clump of bushes, picked off their men by the way. The soldiers, in turn, sacked and pillaged the villages of Partanico and Borghetto. The Neapolitan officers complained bitterly that their mercenaries preferred pillage to fighting. Garibaldi, ever seeking to draw all Italians to himself, praised the bravery of the Neapolitans while congratulating his own army on its victory. It had cost him dear. There were eighteen of the Thousand among the killed, and 128 were wounded.

After a day of rest. Garibaldi marched forward, and on the 18th he was already on the mountains in sight of Palermo. There his men bivouacked in the rain. On the 20th he advanced his outposts to within a mile of Monreale, whence the high road leads directly down to Palermo, not five miles away. He now decided not to try to force an entrance into the city from the side of Monreale. He could not hope to make his way across the plain and past the headquarters of the royal army, even by night, without sacrificing half his men.

He chose instead a movement that, perhaps, no other military man of the age would have attempted. Garibaldi himself said ever after that it could have been executed only in Sicily, under the circumstances of the time. To its success, it was essential that the enemy, lying below in sight of his own camp fires, should have no knowledge of what was going on until all was over. The *picciotti* may not have been able to take their part in regular battle; but there were no traitors among them, nor in the mountain villages through which the expedition was to pass.

The evening of the 21st fell dark and rainy. With nightfall, the Thousand set out on a toilsome march by unfrequented paths over three mountain tops to Parco. Garibaldi wished to move round from the west to the south of Palermo, nearer to the sea. Their few pieces of cannon were dismounted and carried on the backs of the men. At three in the morning the little army was at its destination, wet, and worn out with fatigue, but without a man or gun or precious cartridge missing. The *picciotti* had kept the camp fires blazing above Monreale. General Lanza, who had just been appointed the king's alter ego in Sicily, was not to learn of the stolen march for many hours to come.

The day was passed in taking up positions along the zigzag mountain road leading up to Piana dei Greci, six miles further back from Palermo. Only then, after a night and a day of toil, the men bivouacked around their works.

At day-dawn of the 23rd Garibaldi and Türr—the Hungarian, who was his other self in the expedition—climbed a summit whence they could command a view of Palermo and the plains around. The mayor of Parco had just provided the dreaded leader and his companion with sorely-needed trousers. They looked down on a gallant display of arms. With the exception of the necessary garrison for the forts and a few posts in the city, the royal troops were all in camp on the plains to the west and north of the city or by the headquarters of the general in the great place before the royal palace. Garibaldi's practised eye estimated their number at 15,000 men, and new reinforcements were arriving. To oppose them in serious conflict he could count on not 800 valid men.

Even as they looked, a body of troops, 3.000 to 4,000 strong, began its march on Monreale. When they reached the hills, their movements were impeded by the ceaseless fire of the *picciotti* sheltered behind the positions left by the Thousand. The firing continued during the day and into the night.

When the morning of the 24th came, Garibaldi could see that General Lanza, with thousands of men at his disposal, was carrying out a plan of attack skilfully designed to envelop and sweep away his little army. Beyond Monreale the corps which had marched out yesterday was rapidly advancing toward Piana to surround his left. From below another strong body of troops was marching directly on Parco. Türr was at once sent to save their few pieces of artillery, and, with the help of the Carabineers and *picciotti*, to guard the left. Garibaldi began hurrying on the march to Piana. Türr's men were soon attacked by three times their number, and the *picciotti* fled in dismay. The *Carabineers* succeeded in escaping amid the hills, while Türr, with two companies, held the enemy with his cannon.

At half-past two in the afternoon the whole army arrived safely in Piana. In the evening, General Garibaldi held a council of war with his colonels, Türr, Sirtori, and Orsini, and with Signor Crispi, a long-exiled Sicilian lawyer whom he had made his Secretary of State. He proposed his final plan, which was to deceive again and divide the forces of the enemy. It was put in operation on the spot.

Orsini, with the artillery and baggage and fifty men for escort, began an ostentatious retreat along the road leading to Corleone, many miles further in the interior. For one half-mile, the general and the bulk of the army followed after. The royal outposts on the left hastened to bring the information to General Lanza, who was commanding in person, and he at once sent his whole body of troops in cautious pursuit. In the dense wood of Cianeto, Garibaldi and his men left Orsini to draw the enemy further and further away, while they turned into a path that led to Marineo.

The night was clear, and Türr and Garibaldi, as they marched side by side, looked to the star of the Great Bear, which the latter had connected with his destiny from a child. "General," said the Hungarian, "it smiles on you. We shall enter Palermo."

At midnight, the little army bivouacked in the forest. At four o'clock they were again on foot, and at seven they were at Marineo, where they passed the day. With the night, they took up again their secret march, and at ten they reached Misilmeri. La Masa was there with a few thousand *picciotti*, and there were a few members of the Committee of Sicilian Liberties. These were told to notify their friends in the city that the attack would be made on the morning of the 27th. Türr sent word to Colonel Ebers, his compatriot and correspondent of the London *Times* in Palermo, to come out and share in the adventure.

The day of the 26th was employed in making ready. Garibaldi passed the *picciotti* in review at their camp of Gibilrossa. Then he ascended Monte Griffone to study the city and plain beneath. The royal guards along this southeast side of the city were almost within hearing of a trumpet blast from his mouth. They did not dream that he was nigh.

3.—The Descent of the Thousand.

The sun set on the evening of the 26th in a mass of red vapours, portending the heat of the night. The army of Garibaldi was already forming on the table land of Gibilrossa, in the order which they were to follow in their attack on the Porta di Termini of Palermo.

First came the leaders, with Captain Misori at their head, and three men from each company of the Thousand under the command of Colonel Tukery. They were in all thirty-two men. Immediately behind them was the first corps of the *picciotti*. The first battalion of the Thousand fallowed, under the command of Bixio, who was afterwards a famous general. Garibaldi came next, with Türr and the remainder of his Staff, followed by the Second battalion under Carini. Last of all was the second corps of *picciotti* and the Commissariat. In all they were 750 trained and veteran soldiers—all that was available of the original

GENERAL, IT SMILES ON YOU.

1,065—with two or three thousand *picciotti*, preparing to face 18,000 regular troops of the King of Naples.

It was essential to the success of their enterprise that the alarm should not be given in Palermo until as late as possible. Even if they had wished to follow it, there was no direct road to the city. With as much order as might be, they clambered down the sides of a ravine which led to the valley opening on the highway. It was eleven o'clock when they arrived at this point. Tukery halted his men to see if order was being kept in the rear. The *picciotti* had completely disappeared. A false alarm on the mountain-side had sent them flying. Two hours were needed to re-form the line, when it was found that their numbers were now reduced to 1,300 men. With all these delays, at half-past one in the morning they were still three miles from the city.

They marched forward in close columns until they came up with the Neapolitan outposts. It was now half-past three, and still dark. The soldiers fired three gun-shots and retreated to their guard-house. This was enough to disperse two-thirds of the *picciotti* who remained.

The thirty-two men composing the vanguard of Garibaldi now dashed forward to the bridge over the Oreto. This Ponte dell' Ammiraglio, by a strange coincidence, was the scene of the first combat of Robert Guiscard, the Norman, with the Saracen lords of Palermo, nearly 800 years before, and of Metellus with the Carthaginians 1,200 years before that. It was now defended by some 400 men. The soldiers of Garibaldi first attacked them by a running fire from behind the trees along the road, and then entered on a hand-to-hand fight. A single captain, Piva, was able to bring down four Neapolitans with six shots from his revolver. Misori hastened back to summon Bixio. The first battalion charged, followed by Türr at the head of the second. The bayonets now came into play, and the Thousand had won their first position.

The alarm was now thoroughly given. While the defenders of the bridge were fleeing to the right, a strong column of the royal troops advanced on the left. Türr sent thirty men to stop their advance, and the rest of the Thousand charged past with fixed bayonets.

The Neapolitans now fell back on the street leading to the gate of Sant'Antonino, at the end of the Via Maqueda. This road was lined with the houses of a small suburb, and cut across the street of Termini, by which Garibaldi's men hoped to enter the town. The old gate of Termini had been torn down by King Bomba, and the street leading to the bridge widened to facilitate the movement of his troops. It

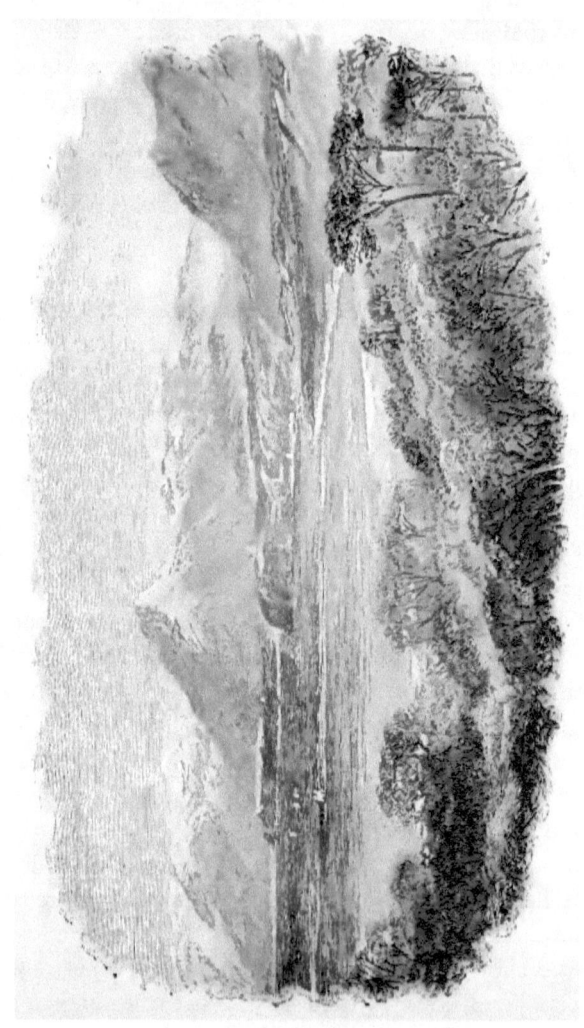

The Coast of Palermo, Looking Towards Termini.

now served the purpose of those who were trying to overthrow: the rule of his son. The Neapolitan commander had already placed two cannons in the Via Sant' Antonino, and at every moment their shots swept across the path of Garibaldi. Even his veterans held back for a moment. A carabineer seated himself in a chair in full line of the firings to persuade the *picciotti* to go on.

Garibaldi now came up, just as his faithful Tukery fell mortally wounded. As if animated by his death, one of the leaders seized the banner of United Italy, and bore it unharmed through the enemy's fire. He was followed by five others, and, little by little, the whole line passed under the eyes of their general. He alone was on horseback, and the most exposed, as he urged his men forward.

Two hundred men were soon scattered through the different streets of the city, nearest to the gate; and their leaders penetrated to the old market, which had been the place of the revolution in 1848. Garibaldi soon arrived in the midst of the fire which the royal troops were keeping up on the rear of the little column. The members of the Committee of Palermo were waiting to receive him. He at once gave orders to make barricades behind, and thus entrenched himself in the midst of his enemies.

The people in the houses remained deaf to his first appeal; but by dint of calling they were at length induced to appear at the windows, where the sight of their deliverers gave them courage. Mattresses were flung from every window, and soon piled up over the barricades most exposed to the royal artillery. Then a few of the inhabitants began showing themselves in the streets. They had but one answer to give to the invitation to join with the invaders:

"We have no arms."

But they lent themselves bravely to the tearing up of paving-stones for the barricades, and the soldiers of Garibaldi found places of vantage in their houses.

With a part of his men Garibaldi now made his way to the centre of the city, where the Via Maqueda is crossed at right angles by the long Via Toledo (now the Corso Vittore Emanuele), leading from the port through the whole length of the city to the Royal Palace. The number of his men was greatly exaggerated in the imaginations of his opponents, and he easily drove back the royal troops close to their general's headquarters at the Palace. The Bourbon Government had just been paving this street with large flags. These were now torn up and built into barricades, while waggons and obstructions of every kind were thrown across the neighbouring streets.

At this moment, the bombardment of the city began from the Fort of Castellamare, in the bay, and from the Royal Palace. The war-ships with their great guns swept all the streets within line of their fire. Three days were next taken up with the constant advancing and retreating of the now infuriated soldiers of the king, aided by the steady downpour of shot and shell on the quarters where the men of Garibaldi—the Italians, as they were now called, even by their enemies—had entrenched themselves. But the crumbling of walls only aided to the making of new barricades, and impeded all the movements of the regular troops.

As the royal mercenaries abandoned their positions, they set fire to the buildings they had left. The convent of the White Benedictines was burned, with fifty of the prisoners who had been confined in it. All Palermo worked actively with Garibaldi and his men, in a fury of rage against the royal army. Soon there remained to the latter only the two forts of the harbour, the Royal Palace, and the post at the Flora below the Porta di Termini, by the bay. Even these could no longer communicate with each other nor receive provisions.

Garibaldi had now conquered once more. On the fourth day, the king's general asked for an armistice—to bury his dead. It was prolonged, and at last the king ordered that the troops should evacuate the city, provided that the garrison in the forts might depart with the honours of war. To save the lives of the prisoners still confined, this was granted. On the 20th of June, the last Neapolitan soldier had left Palermo. Two days later the Thousand of Garibaldi were on the way to deliver Messina, the last hold of the Bourbons in Sicily.

WARS OF ITALIAN UNIFICATION

The Battle of Castelfidardo
September 18, 1860
By John Augustus O'Shea

When Lombardy reverted to Italy after the war of 1859, the idea of a free and united peninsula became robust.

In the kingdom of the Two Sicilies the popular dissatisfaction rose until it came to a head on the landing of Garibaldi at Marsala, and it was felt that the seizure of Umbria and the Marches was the complement of the annexation by popular vote of the Duchies and the Romagna to Victor Emmanuel, pending the time when Venice could be wrested from the Austrians and Rome could be entered by the dynasty of Savoy.

The first overt act of hostility against the Pope had showed itself at Perugia, the chief town of Umbria, where Joachim Pecci, now Leo XIII., was bishop, by a street rising of the discontented on the 20th of June, 1859. This was put down by General Schmid, of the Pontifical army, and picked Swiss troops, with rigour and, some said, with a needless severity.

When the undreamt-of success of the Red Shirts in the South the following year startled the world, Cavour saw that to Garibaldi the credit would accrue of conquering Francis II., if Victor Emmanuel did not intervene to overawe the revolution and tie it to his own leading-strings. But the French were in Rome, and pledged by the Emperor Napoleon to hold the patrimony of Peter against all assailants; and to join the followers of Garibaldi it was imperative to transport a costly expedition by long sea, or to make a shorter journey overland by crossing the Papal territory in Central Italy.

La Moricière was entrusted with the defence of this territory. On the 3rd of May, he had responded to an appeal of Pio Nono and had put himself at the head of the Papal army, which he at once proceeded to organise and strengthen for all adequate services, by which he did not contemplate resisting an invasion by a regular Power, but simply the maintaining of peace within and the guarding against revolutionary incursions.

La Moricière was a Breton, and a soldier of high military repute. He was the comrade of Bugeaud, Pélissier, and others in Algeria; had compassed the downfall of Abd-el-Kader in 1847; led the troops who drove the Red Republicans to the left bank of the Seine at Paris in June, 1848, but in the Assembly, had voted against the expedition to Rome. However, when he was imprisoned for objecting to the *coup d'état* by the Prince-President, he seemed to have acquired an austere religious bias and a bent towards the Vatican.

As soon as Victor Emmanuel resolved to send his homogeneous and seasoned troops to invade the Pope's country. La Moricière saw that his task was hopeless. His heterogeneous levies were ill-equipped and badly-disciplined, and in far weaker numbers. His forces consisted of a few hastily-improvised batteries of artillery, on foot and mounted; some regiments of Swiss and Italian infantry (the latter of a sorry, scarecrow type); Austrians, who could be depended upon; a corps of Franco-Belgians, uniformed as *Zouaves*; dragoons, *gendarmes*, guides formed into a *corps d'élite* of the Legitimist nobility, each private ranking with a lieutenant of the line; and a body of Irish volunteers.

These latter were called mercenaries, but so little of the hireling was in the majority of them that they refused the bounty of twenty *scudi* and were free-handed with their own small money. They were mostly peasants, with a sprinkling of students, clerks, and artisans, ex-policemen and be-medalled veterans of the Crimea and the Indian Mutiny. Beyond their not very luxurious rations they received only about two-pence each day. The control of these men was given to Mr. Myles O'Reilly, a former captain in the Louth Militia, and under him served such captains as O'Mahoney and Murray of the Austrian Army. Count Russell de Killoghy, and O'Carroll, a former subaltern of the 18th Royal Irish. A Baron de Guttenberg, a Bavarian, acted as adjutant-major.

La Moricière hated the revolution, which he compared with Islamism, against which he had been arrayed for the greater portion of his previous career; but he bluntly admitted that to send him against a standing army with such resources as he had was like pitting one against ten, or asking a man with a pistol at 150 paces to match himself with an adversary armed with a carbine. And yet that was the task that was set him and his army of 11,000 men, many dispersed over widely separate stations.

On the afternoon of September 10th, Captain Farini, *aide-de-camp* to General Fanti, Minister of War and Commander-in-Chief of the Piedmontese Army, arrived at the headquarters of La Moricière, at Spoleto, bearing a message from his chief intimating that by order of the king he would occupy Umbria and the Marches m any of three cases; Firstly, if the Papal troops had to use force to put down national manifestations (that is, manifestations on behalf of United Italy or Victor Emmanuel himself) in the cities held by them; next, if the Papal troops were ordered to march upon any city where manifestations had taken place; and lastly, if, such manifestations having been repressed, the Papal troops were not forthwith withdrawn, so as to leave the locality free to express its will.

La Moricière was indignant at this summons, and replied that he had no authority to reply to such a communication without reference to Rome, and explained to Captain Farini that he might have been spared the humiliation of being asked to evacuate the provinces without striking a blow. An open declaration of war would have been franker.

After dinner, a telegram from Fanti arrived ordering Farini back without waiting for a reply, which was equivalent to the desired formal outbreak of hostilities; and on the following day a Piedmontese general—Cialdini, who led a brigade at the Tchernaya, in the Crimea—crossed *la Cattolica*, the imaginary frontier-line between Rimini and Pesaro, and advanced to the attack of the latter Papal fortress.

At the same time that this invasion was made by the coast, Fanti pushed into Umbria by a mountain pass and descended along the west of the Apennines, and a third column, spreading fan-like in the middle, preserved the connection between both. On the same evening Monsignor de Merode sent a despatch that Napoleon had written to Victor Emmanuel, broadly hinting that he would find France opposed to him if he entered the dominions of the Pope. A proclamation to this effect was made to the Papal army, by whom it was believed and hailed with satisfaction.

Pesaro was held by Colonel Zappi with about 400 men, including a half-battalion of Germans under Count Zichy, detached from Ancona, and three guns. For two-and-twenty hours he offered a stout resistance, and then, driven to the last extremity by the number of the enemy, computed at 8,000, he was compelled to surrender.

It leaked out that bands in the interest of the Piedmontese had broken in on the morning of the preceding 9th on the Pontifical territory at Fossombrone, Urbino, and Città del Piève, to the north of Ancona. A brigade of Papalini under General de Courten, a Swiss officer, was directed on Fossombrone, with orders to push on to Urbino, manoeuvring to keep in touch with Ancona, which was the base of operations. This column, discovering that Senigaglia was occupied by a Piedmontese division, made a slight retrograde turn so as to pass the Misa stream at about two leagues from its mouth; and here occurred the first affair in the open in the brief campaign, which was brisk and nowise discreditable to the weaker side.

The Piedmontese, consisting of artillery, cavalry, and infantry, bestirred themselves and attempted to intercept and enmesh the Papalini. The leading column of the latter, mostly Austrians, which was commanded by Colonel Kanzler, were not to be cowed without a stiff fight. Shortly after midday on September 13th they seized a position at Sant' Angelo, and, with their small force of 1,200 men and a couple of field-pieces, gave challenge to the enemy. Coherent accounts by eye-witnesses of this encounter are lacking, but it is agreed that it was sharp, that some brilliant onsets by the Piedmontese cavalry were baffled, and that the Papalini, having received word to fall back before the overwhelming clouds of the Piedmontese, retired doggedly until they finally wore out the pursuit.

It was an overthrow most obstinately denied, not a rout; but 150 of Kanzler's force were left behind, after four hours' unequal strife. It was five before the last discharges died away, and the heated and tired combatants took up the line of retreat unmolested further. Harassed and leg-wearied, they entered Ancona, after their fatiguing trudge over hilly paths to the coast-road, where their hot cheeks were fanned by the Adriatic breezes. As the garrison was roused in the darkest small hours to the martial strains of their band, the writer, who was with those who welcomed their entry, is bound to say they stepped out with the elation of men who had done their duty.

As an example of how trivial matters, at such a moment, will impress themselves on the memory, the recollection of a great shaggy dog, with lolling tongue, shuffling under the big drum, will never be effaced.

In the meantime, La Moricière, with the bulk of his small army, was prosecuting his way from the interior to the sea, under a sweltering sun, by steep and dusty courses. Of a necessity, his progress was

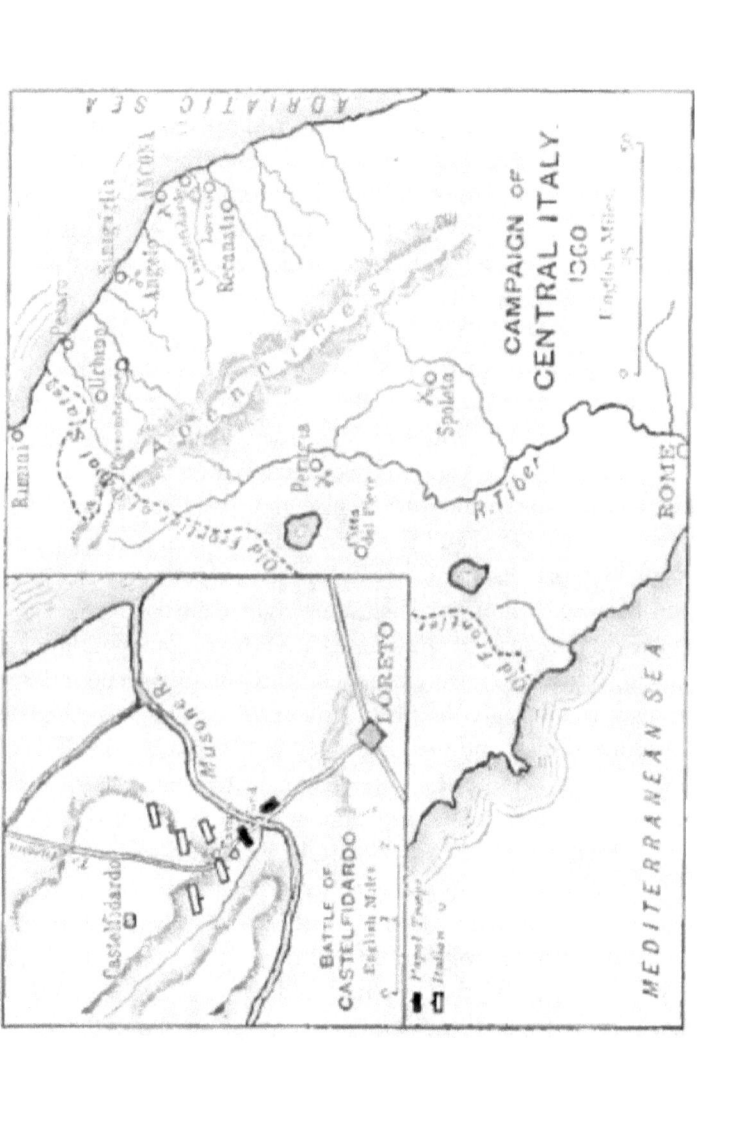

slow, as his guns were feebly horsed, he was without regular baggage train, and his vanguard had to be vigilantly warded from ambuscade. Perugia and Spoleto, in his rear, were both gobbled after short bites. Perugia was occupied by a company of the Irish and a battalion of the 2nd Regiment of the line. The germ of mutiny showed itself in a portion of the latter. After three hours' interchange of gunpowder—desultory skirmishing under cover in the streets for the most part—De Sonnaz, the Piedmontese general, sent word to General Schmid that it was useless to prolong resistance, as Fanti was nigh and would speedily reinforce him. A suspension of arms for five hours was stipulated, and at its expiration, Fanti having in the meantime arrived, terms were arranged and the fortress was handed over to the Piedmontese.

Spoleto, with 580 of a garrison more than half of whom were Irish and the rest Italians, Swiss, and Austrians, with a handful of invalided Franco-Belgians sustained a well-concerted attack almost from breakfast-hour to dusk. Major O'Reilly was in command, and although unaccustomed to fight, and allowed a truce early, made excellent play with his untried soldiers and his two old iron guns with worn carriages. He placed his own corps at the gate and a wall near it and a breach covered with palisades, and the Franco-Belgians in a post of vantage adjacent. General Brignone, having established four batteries, opened on the keep with shot and shell after eight o'clock on the 17th, his rifles keeping up an incessant peppering from the surrounding hills.

Having exhausted seven hours with this preliminary pounding and popping, it was thought that the moment for assault had arrived, and a column of *bersaglieri* and grenadiers, led by Brignone himself, formed in the causeway before the gate. O'Reilly had but one of his iron guns available now, and having drawn it to the entrance, and loading it to the muzzle with grape-shot, he banged twice at the nearing Piedmontese, and a furious sheet of musketry swept their front and laid so many of them low that the rest had to seek shelter in retreat. The corpses of nine *bersaglieri* littered the soil. So vigorously had the offensive been pushed, that one Irish officer at the barrier. Lieutenant Crean, a burly stripling from Tipperary, was wounded in the arm by a bayonet-thrust from a pioneer.

The assault was not renewed, but the batteries, to which another had now been added, resumed their attentions, some companies of *bersaglieri* aiding with a well-nourished fusillade. Twice had the roof and the rooms near the powder magazine been set in flames by shells, and twice had the kindling conflagration been got under with some

Ancona

trouble. About seven o'clock, as the torrid warmth of the day was declining, capitulation was offered, the defences being much shattered and the ammunition beginning to fail. O'Reilly saw the wisdom of yielding, although he had had comparatively few casualties; for his own men needed rest and food, and the Italians, who had been hiding in cellars during the hurly-burly, were not to be trusted in a night attack. But he was granted honourable conditions, in token of his valiant defence.

Fanti by this was in undisputed possession of the entire upper valley of the Tiber. Returning to La Moricière, he managed to send a despatch to Ancona, which was received there on the 15th, confirming his advance thither, and terminating with this warning:

Defend the approaches of the place courageously, and rally to the sound of my cannon.

A proclamation was simultaneously posted in the town stating that the Marches had been invaded, that Zappi had been beaten, that a great battle was imminent, and that in prevision of emergencies the church of St. Dominic was about to be converted into a hospital for 400, to which the inhabitants were requested to contribute bedding.

On the very day that Spoleto fell, news was brought that Ancona was likely to be beset by a powerful fleet under the Piedmontese admiral, Persano; therefore, it was more than ever imperative for him to penetrate to that, the last stronghold of the Papal power outside of Rome. The Emperor of the French might at last relent, or Austria might interpose. To Ancona he was trending; that was his objective point all through. It could hold out against a large force on the land side. It was essential that he should get in there. But here, close to Loreto, at the point of effecting the hoped-for junction, he found that Cialdini had been beforehand with him.

This advance guard of dragoons clattering into Loreto, a squad of Piedmontese lancers hurried off like hunters caught napping. De Paz, of the Guides, with a *gendarme*, having ventured as far as a barricade on the high road, was halted by a point-blank discharge of canister, fatal to himself and wounding his comrade. He calculated that the Piedmontese general had hastened up three divisions of his army, and had lodged them in parallel lines on the direct passage between him and the tongue of land, with its circling eminences, on which Ancona was situated.

The enemy was lying in strength, comfortably occupying the rising ground between the mamelon or mound of Castelfidardo, in front, and the plain spreading at the feet of Loreto. He mustered his weak columns, and took thought of his plan of action. The plain was within 500 yards of the Musone River, then run so dry as to be practicable for artillery. There was a ford here, and on each side a good country road. On the 18th it appeared to him that this point had been reinforced. A strong detachment rested on a farm midway, and a second farm about 500 yards to the rear, on the crest of a hillock crowning the first position. A wood was near, and there were numerous rifled cannon on the slopes in the neighbourhood.

The ford of the Musone, by which the Papalini must pass to reach Ancona, was less than a mile and a quarter from the outmost ground of the foe, but to enable them to pass it was necessary to take and hold the two farms. The banks of the river were high, but might easily be climbed, and the bed of the stream was very shallow—nowhere knee-deep.

La Moricière, before engaging in the action, went to the shrine of Our Lady of Loreto, the holy house of Nazareth—said to have been wafted through the air by angels—and performed some devotional exercises.

De Pimodan, his second in command, who was no stranger to powder, got the order to cross the river, seize the first farm—the Crocetta—bring his guns to play upon the wood and the second farm—Cascina—and thus clear the way for the remainder to advance. For this arduous task, he had at his disposal about 2,300 men—that is to say, four battalions and a half—8 pieces of light artillery 6-pounders, and 4 mortars, with about 250 cavalry, consisting of two squadrons of light dragoons, the troop of guides, and a section of *gendarmes*.

D'Arcy's company of Irish—who were inefficiently equipped, having neither pouches nor knapsacks, carrying their cartridges in their haversacks— were attached to the artillery, to help them in moving the guns and afford them ill necessary protection.

The battle began well for La Moricière. The first farm was assailed at a scamper, and gallantly carried in spite of a gallant defence, and 100 prisoners captured. Two guns were moved forward to the bottom of the slope, and the Irish, under a hot fire, helped to place two of the mortars in front of the farmhouse. Then, having fulfilled their mission, they mixed with the sharpshooters and fought with them till the close of the engagement.

Then an advance on the second farm was essayed and spiritedly made by a column of Franco-Belgians, headed by Commandant Becdeliévre; but it was repulsed by a murderous fire, and though they rallied and faced the enemy with bullet and bayonet, it was useless. The Franco-Belgians—bare-throated, vain of their loose picturesque garb of silver-grey braided with scarlet, their wide scarlet waistcloth, and the isthmus of gamboge buskin between *Zouave* trousers and gaiters—were as conspicuous by their eager martial bearing as by their cool resolution. Having gained their ground with a rush and a rallying cheer, they dropped on their knees and kept up a sputter of independent shots from behind a hedge.

The Piedmontese held fast, and by smiting them with a steady but rapid flame of rifle-shots checked them, and, keeping up the rattle of death persistently, compelled their shattered ranks to fall back. To the shouts of defiance of onset succeeded a sullen retirement. Such was the impetuosity of these young warriors and the firmness of their bearing that many came to the white arms, and the onset was repelled with steel. The Viscount de Poli received a desperate bayonet-wound in the breast.

The troops sent to their assistance, several thousand led by La Moricière in person, behaved with shameful weakness. They occupied the centre, and carried with them on their flanks a battalion of Swiss Rifles and a boyish Roman corps. The indigenous regiment wavered as it deployed, and finally sought safety under the reeds by the river. Its want of steadiness was charitably attributed to youth and indiscipline. The drivers attached to one battery of guns cut their traces and fled, leaving their cannon behind them. The Franco-Belgians, with Major Fuchman's half-battalion of Austrian sharpshooters in support, were the only troops who did not show symptoms of resorting to leg-bail.

The tough Piedmontese were very stubborn, especially that crack light infantry the little blue-jacketed *bersaglieri*, to be marked by the constant bursts of smoke from the line defined by glazed round hats tipped with jaunty cocks' feathers. The haycocks and farm-steadings of Crocetta were clung to with tenacity while a chance remained, but reinforcements poured down from the ridges opposite, and soon a general panic was caused, bearing away the brave with the fainthearted. To add to the confusion, De Pimodan, who was mounted and daringly encouraging his men, was shot in the face and subsequently in the back—some said by his own followers, either through mistake or treachery—and fell from his saddle bleeding from four wounds. La Moricière gave him a farewell grasp before he died.

THE HAYCOCKS AND FARM-STEADINGS WERE CLUNG TO.

The Piedmontese prisoners captured at an earlier stage of the combat got out of the toils, the captain, Tromboni, preventing retaliations. But the intrepid Franco-Belgians left a third of their 280 on the field, and trenches were dug for them by next day near the spot where they fell on the slopes of the Musone.

La Moricière was powerless to control or infuse courage into his force. There were acts of individual heroism, but what could they avail against the odds in numbers, discipline, and material? The disorder degenerated into something worse, and the mass of the Pope's army sought refuge in flight at the double-quick, while corps and fragments of corps, embracing men of different nationalities, tramped or trotted to Loreto, where some of them laid down arms in a hopeless muddle. The Piedmontese did not pursue: they saw it was not necessary. They had succeeded in their object, which was to prevent the relief of Ancona, and they had barred the road and caught their enemy in a trap from which there was no escape.

The affair had not lasted quite three hours, the actual conflict being confined to one hour. Some of the vanquished made for the mouth of the Musone, and twenty Papal artillerymen, with two field-pieces, the military chest, and a flag of the Swiss, succeeded in coasting in a fishing-boat to Ancona. A few guides and a Swiss sapper also reached the same harbour in a skiff. But the army which had left Loreto in the morning—preceded by some of the banners of Don John of Austria, the hero of Lepanto, removed from the shrine of Loreto—was "ground down and beaten to pieces" before shades of evening fell.

A few bold spirits talked of defending the town, but the majority were too much demoralised, and continued the retreat to Recanati, where formal surrender was made. The Papalini marched out by torchlight to give up their arms, with bayonets fixed and bands at their head, between lines of Piedmontese infantry, who presented arms as they passed.

When the names of the Franco-Belgian prisoners and the guides—such as Rohan Chabot, St. Sernin, the Marquis d'Holiand, the Count Bourbon de Chains, and Prince Edward de Ligne—were being ticked off from the roll-call, before being sent into detention in the interior, General Cugia remarked with surprise that it was just like reading a list of invitations to a court ball under Louis Quatorze.

But La Moricière, who had directed the operations of the day on horseback with a cane, had disappeared. It will be seen that there was no strategy on his part in this brief, disastrous campaign. His plan was

A Pontifical Zouave.

the obvious one of plain, straightforward fighting; and had he been seconded by the due valour and numbers the result might have been adjourned, but ultimate defeat could not have been averted. He had no allies whom he could trust. The Emperor Napoleon III. dared not stir out of Rome; in fact, he had advised his allies of the former year to "strike hard and promptly" if they would lift him out of embarrassment.

La Moricière, with his purpose grimly set, took the opportunity of the smoke and turmoil to assemble about 300 infantry and what remained of an escort of dragoons, and bent by a devious mountain path to Ancona. A peasant acted as guide, having first been sworn by all he prized as most sacred to point the right direction. At dusk attended by the horsemen he entered the ramparts and went to his countryman, the Count de Quaterbarbes.

"You are welcome," said the governor; "and your army?"

"You see it," said La Moricière, pointing to the few fugitives outside. "I have no longer an army."

It was his earliest experience of failure in war, but he did not expect miracles. He did not count on beating a well-armed force of 40,000 men, eager and inured to the field, with some thousand volunteers who were weighed down from want of rest and the long, forced marches. But all was not lost, although Persano's fleet of thirteen vessels, carrying 400 guns, was in the offing and had started the bombardment that day, without notice, contrary to the usages of war. After a stout defence of Ancona for over a week, Persano forced the boom at the entrance of the harbour, and blew up the battery at the lighthouse.

La Moricière hoisted the white flag upon the citadel, and repeated the signal of capitulation in the forts. The garrison ceased fire. Shortly after, the Piedmontese army resumed the offensive all along the line, and up to nine in the following morning the din of cannon lasted, notwithstanding the despatch of *parlementaires* and the landing of Piedmontese naval officers and marines. The garrison marched out of the city with the honours of war in the dusk of the following evening, gave up their arms, and were led under escort to Alessandria, where they were liberated under condition of not serving for a year against the king. La Moricière gave his sword to Persano, who handed it back to him, and the officers were embarked on a vessel for Genoa. Victor Emmanuel was free to advance to the Neapolitan border, and lend the prestige of his name and the aid of his arms to Garibaldi; in short, he was allowed the occasion of tipping the lance-shaft with a sharp steel head.

The Pope dismissed his troops to their homes, giving the Irish auxiliaries, in an order of the day, the highest praise. A medal of silvered bronze, girdled with a serpent with tail coiled in mouth, symbolising eternity, was issued to his *legionaries*, with an inverted cross on the hollowed middle in commemoration of the crucifixion of St. Peter, and the inscription on one side. *Pro Petri Sede* ("For the See of Peter"), and on the other, *Victoria quae vincit mundum fides nostra* ("The victory which overcomes the world is our faith"). Thus, ended with a decoration the tale of defeat not entirely without dishonour.

The Battle of Volturno
1st Oct: 1860
By Jesse White Mario

The liberation of Sicily completed by the victory of Milazzo on the 23rd of July, 1830, Garibaldi, bent on freeing the Italian mainland, sent across the straits 210 pioneers to raise the flag of revolution there, intending to proceed across the frontier into the Papal territory, give battle to the Papal and French troops, and crown Victor Emmanuel King of Italy in Rome.

This last part of his programme was opposed by Cavour, who, however, obtained permission from the French emperor to invade Umbria and the Marches, and attack and defeat La Moricière's legion, on the understanding that all conflict with the French troops would be avoided and the Pope's authority respected.

Garibaldi, after a triumphal march through the Calabrias, entered Naples on the 7th of September, accompanied by General Cosenz, Dr. Agostino Bertani, the surgeon-soldier and organiser of the volunteer expeditions, nine staff-officers and orderlies.

The young king, with some 50,000 troops who remained faithful to him, retiring to Gaeta with the royal family, on board a Spanish warship, as his own fleet refused to leave the Bay of Naples, Garibaldi at once realised that the final duel would have to be fought out by the royal and revolutionary forces between Gaeta and Capua. He took up his position, therefore, between Naples and the Volturno, and after a slight reverse, due to the imprudence of the officers left in charge during his brief absence, he fixed his watch tower on the summit of S. Angelo, never quitting it save to sleep at headquarters in Caserta.

Towards the end of September, 1860, Garibaldi's army of volunteers, numbering in all some 21,000, were distributed between Caserta and the River Volturno, as follows: At S. Angelo, the centre and key of his position, was Medici (the man who had held the Vascello against the French throughout the siege of Rome), with 4,000 infantry and nine guns in position. At Sta. Maria, Milbitz (also a Roman veteran) commanded the left wing, instead of Cosenz (now Minister of War), with 5,000 men and four guns, Corte and 1,500 men being on his extreme left towards Aversa; at Maddaloni, Bixio (who, on the 30th April, 184Q, captured 300 French invaders and brought them prisoners to Rome), the commander of the *Lombardo*—which, with the *Piedmont*, had borne the Thousand from Quarto to Marsala—with 5,663, was in charge of the right wing; while isolated at Castel Morone stood Bronzette with 227 sharpshooters, and at S. Leucio and Gradillo, Gaetano Sacchi, Garibaldi's Montevidean comrade, whom he had carried off wounded from the victorious field of Salto and nursed on the return voyage with tenderest care.

All the generals and superior officers had fought under him in Lombardy in the "Hunter of the Alps" volunteer corps, pioneers of the Franco-Piedmontese allies against the Austrians.

At Caserta, under Sirtori, now chief of his staff, were the reserves, to the number of 4,500 and thirteen guns, the Guides, and a few Hussars for all cavalry. Such was the "twelve-mile" Garibaldian line extending from Aversa to Maddaloni. "A defective line," wrote the general later, "irregular and all too long for the troops at my disposal." But their defects were unavoidable considering the formidable positions of the Neapolitans in Capua, whose fortifications forming the *tête-de-pont*, were surrounded on three sides by the Volturno, with the one solid bridge across the river in their hands, together with all the *scafi*, or boat-bridge ferries, with 50,000 troops; numerous well-supplied field-artillery with sixty-four rifled guns, besides batteries in position in the front of the fortress and on the heights of Jerusalem, and 7,000 splendid cavalry, which daily performed their evolutions on the exercise-ground of Capua.

Seeing that seven roads issuing from the Volturno converge on Naples, the enemy's objective point, it behoved indeed that he who held the city in trust for Victor Emmanuel should keep hourly watch and ward along the left bank of the tortuous, snake-like river which, in its course from its source in the mountains of the Abruzzi to its mouth in the Gulf of Gaeta, crawls here at a snail's pace, there runs with hare-like velocity. On September 27th appeared in the official *Gazette* Garibaldi's proclamation of Cialdini's victories over La Moricière and of the taking of Ancona, ending thus:

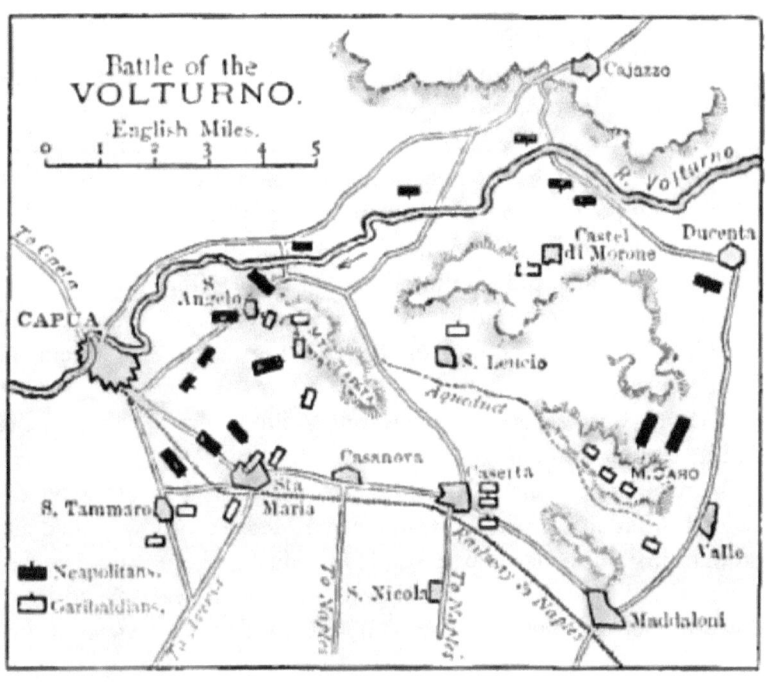

The valiant soldiers of the army of the North have passed the frontier and are on Neapolitan soil. We shall soon have the good fortune to grasp their victorious hands.

Probably this unwelcome news decided King Francis, who with his stepbrothers had joined the troops at Capua, to consent to his general's plan for attacking Garibaldi along all his line, so that the king should "spend his birthday in Naples."

Garibaldi—who, from his eyrie on Mount Angelo marked, pondered, and understood the movements in front of Capua and along the river—divined their intention, and on the 30th September, warning Medici to repulse but not to follow Colonna's column of 3,000, which attempted to cross the Volturno at the Triflisco ferry, he started for Maddaloni, telling Bixio that the Royalists would pour down on him from Ducenta, and advising him to withdraw from Valle, concentrate his forces round Maddaloni, occupy the Caroline Aqueduct, and to hold Monte Caro at any cost. "If you lose that, I shall be cut off from Naples."

"Monte Caro shall be yours as long as life is mine," answered the daring, dashing veteran.

Returning to S. Angelo, Garibaldi gave his last instructions to Medici, then to Milbitz at Sta. Maria, and seeing Medici's forty wounded just brought in, said to old Ripari, surgeon-soldier at Rome and detained there after the siege in the Papal galleys for seven years, "Send them down to Naples, empty the Caserta hospital, and mind that you all *sleep on the wing*."

At three a.m. on the following morning, leaving strict orders with General Sirtori to keep the reserves at Caserta till he should summon them, he again alighted from the railroad at Sta. Maria just as the battle had commenced, as he had foreseen, "along all the line."

From Capua two brigades—10,000 men—under Afan de Rivera, marched against Medici's 4000. Another column, 7,000 strong, attacked Milbitz and his 4,000, and a detachment under Sergardi, going towards Aversa to find Corte De Mechel, with 8,000, poured down by the Ducenta road on Bixio's 5,600—Perrone starting to rejoin him with 2,000 more. Colonna, repulsed by Medici the day before, was at the Triflisco ferry, now with 5,000 men, and 7,000 reserves at Capua, all the columns well supplied with batteries and horse, 2,500 cavalry still remaining in front of the fortress ready to be despatched where needed—40,000 regulars pitted against 20,000 irregulars! So sudden

Naples from Posillipo

was Tabacchi's attack on Milbitz that his outposts at the brick-kiln and convent fell back, and S. Tammaro was evacuated; the little battery of four pieces on the railroad answered bravely to the enemy's battery of eight on the Capuan high road.

After an hour, the infantry duel commenced, and the Neapolitans were driven back behind their pieces, the bright *picciotti* of Corrau's brigade badly mangled. Garibaldi at once summoned Assanti's brigade—1,100—from Caserta, then leaving Milbitz to shift for himself, he dashed off in a carriage towards S. Angelo to see how it fared with Medici. He was greeted by a hail of bullets; his coachman being killed and an *aide-de-camp* and the correspondent of the *Daily News* wounded. He and his staff sabred their way through till they reached Mosto's crack corps of Genoese sharpshooters, who, with Simonetta's Lombards, were in the thickest of the fray.

Medici, with his centre in the village of S. Angelo in Formis, his extreme right extending to the S. Vito wood, his left to the Sassano and Di Napoli villas, loop-holed, barricaded, and fortified on the Sta. Maria road, with his guns on the heights, a battery constructed on the Capua—S. Angelo cross-roads, had stationed his outposts to the north on the river banks, to the south, within 2,000 paces of Capua, with a loose line of skirmishers thrown across to Sacchi's Brigade at S. Leucio. At dawn Afan de Rivera, with two brigades, invested his entire front; the outposts fell back, nor could two battalions led against the enemy's right, to prevent their occupying the road, prevail against the number of the assailants and the superiority of their guns: the Garibaldians were driven back to the slopes.

At the same time the Sassano and Di Napoli villas were attacked and taken; then the battery on the cross-roads, when the grape from Torricelli's battery stopped their progress. Simonetta, Ramorino's battalions, and the English (Dunn's two companies of *picciotti*), after a fierce fight, recaptured the guns; then Dunn's ammunition failing, "To the bayonet!" he cried, and gallantly his boy-soldiers charged under the fire of the guns till, Ramorino killed and Dunn's thigh smashed, the Bourbons scored another success and retook the guns. Medici, Guastalla, his staff chief, and Major Castellazzi, leading an onslaught at the bayonet, arrested their progress but could not then re-capture their guns.

It was at that moment that Garibaldi appeared on the scene of action, and, gathering together all the forces at hand, made them charge the fourfold foe with the bayonet, repulsed, routed, and retook the

IT WAS AT THAT MOMENT THAT GARIBALDI APPEARED.

two houses; then, believing the enemy to be "only on his left," made for S. Angelo. To his surprise, he found several battalions in his rear, stationed on the formidable heights of Tafata, actually dominating Mount S. Angelo. Better acquainted with the country than he or his, the Colonna brigade had, during the night, penetrated Medici's lines by one of the sunken roads—old military routes or watercourses, now dry and so deep that "even cavalry and artillery can occupy them and remain invisible."

With his Genoese and a portion of Sacchi's brigade, he, from the top of S. Nicola, succeeded in dislodging them, but, surveying the battlefield, saw Medici still encompassed by his foes. Dashing down he expelled them from a villa, collected all the troops he could lay hands on from a battery to the west, opened a rattling fire, electrifying officers and men by his presence, saw them recover the villa on the Capuan road, the barricade, and three lost pieces, taking two companies prisoners.

At noon, there was a lull. Medici ordered his men to "halt and eat," when, just as they were falling to, Afan di Rivera brought up fresh troops who devoured the rations, seized two pieces, and, setting fire to several houses, possessed themselves of S. Angelo in Formis. Medici—cool and imperturbable as ever, with his men perfectly in hand—slowly retired to the slopes, keeping up a steady and constant fire; still Garibaldi saw that without fresh troops he must be cut to pieces. But how to summon the reserves?—the road and telegraph lying between S. Angelo and Sta. Maria in the enemy's hands, no news as yet of Bixio, no certainty of Milbitz's fate.

Putting in practice his favourite proverb, "*Who wills goes, who wills not sends*," alone with his faithful Basso, that inseparable comrade, orderly, sick-nurse, and friend, taking care that the soldiers should not see him depart, by goat-paths and watercourses across country, he regained Sta. Maria, where Milbitz, himself wounded, his troops decimated, still held the post-road, the rail, and the town of Sta. Maria against tremendous odds, as Tabacchi, with ever fresh forces and well-supplied artillery, kept up a ceaseless fire.

Bixio's news had varied from hour to hour. Attacked by three columns on his front, on Monte Caro, and on the aqueduct, a lively fire was interchanged; a rifled battery of eight guns sent the Eberhard brigade flying, leaving the aqueduct in possession of the enemy. Boldrini, with seven officers and most of his soldiers wounded, fell mortally wounded on the summit of Monte Caro.

Dezza, in command of that "precious gem," sends up Menotti Garibaldi with two companies, but the enemy had scaled the heights; Taddei, under cover on the left, surrounds them in the rear, waving his cap as he reaches the summit. Dezza, with Menotti reinforced, charges at the bayonet on their front; they retreat with a run, and Monte Caro is saved.

Bixio, relieved of this anxiety, rallies his forces, drives the enemy along the road, sends back to Maddaloni his two howitzers, with their commanders killed, other two from the aqueduct; then a general charge at the bayonet, and two of the enemy's columns retire behind their own battery. Dezza and Menotti charge four times at the bayonet, and the third column, which, protected by a wood, has aimed at cutting off communications with Caserta, is sent to join the others.

This success was owing in great part to the heroic resistance of Bronzetti, who for ten hours "detained" Perrone, with 2,000 men, marching to the assistance of Von Michele Pilade—twin brother of Oreste, killed at Tre Ponte in 1859—alone sustained the shock of the guns on a height and of the enemy's musketry. When ammunition failed, they rushed on to the bayonet—just fifteen, the rest killed or wounded on the slopes.

"Surrender, oh brave ones!" cried Perrone; but, marching on to death, Bronzetti fell with a bullet through his heart. The rest were carried wounded into Capua, Bixio, who at noon had telegraphed to Caserta for reinforcements, at 3 p.m. sent word that he could hold his own.

Garibaldi having summoned all the reserves from Caserta, reanimating the troops at Sta. Maria as he had done at S. Angelo, went himself to watch for their arrival.

Guessing his fasting condition, some friends (amongst them the writer), who were present, conveyed to him by two British tars, with "H.M.S. Hannibal" on their caps, who had been pleading "for muskets to join in the fray," a pail of water, a basket of fresh figs, and a tin of English biscuits. The inhabitants of Sta. Maria, having quitted or shut up their houses, no more solid fare was obtainable. As we reached him with these, a bright, sunny smile lit up his serenely serious face.

"What!" he said, "are you encouraging your Queen's sailors to desert?"

"Never a bit," we replied. "They are out for a holiday, and want some fun."

Then as, after drinking eagerly from the pail, his hand was stretched out for the biscuits, a shell, ricocheting from the field, burst at his feet. A splinter, as he told us afterwards, grazed his thigh, but this he heeded not, his eyes now sparkling with delight as they rested on the head of the reserve column, and the *bersaglieri* of the Milan brigade recognising him, dashed forward shouting "*Evviva!*"

"The day is ours," he said; and, despite the heavy fire on the left and the fact that two battalions sent across the fields to Parisi were surrounded, he bade them halt for five minutes. Then, forming them in column of attack, he sent the Milan brigade to "clear the road" of the Bavarese who divided him from Medici, where they were assailed by a galling fire, Tabacchi, determined to seize the Capuan gate, shelling the S. Angelo road and the Eber column in the shelter of the trees.

On were sent the gallant "Calabrians" under Pace, and as the trumpet sounded the charge the Milanese sharpshooters rushed on the enemy, followed by another battalion, charging, as ordered, without firing a shot.

The corps of Tabacchi and Afan de Rivera were now pursued on flanks and rear. Medici, who, with his inflexible obstinacy, had held his own against such overpowering numbers, rallying all his men for a last assault, Tabacchi began to beat a retreat, and to cover this charged the Milan brigade with four squadrons of cavalry, but, greeted with a hail of bullets, they turned tail and fled. Milbitz sent out of the Capuan gate some seventy hussars, and Tabacchi left three pieces behind him.

Then the Hungarian legion arrived, and Garibaldi, pointing to the wooded plain to the left, whence the Bourbons were firing volley after volley, called out: "Welcome, my brave Hungarians; drive away those rascals for me—*chassez-moi ces coquins*." Said and done. Up came Eber (who was acting, it may be mentioned, as correspondent of the *Times*) with his brigade, and the French company De Flotte, which had been under fire since dawn, and the remnant of the *picciotti*—Corran, the fellow-pioneer of Rosalino Pilo, badly wounded, shouting with joy at the sight of *Galibardo*.

Medici, with old Avezzanós (Guastalla wounded), cleared their end of the road, Türr's battery shelled from the rail, he charging brilliantly at the head of his hussars.

A little band of Englishmen maintained the reputation that Peard, Wyndham, Dowling, and the wounded Dunn had created. The so-called British legion had not yet arrived.

Vainly the Bourbon cavalry charged across the plain: the cavaliers turned tail as the home thrusts of the bayonet touched them. The very gunners seemed to miss their range—perhaps because the Garibaldians rushed too close under the muzzles of their guns. Clear, audible above the battle din, rang out from time to time the Duce's clarion voice: "Bravo, my Calabresie!" "Hungary, well done!" "Charge, Milan, charge!" "What heroes are my *picciotti!*"

Suddenly one "heard the silence": the enemy, after fighting obstinately for twelve mortal hours, re-entered Capua, protected by the guns of the piazza. Bixio telegraphed that Von Mechel had returned to Dugenta. The Garibaldians lost one-tenth of their numbers—306 killed, 1,717 wounded, all of whom were brought into ambulance or hospital, tended and their wounds dressed before midnight. Of the Bourbon killed and wounded we have no list on that day and the morrow. Garibaldi took 2,070 prisoners, chiefly of Perrone's column; so Bronzetti was avenged. At 5 p.m. on the 1st October the field battle of the Volturno was fought out and won, the Bourbon dynasty for ever doomed and Italian unity assured by that Garibaldian "*Victory along all the line.*"

GARIBALDI'S AUTOGRAPH

The Battle of Aspromonte
August 29, 1862
By Charles Lowe

Giuseppe (or Joseph) Garibaldi was for many years the most picturesque and interesting figure in all Europe. He might be called the William Wallace, or the William Tell, of Italy. His name (which is still a common enough one in Genoa among all ranks of life) is said to have been a corruption of Garibaldo, *i.e.* "Bold in War." At any rate, a warlike star presided over his birth (at Nice in 1807), for he first saw the light in the very house where, forty years before, Massena, one of the Great Napoleon's greatest generals, was born.

At the time of his birth his native country—Italy—was in a woeful state of disunion, and much of it was under the yoke of the foreigner—the Austrians in particular. It was cut up into several conflicting monarchies; while the Pope, the spiritual head of the Roman Church, also claimed—and had his claim allowed—to be temporal sovereign of Rome. But as the century grew older, the Italian people began to be stirred with a deep desire for national unity, without which they knew they could never become great, strong, or respected; and of all who threw themselves into this movement, none did so with more ardour than the son of the humble Nice skipper who sailed his own little vessel all over the Mediterranean.

This son, Giuseppe, took to his father's calling, and began life as a sailor. Once, when second in command of a brig, he was attacked by Greek pirates, after which he landed at St. Nicholas to re-victual without so much as shoes to his feet. An Englishman, taking pity on him, offered him a pair, and this touched him to the heart.

Garibaldi wrote in 1870 to *Cassell's Magazine:*

When I look back upon it now, I cannot help remembering that it was the first of the many acts of kindness which bind me with such strong and lasting ties of gratitude to your noble nation.

In 1836 he had joined a revolutionary movement, which failed; and, after many privations and vicissitudes, he finally sailed for South America, where for the next ten years he led a life of the most stirring excitement and adventure among the quarrelsome young Republics of that continent—fighting now on one side and then on the other, like Rittmeister Dugald Dalgetty in the Thirty Years' War, and gaining a name for the greatest personal bravery. The wanderings and adventures of Ulysses were nothing to those of Garibaldi, which would fill volumes of as fascinating reading as can be found in the pages of a novelist.

When the revolutionary movement of 1848 swept over Europe—including Italy—Garibaldi returned home with a knowledge of guerilla—or irregular—warfare such as was possessed probably by no other man alive; and then, with his volunteers, he threw himself heart and soul into the movement for "making Italy free," as the phrase ran, "from the Alps to the Adriatic."

With his Red-Shirt Volunteers, Garibaldi took a prominent part in the fighting of 1848 and 1859, and with his "Thousand"—as famous a fighting force as Xenophon's "Ten Thousand"—he, in 1860, attacked and conquered the Two Sicilies (*i.e.* the island of Sicily and Naples), and made a present of these kingdoms to his sovereign Victor Emmanuel, after which he returned to his solitary farm on the little island of Caprera. Here, on this rocky island—fifteen miles in circumference, and five in length—Garibaldi was monarch of all he surveyed. He wrote:

> The absence of priests, is one of the especial blessings of this spot. Here God is worshipped in purity of spirit without formalism, free from mockery, under the canopy of the blue heavens, with the planets for lamps, the sea winds for music, and the green sward of the island for altars.

This was the den, so to speak, into which the lion-patriot retired when no political prey was stirring. But no sooner did he scent the opportunity for action than out again he would rush with a roar, which was sometimes just as disquieting to his friends as to his foes. This was more particularly the case on the occasion which led to Aspromonte. But, before proceeding to the tragic scene of this encounter, let us see what sort of fighters Garibaldi and his red-shirted

GENERAL GARIBALDI

KING VICTOR EMMANUEL

followers were. A correspondent of *The Times* wrote:

Garibaldi, was a middle-sized man, and not of an athletic build, though gifted with uncommon strength and surprising agility. He looked to the greatest advantage on horseback, since he sat in the saddle with such perfect ease, and yet with such calm serenity, as if he were grown to it, having had, though originally a sailor, the benefit of a long experience in taming the wild mustangs of the Pampas.

But his chief beauty was the head and the unique dignity with which it rose on the shoulders. The features were cast in the old classic mould: the forehead was high and broad, a perpendicular line from the roots of the hair to the eyebrows. His mass of tawny hair and full red beard gave the countenance its peculiar lion-like character. The brow was open, genial, sunny; the eyes dark grey, deep, shining with a steady reddish light; the nose, mouth, and chin exquisitely chiselled, the countenance habitually at rest, but at sight of those dear to him beaming with a caressing smile, revealing all the innate strength and grace of his loving nature.

His garb consisted of a plain red shirt and grey trousers, over which he threw the folds of the Spanish-American *poncho*—an ample upper garment of thin white woollen cloth with crimson lining, which did duty as a standard, and round which his volunteers were bidden to rally in the thick of the fight, as did the French Huguenot chivalry round Henry of Navarre's '*panache blanche*.' His sword was a fine cavalry blade, forged in England and the gift of English friends, and with it he might be seen at his early breakfast on the tented field cutting his bread and slicing his Bologna sausage, and inviting those he particularly wished to distinguish, to share that savour fare.

The sabre did good slashing work at need, however, and at Milazzo, in Sicily, it bore him out safely from the midst of a knot of Neapolitan troopers who caught him by surprise and fancied they had him at their discretion. Garibaldi carried no other weapons, though the officers in his suite had pistols and daggers at their belts; and his negro groom, by name Aguyar, who for a long-time followed him as his shadow, like Napoleon's Mameluke, and was shot dead by his side at Rome, was armed with a long lance with a crimson pennon, used as his chief's banner.

His staff officers were a numerous, quaint, and motley crew, men of all ages and conditions, mostly devoted personal friends—not all of them available for personal strength or technical knowledge, but all to be relied upon for their readiness to die with or for him. The veterans he brought with him from Montevideo, a Genoese battalion whom his friend Augusto Vecchi helped to enlist, and the Lombard Legion, under Manara, were all men of tried valour, well trained to the use of the rifle, inured to hardships and privations; and they constituted the nucleus of the Garibaldian force throughout its campaigns.

The remainder was a shapeless mass of raw recruits from all parts of Italy, joining or leaving the band almost at their pleasure—mere boys from the Universities, youths of noble and rich family, lean artisans from the towns, stout peasants and labourers from the country, adventurers of indifferent character, deserters from the army, and the like, all marching in loose companies, like Falstaff's recruits, under improvised officers and non-commissioned officers; but all, or most of them, entirely disinterested about pay or promotion, putting up with long fasts and heavy marches, only asking to be brought face to face with the enemy, and when under the immediate influence of Garibaldi himself or of his trusty friends seldom guilty of soldierly excesses or of any breach of discipline.

The effect the presence of the hero had among them was surprising. A word addressed to them in his clear, ringing, silver voice electrified even the dullest. An order coming from him was never questioned, never disregarded. No one waited for a second bidding or an explanation. 'Your business is not to inquire how you are to storm that position. You must only go and do it.' And it was done.

One of his Lombard volunteers, Emilio Dandolo wrote:

> On the approach of a foe, Garibaldi would ride up to a dominating point in the landscape, survey the ground for hours with the spy-glass in brooding silence, and come down with a swoop on the enemy, acting upon some well-contrived combination of movements by which advantage had been taken of all circumstances in his favour.

And as this was his custom in the field of war, so it was ever also

EVERYWHERE THIS FREE-LANCE EVOKED ENTHUSIASM

his habit in what must be called the field of politics. After finishing a campaign, he would sheathe his sword and return to Caprera, there to stand and strain his eyes towards the mainland, watching for his next opportunity of action. Not an event escaped his notice, and he heard with a smile of contentment how Victor Emmanuel had stormed the fortress of Gaeta, and the two crowns of the Sicilies had been placed upon the head of the Piedmontese King. But the national unity was still far from complete. Above all things, Venice still remained under the yoke of the Austrians, while Rome was equally in the power of the French, who remained there to champion with their bayonets the pretensions of the Pope.

They had been there ever since 1849, when the Romans rose against the Pope, declared a Republic, and were supported by Garibaldi and his Red Shirts. But then the French rushed to the assistance of the Pope, and after a three months' siege—during which the Garibaldians behaved with splendid bravery—at last stormed the city, restored the authority of the Pope, and compelled the Hero of Caprera to retire to the mountains.

He had said, on leading his men away from the Eternal City:

> Soldiers! that which I have to offer you is this: hunger, thirst, cold, heat; no pay, no barracks, no rations; but frequent alarms, forced marches, charges at the point of the bayonet.

And 4,000 men had readily answered to this appeal.

The memory of this defeat rankled ever after in Garibaldi's mind, and he determined to seize the first opportunity of retrieving it. This opportunity, he deemed, had at last come in the year 1862, soon after the death of the great statesman Cavour, who had been the Bismarck, so to speak, of Italian unity, as Victor Emmanuel had been its King William. But while Garibaldi had been their greatest support, he had also been the source of their greatest weakness. For he was not a regularly appointed servant of the government, but the self-constituted soldier and champion of his country. He chose his own time for fighting, irrespective of what the king and his ministers wished, and thus often placed them in the greatest difficulty.

So little, indeed, did Garibaldi consider his times and seasons for action, that he was said by many to have "an ass's head linked to a lion's heart." He was nothing but a headlong soldier, who scorned the arts of statesmen; and his head was turned with his extraordinary popularity among the masses of the Italian people, who paid him something like

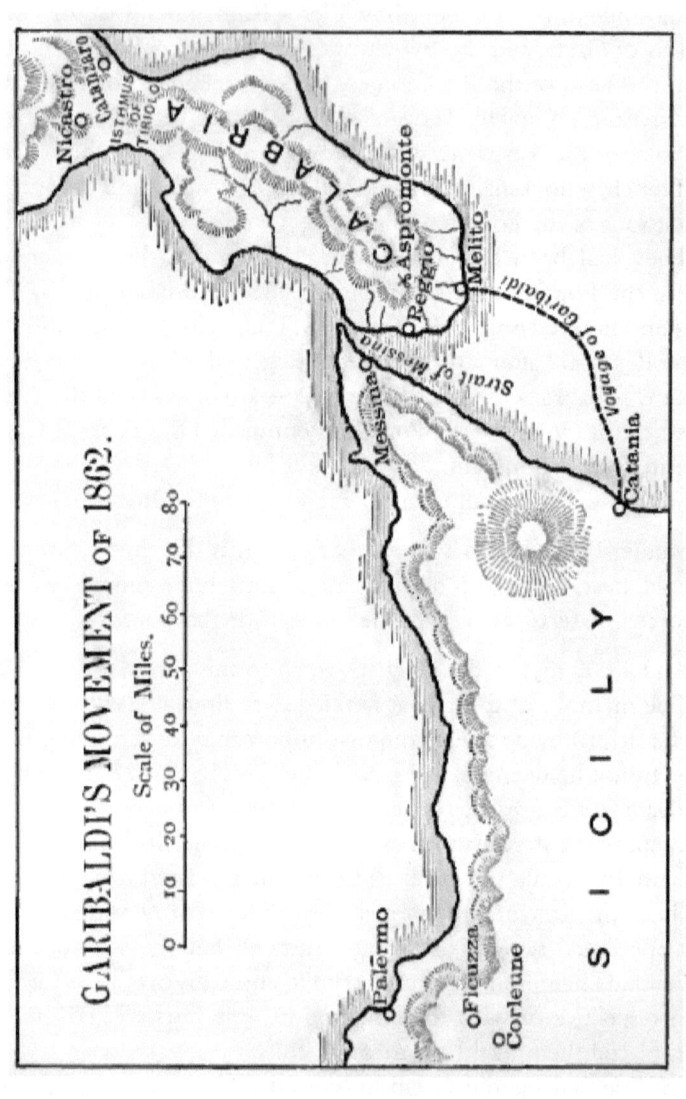

Divine honours.

Everywhere this free-lance hero evoked far more enthusiasm than was even shown the king, who, naturally enough, followed Garibaldi's movements with the greatest solicitude, whilst recognising that he had done so much for his country that the very greatest indulgence and forbearance had to be shown him.

But there came a time when it was thought that Garibaldi should not be allowed the free hand which had hitherto been granted him. This was when he announced his intention of placing the national flag on the walls of Rome, which still owned the dominion of the Pope, and was garrisoned by the French. However much Victor Emmanuel desired to see Rome become the capital of Italy, he could not forget the debt of gratitude which he owed the French, who had been his allies in the successful war against Austria in 1859; and when he heard of Garibaldi's proposed enterprise, he issued a proclamation to his subjects, saying:

> It is painful to me to see deluded and inexperienced young men forgetting their duties and the gratitude we owe our best allies, and making the name of Rome a watchword of war. . . . Italians! beware of guilty impatience and incautious agitation. When the hour to finish the government work shall have come, the voice of your king will be heard among you. A call which does not come from him is a call to rebellion and to civil war. The responsibility and the rigour of the law will fall upon those who do not listen to my words.

But this warning had no restraining effect on the eager Garibaldi, who only panted to recover for his country the Eternal City, exclaiming: "Rome! Rome! Who is not urged by thy very name to take up arms for thy deliverance?" At the same time, there is considerable reason for believing that the king and his government had given secret encouragement to Garibaldi to embark upon his mad enterprise, in order to have a pretext for arresting the lionhearted but inconvenient rebel. In any case, away to Sicily he went to make preparations for his Quixotic expedition. He probably calculated that the news of his enterprise would induce his countrymen to rise *en masse*, and that the French Emperor, seeing the enthusiasm of the Italian people, would withdraw his troops from Rome.

He landed at Palermo, whence a body of his volunteers marched to Corleone, a town of the interior, where they overpowered the National Guard and armed themselves with their muskets. Then they took up their quarters in a camp at Ficuzza, a forest district about twenty miles from Palermo. Here they were visited on August 1st by Garibaldi, who thus addressed them:

> My young fellow-soldiers! Today again the holy cause of our country unites us. Again today, without asking whither going, what to do, with what hope of reward to our labours, with a smile on your lips and joy in your hearts, you hasten to fight our overbearing dominators, throwing a spark of comfort to our enslaved brethren. . . . I can only promise you toils, hardships, and perils; but I rely on your self-denial. I know you, ye brave young men, crippled in glorious combat! It is needless to ask you to display valour in fight. What I ask is discipline, for without that no army can exist. The Romans were disciplined, and they mastered the world. Endeavour to conciliate the goodwill of the population we are about to visit, as you did in 1860, and no less to win the esteem of our valiant army, in order, thus united with that army, to bring about the longed-for unity of the country.

Garibaldi now went to Catania, where the royal troops already began to close round him with intent to take him prisoner. But many deserted to his side in the hope of sharing the martial glory which they believed to be again in store for the wayward Hero of Caprera. His force soon swelled to a very considerable body; but here it was on the island of Sicily, and how was it to get across to the mainland in order to commence its march on Rome? Garibaldi had no ships; but in the harbour of Catania there were lying three vessels—a French frigate, the *Marie Adelaide*; a French steamer, *Le Général Abbatucci*; and an Italian steamer, *Il Dispaccio*, belonging to the Florio Company. In addition to these vessels there was a royal Italian man-of-war—*Il Duca di Genova*—the commander of which gave out that he would fire on any of the other three ships which made bold to carry over Garibaldi and his Red Shirts to the mainland.

One day, however, the *Duca di Genova* took it into its head to go for a little cruise outside the Straits of Messina—probably, indeed, because it had received secret orders to do so, in order the better to lure Garibaldi into the trap which had been laid for him. On the disappearance of the *Duca di Genova*, Garibaldi stepped into a boat with several trusty followers, and was rowed off to the other three vessels above referred to, when he put their respective captains under arrest, and then proceeded to fill them up with his impatient Red Shirts.

One of his biographers says:

> At five o'clock in the afternoon, the embarkation commenced, and the good people of Catania crowded the harbour, waving handkerchiefs and cheering. Menotti (Garibaldi's son) and his 'Guides,' the Tuscans, and the flower of the Sicilian volunteers, moved off for *Il Dispaccio*; General Corrao, with some more Sicilians, occupied *Le Général Abbatucci*; whilst Garibaldi took the command of the former and put Burratini in command of the *Marie Adelaide*, with orders to get her filled with troops as soon as possible. During this time, it had been growing dark, and each ship was filled to suffocation, no one being able to lie down, or get any rest, as boats were for ever arriving with their cargoes of men. About midnight the ships were got under way; and after crossing the Straits in the dark, without any mishap, the troops were all safely landed at Melito next morning, on the spot celebrated as the one on which the former expedition had gone ashore.

Garibaldi landed in Calabria with a force of about 3,000 men—a very insignificant body, one would have thought, to march against walled and embattled Rome with its formidable French garrison. But by the time he came into collision with the royal troops, who had been sent after him to arrest his progress, his little army of Red Shirts had dwindled by about a half on account of the privations to which it was exposed and the rapid marches which had been exacted of it.

On hearing of Garibaldi's naval *coup-de-main* at Catania, and his crossing over to Calabria, General Cialdini at once gave chase, and in order to catch the Hero of Caprera, he sent two of his generals—Revel and Vialardi—with a body of royal troops to draw a cordon across the isthmus of Tiriolo at its narrowest point, between Nicastro and Catanzaro, so as thus to bar the Rome-ward march of the Red Shirts. Having done this, he next ordered three vessels of war to cruise about the Straits so as to prevent Garibaldi from reembarking, and then despatched Major-General Pallavicini, at the head of a considerable force, from Reggio, with instructions to drive the Red Shirts northwards in the direction of the aforesaid cordon on the isthmus, as game is driven by the beaters towards the sportsmen—Pallavicini's instructions being to attack Garibaldi "anywhere and anyhow," unless he consented to an

CATANIA

unconditional surrender.

Things had thus assumed a very serious aspect indeed for the disillusioned Hero of Caprera, who, on the evening of the 28th August, after a long and tiring day's march, had pitched his camp on the brow of the far-famed hill of Aspromonte, on a plateau overlooking the sea, with a wood behind which connected it with a high range of the Apennines, and would afford ample shelter for his troops. The men were encamped *al fresco* under cover of this wood, whilst Garibaldi occupied one of two woodmen's huts which were on the plateau, and gave the spot the name of "*i forestalli*." It was wet and gloomy, the rain put out the bivouac fires, every rag on their backs was soaked, and they had no provisions with them; so that the position of the volunteers was far from enviable.

Next morning General Pallavacini came up with the Red Shirts, and at once proceeded to carry out his orders. How he did this let us see from his own pen:

> On the morning of the 29th I set forth early, directing my course towards San Stefano, where I arrived at about half-past eight a.m. There, from secret information received, I knew that General Garibaldi had encamped with his force during the night on the plateau of Aspromonte. I ordered the troops to pursue the march until within a short distance of the plateau, and before allowing them to proceed I caused the troops to rest themselves, as they were excessively fatigued by a long march by abrupt paths. In the meantime, I learned that only two hours previously General Garibaldi had encamped at the foot of the plateau of Aspromonte, and I saw that by two paths I could descend towards his camp.
>
> I then divided my troops into two columns, which arrived at the same time in view of the Garibaldian encampment, already abandoned by him, he having taken up a position on the crest of a rugged hillock to the east of the plateau of Aspromonte. I then sent an order to the *commandant* of the left column, while making the right column fall back by a rapid movement. I attacked the left flank of the rear of the rebels, in order to cut off their retreat. In the meantime, with a battalion, I caused the entrance of the valley to be occupied, that they might not regain the plateau.
>
> The left column, with the 6th Battalion of the *Bersaglieri* at their

head, then attacked the rebels, and after a smart fire carried the position at the point of the bayonet with cries of '*Viva il Re!*' '*Viva Italia!*' while the left side was also attacked by our troops. General Garibaldi and his son Menotti (who had written to a friend in Liverpool, "In three weeks we shall be in Rome!") having been wounded, and the rebels being surrounded on all sides, resistance became useless, whereupon the Garibaldians gave the signal to cease firing.

Their own account of the engagement was somewhat different. Garibaldi himself wrote:—

> They thirsted for blood, and I wished to spare it. . . . Yes, they thirsted for blood. I perceived it with sorrow, and I endeavoured, in consequence, to do my utmost to prevent that of our assailants from being shed. I ran to the front of our line, crying out to them not to fire, and from the centre to the left, where my voice and those of my *aides-de-camp* could be heard, not a trigger was pulled. It was not thus on the attacking side. Having arrived at a distance of two hundred metres, they began a tremendous fire, and the party of *Bersaglieri* who were in front of me, directing their shots against me, struck me with two balls—one in the left thigh, not serious; the other in the ankle of the right foot, making a serious wound.
>
> As all this happened at the opening of the conflict, and I was carried to the skirt of the wood after being wounded, I could see nothing more, a dense crowd having formed round me while my wound was being dressed. I feel certain, however, that up to the end of the line (of troops) which was at my litter, and to that of my *aides-de-camp*, not a single musket shot was fired. . . . It was not so on our right.
>
> The *Picciotti*, attacked by the regular troops, replied by a fire along the whole line, and, although the trumpets sounded to cease firing, there was at that spot a smart fusillade, which lasted not more than a quarter of an hour. My wounds led to some confusion in our line. Our soldiers, not seeing me, began to retreat into the woods, so that, little by little, the crowd around me broke up, and the most faithful alone remained.

A Garibaldian officer who was present thus wrote:

> When the general received the bullet, he was passing along our

front, ordering the men not to fire. I saw a slight shiver pass through his body; he took two or three steps, and then began to stagger. We ran to him, holding him up; he was regardless of his sufferings. Raising his cap in the air, he cried '*Viva l'Italia!*' I had his poor foot resting on my thigh; he called out to his assailants, and asked what they were doing with his people. I felt a shivering in all his limbs; and, reminding him of his wounds, I implored him to be quiet.

While the surgeon was dressing his wounds, the sturdy soldier calmly produced a cigar and began to smoke, inquiring of the doctor whether he thought amputation would be necessary. Twenty minutes later he had an interview with his conqueror and captor, General Pallavacini, who assured him, with tears in his eyes, that this was the most miserable day of his life. Yet he had received certain orders, and he had no choice but to obey.

It was the bitterest of all moments for the hero of Italian unity when, staggering from the effects of his double wound, he fell forward upon the Italian soil to which he had devoted his whole life. Generals Cialdini and Pallavacini had been his friends and comrades, their troops were his compatriots and brothers-in-arms.

Two bullets had thus put an end, sudden and complete, to Garibaldi's march on Rome, though he was to live to make another and an equally unsuccessful attempt upon the Eternal City. Meanwhile, the illustrious rebel was carried to prison at Spezzia, where he was, however, kept but a short time, and then removed to Pisa. There Dr. Nélaton, of Paris, who came all the way for the purpose, succeeded in extracting the bullet from Garibaldi's ankle, for which bullet a hero-worshipping Englishman offered as much as 30,000 *francs*.

Two years later, when he had recovered from his wounds, he visited England, a country which had always taken the keenest interest in his adventures, and even sent him volunteers, as well as a doctor to attend him in his illness. High and low welcomed him with the warmest enthusiasm, and the attentions that were rained upon the Hermit of Caprera culminated in a grand banquet given in his honour by the Lord Mayor and City of London.

Raising his cap in the air, he cried 'Viva L'Italia!'

www.ingramcontent.com/pod-product-compliance
Lightning Source LLC
Chambersburg PA
CBHW031559170426
43196CB00031B/202